RETHINKING THE FAMILY
Some
feminist
questions

RETHINKING THE FAMILY

Some feminist questions

EDITED BY
BARRIE THORNE

WITH
MARILYN YALOM

*Prepared under the auspices of
The Center for Research on Women
Stanford University*

Longman

New York & London

In memory of Shelly Rosaldo, *our friend and colleague, whose intellectual presence infuses this book*

RETHINKING THE FAMILY Some Feminist Questions

Longman Inc., 95 Church Street, White Plains, N.Y. 10601
Associated companies, branches, and representatives
throughout the world.

Developmental Editor: Nicole Benevento
Interior Design: Angela Foote
Cover Design: Dan Serrano
Manufacturing and Production Supervisor: Robin B. Besofsky
Composition: Book Composition Services, Inc.
Printing and Binding: Fairfield Graphics

Library of Congress Cataloging in Publication Data

Main entry under title:

Rethinking the family.

Includes index.
1. Family—United States—Addresses, essays lec-
tures. 2. Feminism—United States—Addresses, essays,
lectures. I. Thorne, Barrie. II. Yalom, Marilyn.
III. Stanford University. Center for Research on
Women.
HQ536.R454   306.8'0973   81-2427
ISBN 0-582-28265-9   AACR2

Manufactured in the United States of America

9 8

About the Authors

RENATE BRIDENTHAL is associate professor of history and director of women's studies at Brooklyn College and editor of *Becoming Visible: Women in European History*, with Claudia Koonz.

CLAIR (VICKERY) BROWN is assistant professor of economics, University of California, Berkeley.

NANCY CHODOROW is associate professor of sociology at the University of California, Santa Cruz, and the author of *The Reproduction of Mothering*.

JANE COLLIER is assistant professor of anthropology at Stanford University.

SUSAN CONTRATTO is a psychologist and coordinator of the Women's Studies Program at the University of Michigan.

WILLIAM J. GOODE is professor of sociology and senior research fellow, Hoover Institution, Stanford University.

LINDA GORDON is associate professor of history, University of Massachusetts, and author of *Woman's Body, Woman's Right*.

SUSAN WESTERBERG PRAGER is associate dean and professor of law, University of California, Los Angeles.

RAYNA RAPP is associate professor of anthropology at the New School for Social Research and editor of *Toward an Anthropology of Women*.

MICHELLE Z. ROSALDO is associate professor of anthropology at Stanford University and editor of *Woman, Culture and Society*, with Louise Lamphere.

SARA RUDDICK teaches philosophy and literature at The New School for Social Research in New York and is editor of *Working It Out*, with Pamela Daniels.

DAVID SPIEGEL is assistant professor of psychiatry and behavioral sciences, Stanford University, and author of *Trance and Treatment*, with Herbert Spiegel.

BARRIE THORNE is associate professor of sociology at Michigan State University and editor of *Language and Sex: Difference and Dominance*, with Nancy Henley.

MARILYN YALOM is associate director of the Center for Research on Women, Stanford University, and former professor of foreign languages and literature, California State University, Hayward.

SYLVIA YANAGISAKO is assistant professor of anthropology at Stanford University.

ELI ZARETSKY is a member of the Core Faculty at the Wright Institute, Berkeley, California, and author of *Capitalism, The Family and Personal Life*.

Preface

Most of the essays in this book were presented as public lectures at Stanford University during the spring of 1979. Under the sponsorship of the Center for Research on Women, nationally known scholars from different disciplines were invited to identify and address questions about the family that are of particular concern to feminists. Subsequently, most of the essays were considerably revised, and four were added, including an introductory essay by one of the editors.

These revisions and additions reflect the lively interchange of ideas among the original contributors that continued long after the public presentations. They also reflect contact with other feminist thinkers whose work was ultimately deemed essential to the collection. Thus the book represents both the efforts of individual scholars from the vantage of their respective disciplines and the work across disciplines that is so central to feminist scholarship. Our aim was to produce a cohesive, comprehensive, and thoughtful book on the family that asks feminist questions and suggests a few answers.

The editors wish to thank Marilyn Levy for her moral support and the Rockefeller Family Fund for helping to make this project possible. We are very much indebted to Joanne Kliejunas, graduate student in the Stanford School of Education, for substantive contributions and careful research assistance. We also wish to thank the entire staff of the Center for Research on Women at Stanford for providing a panoply of services such as typing, telephoning, xeroxing, budgeting, chauffering, and all that is characteristically unsung. Jackie Campbell, of the Michigan State University Sociology Department, also provided clerical help. Finally, we wish to thank Jing and Richard Lyman for their interest in this project and their long-standing friendship with CROW.

Barrie Thorne
DEPARTMENT OF SOCIOLOGY
MICHIGAN STATE UNIVERSITY

Marilyn Yalom
CENTER FOR RESEARCH ON WOMEN
STANFORD UNIVERSITY

Contents

1

BARRIE THORNE

Feminist Rethinking
of the Family:
An Overview

Within the last decade the family has emerged as a political issue. Some who claim that the family is in crisis cite as evidence the high divorce rate; the increase in single-parent families and people living alone; and the rising employment rates of married women, especially mothers of young children. There have been calls for new federal policies to "strengthen" the family, while the New Right has played upon fears of family breakdown by using the term "pro-family" to draw together opposition to the Equal Rights Amendment, abortion, and gay rights.

Defenders of the family often locate feminists among those who criticize and would even destroy the family; the conservative "pro-family" movement is explicitly antifeminist. Critical analyses of the family, and efforts to change traditional family arrangements, *have* been central to the women's movement, although trends such as the high divorce rate and the increase in women's employment predated the feminist movement. Of all the issues raised by feminists, those that bear on the family—among them, demands for abortion rights and for legitimating an array of household and sexual arrangements, and challenges of men's authority and women's economic dependence and exclusive responsibility for nurturing—have been the most controversial.

The essays in this book, first delivered in a public lecture series at Stanford University in the spring of 1979,[1] were written in the wake of controversy over the family. The authors affirm the significance of feminist analysis and politics; they also reflect on the content and implications of recent defenses of the family. These reflections bring into sharp

For comments and suggestions on an earlier draft of this essay, I would like to thank Nancy Chodorow, Linda Gordon, Joanne Kliejunas, Karen Skold, Alison Thorne, Susan Contratto, and Marilyn Yalom.

relief the nature and complexities of feminist analysis, as well as fears, needs, and larger issues bound up in "the family crisis."

The authors come from varied disciplines: anthropology, history, sociology, psychology, psychiatry, philosophy, economics, and law. Each essay bears the stamp of its originating discipline, but the papers also contain recurring assumptions and points of ambivalence anchored in feminist thought. Feminism, of course, is not all of a piece, and the authors' assumptions differ in ways that are worth noting. This essay introduces the papers that follow by setting forth five themes central to feminist rethinking of the family:

1. Feminists have challenged prevalent assumptions about the family. They have argued against the ideology of "the monolithic family," which elevates the contemporary nuclear family with a breadwinner husband and a full-time wife and mother as the only natural and legitimate family form. Feminists have challenged beliefs that any specific family arrangement is natural, biological, or "functional" in a timeless way.

2. Feminists have sought to reclaim the family—including topics such as the sexual division of labor, heterosexuality, male dominance, and motherhood—for social and historical analysis. This analysis has been furthered by an analytic decomposition of "the family" into underlying structures of sex and gender, and of generation. By taking gender as a basic category of analysis, feminists have made important contributions to family theory.

3. Because families are structured around gender and age, women, men, girls, and boys do not experience their families in the same way. Feminists have explored the differentiation of a family experience mystified by the glorification of motherhood, love, and images of the family as a domestic haven. Feminists have voiced experiences that this ideology denies: men's dominance and women's subordination within as well as outside of the family, and the presence of conflict, violence, and inequitably distributed work within the "domestic haven."

4. Feminists have raised questions about family boundaries. On the one hand, they have shown the troubled consequences of privatized modern families for women and children who are cut off from outside contact and support. On the other hand, some feminists have argued that family isolation may be partly illusory, since there are close connections between the internal life of families and the organization of the economy, the state, and other institutions. This line of analysis challenges a series of dichotomies—private and public, family and society—that are often taken for granted.

5. These dichotomies are linked to an ambivalence, as Linda Gordon phrases it, "between individualism and its critique," an ambivalence embedded in feminism since the nineteenth century and strongly evident today. The ambivalence is between values of individualism and equality,

which are derived from the capitalist market, values that women have historically been denied and are now claiming; and values of nurturance and collectivity, which are strongly associated with women and the family. These values, which have also been affirmed by some feminists, contain an implicit critique of capitalism. The authors in this volume hold different perspectives toward this ambivalence—the degree to which the division between market-based individualism and family-based nurturance is ideological or factual, and its consequences and possible solutions. The theme recurs in the essays in interesting ways.

The essays are arranged in a sequence that loosely follows these five themes. Jane Collier, Michelle Rosaldo, and Sylvia Yanagisako criticize prevailing ideologies of the family, especially functionalism. Linda Gordon traces the history of women's struggle for control of reproduction—an example of the way in which feminist social and historical analysis, with sustained attention to gender, can illuminate topics often regarded as biological or, in the case of birth control, as simply technological. The next two essays, "The Fantasy of the Perfect Mother" by Nancy Chodorow and Susan Contratto and "Maternal Thinking" by Sara Ruddick, explore an issue central to women's experience of the family: the nature of mothering as embedded in popular beliefs and in actual practice. David Spiegel examines a recurring theme in theories of mental illness—the blaming of mothers. The papers by Susan Westerberg Prager and by William J. Goode explore sources of conflict within families and between the sexes: conflicting legal philosophies bearing on problems of divorce, and the nature of men's resistance to women's demands for equality. Clair Brown addresses the changing relationship of housework to the market economy, a topic that bears on the internal lives of families and on their relation to other institutions. The question of boundaries is also addressed by Rayna Rapp, who argues that while households may be seen as autonomous, in fact they are closely tied to production and have significant variations by social class. Eli Zaretsky challenges a prevalent view that sees the family as opposed to the state; he argues that rather than being usurped by the welfare state, a particular family form has been enforced by state policies. Finally, Renate Bridenthal reviews the history of varying efforts to rethink the family and specifies recent feminist contributions to that undertaking.

Feminist Criticisms of Prevalent Assumptions about the Family

Feminist rethinking of the family begins with a challenge of three widespread assumptions: the ideology of "the monolithic family," beliefs that the family is natural or biological, and analyses that freeze present family ideals in a language of function and roles.

Criticisms of the Ideology of the Monolithic Family

The language often used to refer to kinship, households, and domestic sharing is monolithic and singular: "The family" implies a firm, unchanging entity, always similar in shape and content. Feminists have challenged this assumption. Anthropologists Jane Collier, Michelle Rosaldo, and Sylvia Yanagisako argue that "the family" is a distorting ideological construct that "maps the function of 'nurturance' onto a collectivity of specific persons (presumably 'nuclear' relations) associated with specific spaces ('the home'), and specific affective bonds ('love')." In contemporary parlance, "the family" assumes, in addition, a particular sexual division of labor: a breadwinner husband, freed for and identified with activities in a separate economic sphere, and a full-time wife and mother, defined, in Renate Bridenthal's words, as "*being* the core of the family, rather than simply being one member of it."

In short, the modern nuclear family, with a particular sexual division of labor, has been writ large as The Family and elevated as the only desirable and legitimate family form. A number of critics have set out to demystify the ideology of the monolithic family,[2] but it is feminists who have emphasized the close connection between that ideology and the oppression of women.

Women's subordination is linked to The Family as a specific household arrangement *and* as an ideology.[3] Within households that resemble The Family in composition, boundedness, and division of labor, women are excluded from gaining direct access to valued resources such as income, recognized and status-giving work, and political authority. They are economically dependent on their husbands; their unpaid work at home is generally burdensome and devalued; and the work of mothering is done in relative isolation, to the detriment of both mother and child.

But the ideology of The Family extends beyond families of that specific type to infuse general understandings of women's "proper place." Beliefs that most people live in the nuclear family, that adult women usually have husbands to support them, and that motherhood is women's central vocation are used to legitimate the subordination of women in the economy. Women's lower wages and their disadvantaged position in the labor force are justified by the assumption that their paid work is secondary to that of men. The belief that women are uniquely suited for domestic service and nurturing supports sex segregation of occupations and the confinement of women to jobs that resemble their wife-and-mother roles: clerical and service work, nursing, teaching and care of the young, production and selling of food and clothing. In short, the ideology of The Family reinforces the economic exploitation of all women.

While the ideology of The Family is still strongly embedded in cultural ideals, government policies, the organization of the economy, and "pro-family" political movements, in fact only a minority of U.S. households fully resemble that form. In 1977, of all U.S. households, only 16 percent included a father as sole wage earner, a full-time homemaker mother, and at least one child living at home. In another 18 percent of all households, both parents were wage earners, and there were one or more children at home; 30 percent of all households included married couples who were either childless or had no children living at home. Other households included single-parent families headed by women (6 percent) or men (.6 percent); unrelated persons living together (2 percent); people living alone (21 percent); and households with relatives other than spouses or children (5 percent).[4]

These household statistics offer snapshots at one moment in time. They ignore family life cycles and say nothing about people's experiences of family, which are not always synonymous with household. Nevertheless, in pointing to wide variations in household arrangements, these figures challenge the image of the monolithic family. This image has been especially undermined by trends of the last decade: an overall decline in husband-wife households (although the marriage rate remains high, and this is still the prevalent household type) and an increase in female-headed households, people living alone, and unmarried women and men living together. In addition, the living arrangements of lesbians and gay men have become more visible.

Those alarmed about the current state of the family see these trends as signs of family breakdown and crisis partly because they idealize the family with a male wage earner and stay-at-home wife and children as the normal, most healthy household arrangement. Feminists have read other implications from these statistics, emphasizing the risks and problems experienced by those living in households that do not match up to the monolithic family ideal. These problems include the poverty of families headed by women and elderly women living alone (in 1977 the latter group were a third of single-person households). A scarcity of publicly supported child-care facilities places a heavy burden on parents raising children alone and on two-earner families with young children. And an ideology of heterosexuality, marriage, and pronatalism places burdens on lesbians and gay men, the unmarried, and those without children. In short, feminists have called for recognition of alternative family arrangements in public policy and law, in the organization of the economy, and in beliefs about legitimate choices concerning sexuality and reproduction.[5]

In her essay, Linda Gordon emphasizes the importance of the ongoing struggle for nonoppressive arrangements of reproduction and sexuality. She also notes the complexities involved, since the successful creation of alternative forms of collectivity has not kept up with consciousness raising. Gordon challenges the women's movement "to find a program that equally defends our right to freedom, particularly sexual freedom, and the dignity of our need and capacity for nurturance and being nurtured, with or without biological motherhood."

Challenging Beliefs That the Family Is a Biological Given

The ideology of the monolithic family is tenacious and difficult to demystify, partly because—of all social institutions—the family seems the most natural and biological, the most timeless and unchanging. Families deal with root biological events—birth, sickness, death. They are a place of sexuality, eating, sleeping, and of thick and close forms of relatedness imaged by biological ties of kinship. The rhythms of family life are organized more around bodily needs and the demands of children than are the time-governed rhythms of the work place. Procreation and the raising of children, usually seen as core family activities, seem inextricably linked with biology. And insofar as women are defined by their reproductive and mothering roles, and embedded in the family, their situation too has been made to appear natural. Collier, Rosaldo, and Yanagisako note that this view, "uniting women and the family to an apparently unchanging set of biologically given needs," has infused social theory up to the present.

Contemporary feminists challenge beliefs that family arrangements are biological in any direct or immutable way. They have set out to reclaim the family for social and historical analysis by emphasizing the *social organization* of sexuality, reproduction, motherhood, the sexual division of labor, and the division of gender itself. Several essays in this book demonstrate the rich insight yielded by this approach.

Linda Gordon traces changing feminist attitudes toward birth control, which are part of a long history of conflict over the social control of reproduction. For feminists, the issue of who should control reproduction, and how, has always been closely tied to strategies for improving the situation of women. The essays by Nancy Chodorow and Susan Contratto and by Sara Ruddick pursue a topic recently opened for fresh and provocative analysis: historical changes in conceptions of motherhood and—the focus of Ruddick's carefully reasoned account—mothering as a daily practice that develops distinctive patterns of thought. In her earlier book, *The Reproduction of Mothering*,[6] Chodorow showed that a seemingly obvious question—Why do women mother?—is not so obvious. The sexual division of labor that designates women as primary parents is anchored in social structure, not simply in biology, and has important consequences for the reproduction of gender and of sexual inequality.[7]

Theories of biological determinism of human behavior have recently reemerged on the scientific and political scene in the form of sociobiology. Sociobiologists such as E. O. Wilson[8] and David Barash[9] have argued that there is a strong evolutionary, and hence genetic, basis for male dominance and for the specialization of women in reproduction and child care. These theories have been used to justify existing gender arrangements, including sexual inequality. Many critics have demonstrated the weak status of sociobiology as a scientific theory.[10] For example, "none of these theories can demonstrate, in a way that satisfies the minimum requirements of the scientific method, the extent to which a given behavior is caused by environment or by biology."[11] Biological factors such as genes and hormones interact with environmental factors in complex and variable ways, especially in humans, where culture and learning are paramount. In claiming that there are universal, biologically determined sex differences, sociobiologists ignore or downplay cross-cultural variation. In contrast, feminists emphasize cross-cultural and historical variation and the importance of social organization in shaping gender arrangements and the nature and extent of sexual inequality.

Criticisms of Functionalism and Role Theory

The claim that The Family (or some of its components, such as the connection of women and maternity) is biological conveys one sort of immutability. The argument that the family is "functional" sets forth another. Functionalist theories—for example, those of Bronislaw Malinowski in anthropology and Talcott Parsons in sociology—pervade interpretations of the family. According to Malinowski's account, the nuclear family is a universal human institution because it functions to fulfill a universal human need, the nurturing of children. Collier, Rosaldo, and Yanagisako note the circularity of Malinowski's reasoning, which assumes that an institution exists because it fulfills a given function; they point to an array of cultural arrangements that argue against the claim that The Family is universal.

Talcott Parsons also took the contemporary nuclear family and made it seem inevitable.[12] He theorized that with the development of industrialization and the shift of productive functions out of the home, the small, relatively isolated nuclear family came to specialize in socializing children and meeting the personality needs of family members. He assumed that the family has two basic structures: a hierarchy of generations and a differentiation of adults into "expressive" and "instrumental" roles. Parsons argued that the wife necessarily plays the expressive, and the husband, the instrumental role. Thus, he translated the division of gender into a language of roles.

Although the language of roles seems to allow room for society and culture, in practice the opposite is conveyed. Parsons implies that a particular sexual division of labor, with women specializing in "socio-emotional" activities and men in accomplishing tasks and connecting the family with other institutions, is inevitable. His framework glosses over the complexity of behavior in actual families and falsely assumes that expressive and instrumental activities are mutually exclusive.

The language of roles conveys not only a sense of the fixed and dichotomous but also an image of separate but equal. Parsons acknowledges the primacy of the father over the mother, which he links to Western emphasis on achievement and instrumentality, but he does not emphasize or question male dominance. The influence of functionalism is apparent in widespread, uncritical use of terms like "sex roles," "the female role," and "the male role," terms that obscure not only differences of power between women and men but also the presence of conflict.[13] As Ellen Ross observes, roles "provide the building blocks of the harmonious families and societies which functionalism posits; they are thus pieces of a static and conflict-free social picture."[14]

In short, feminist analysis often begins with a critical perspective on prevalent ways of thinking about the family: the elevation of one family form as "the family"; theories of biological determinism; and emphasis on function and roles. Not all feminists, however, are in full agreement about these points; Alice Rossi, for example, has used a "biosocial" perspective in her recent work.[15] And the language of "roles" is still in widespread use in feminist circles, although there is much debate about the applicability of role theory to sex and gender.[16]

It should be noted that feminist theorists borrowed from functionalism an emphasis on sex and age as underlying axes of family relations. But feminists have taken this insight further by questioning and theorizing about the nature of sex and gender, instead of taking that axis for granted. Moreover, they have rejected the functionalist emphasis on a smoothly working social order and have emphasized power, conflict, and change.

Decomposing "The Family": The Sex/Gender System

In reclaiming the family for full social and historical analysis, some feminists have urged a more structural understanding. Thus, Juliet Mitchell argues that it is essential to discuss "not the family as an unanalyzed entity, but the separate *structures* which today compose it, but which may tomorrow be decomposed into a new pattern."[17] In Mitchell's framework, these underlying structures include production, reproduction, sexuality, and the socialization of children.

This theoretical insight—that fruitful analysis of the family requires differentiating underlying structures—was carried further by Gayle Rubin.[18] Rubin drew several lines of analysis into a coherent theory of "the sex/gender system," a term that has become central to recent feminist theory. A society's sex/gender system consists of "a set of arrangements by which the biological raw material of human sex and procreation is shaped by human, social intervention and satisfied in a conventional manner." [19] Like the mode of production, which is for both Rubin and Mitchell also a basic element of society, the sex/gender system is socially constructed and changes historically.

Kinship and family organization form the core of a given society's sex/gender system. The specifics vary cross-culturally and historically, but the sex/gender system includes

1. *The social creation of two dichotomous genders from biological sex.* This involves an exaggeration of differences—or a suppression of similarities—between women and men.

2. *A particular sexual division of labor.* Although the specifics vary, all societies allocate at least some tasks by sex, a practice that divides men and women, exacerbates differences, and makes men and women dependent on one another.

3. *The social regulation of sexuality.* Although there is wide cross-cultural variation in the forms of sexuality prescribed or repressed, the sexual division of labor works against sexual arrangements other than those containing at least one woman and one man, and thereby enjoins heterosexual union.

Thus Rubin argues that there are close and systematic ties between the creation of two genders, the sexual division of labor, and compulsory heterosexuality—all components of the sex/gender system, a system that underlies family arrangements.

All sex/gender systems thus far have been organized asymmetrically, in ways oppressive to women. In the organization of kinship, men recurringly exercise rights over women's sexuality and reproduction, and "women do not have the same rights either to themselves or to their male kin." [20] Furthermore, the oppression of homosexuals results from the same system that oppresses women. Rubin calls for a transformation of sex/ gender systems based on sexism, socially imposed differences of gender, and obligatory sexualities.

In *The Reproduction of Mothering*, Nancy Chodorow explores the consequences of a specific feature of the sex/gender system: Women mother. That is, women provide primary care to infants and young children. This sexual division of labor sets up a different developmental experience for girls than for boys, creates gender-specific personalities (men tend to undervalue connections with others, while women are excessively preoccupied with relatedness), and encourages men's devaluation of women. Chodorow demonstrates complex relations between gender and generation, the structures that underlie the family. Chodorow's analysis of the social creation of gender—and that of other feminists such as Dorothy Dinnerstein [21]—assumes the structuring of generation, the other basic axis

of the family. Feminists have emphasized gender much more than generation, however. As Chodorow and Contratto suggest in their essay,
feminist theories of the family would both enrich and be enriched by more
careful attention to childhood itself and to other age-defined stages of life.

In developing their analyses, Rubin, Chodorow, Mitchell, and other
feminist theorists have drawn on earlier social theories, especially those of
Lévi-Strauss, Freud, and Marx. But in reworking social theory, feminists
have questioned, rather than assumed or taken for granted, the sexual
division of labor, male dominance, and obligatory heterosexuality. By
pursuing the implications of gender as a basic category of analysis,
feminists have made important contributions to family theory.

The Differentiation of Family Experiences

Because families take shape around underlying structures and interpretations of gender and age, women, men, and children of different sexes do
not experience their families in the same way. This differentiation of
experience, a basic tenet of feminist writings on the family, is distorted or
denied by various conceptualizations that recur in literature on the family:

1. Some studies assume a harmony of interests among all family
members. For example, demographers use the term "family decision"
to refer to decisions about limiting family size, a usage which
obscures the long history of conflict between the sexes over reproductive control, a conflict described by Linda Gordon in her paper.[22]

2. Although they pay attention to the behavior of individuals within
the family, some studies do not consider the relevance of gender and
age. For example, "family violence" is sometimes portrayed as "a
series of assaults perpetrated by one individual upon another,"[23]
ignoring the crucial fact that violence runs along lines of power, and
that adult women and children are more often the victims of "family
violence" than are adult men.

3. Gender is sometimes mentioned incidentally without regard for its
systematic relevance. In *Critical Theory of the Family*, Mark Poster
defines age and sex as central axes of the family, but most of his book
focuses on relations of parents and children without taking account of
gender.[24]

4. Specific gender assumptions are often masked beneath non-
genderized language. In *Haven in a Heartless World*, Christopher Lasch
usually means "father" when he writes "parent," and "son" when he
writes "child."[25]

5. "Family" is sometimes tacitly equated with "mother," neglecting
the presence of varied family members and their relations with one
another. Thus, David Spiegel observes that in much of the literature

on families and mental illness, "family is a code word for mother," and father-child interactions are ignored.

Feminists argue that the specifics of daily family living—the allocation of tasks, experiences of work and leisure, the giving and receiving of nurturance, conflicts and episodes of violence, decisions about employment or moving or consumption or family size—cannot be adequately understood without systematic attention to underlying structures of gender and age. Women's experiences of the family have been buried by the use of overarching, homogeneous units of analysis such as "the household" and "the family"; by a tendency to equate women with family, while men are allowed a separate and individualized status; and by the hegemony of male experience of families, as evidenced in Lasch's book and in much of the writing of Freud and Horkeimer.[26]

It is not that women have been invisible in studies of the family, as they have been in past studies of politics and paid work, but that women's experiences of the family have been distorted. Three themes that infuse popular and academic portrayals of contemporary families have especially mystified women's experiences: the glorification of motherhood, the emphasis on love and consensus as the basis of family relations, and the notion of the family as a domestic refuge and haven.

Motherhood and the Experiences of Mothering

At least since the nineteenth century, motherhood has been glorified as women's chief vocation and central definition.[27] The tie between mother and child has been exalted, and traits of nurturance, selflessness, and altruism have been defined as the essence of the maternal, and hence, of the womanly. Nineteenth-century feminists, as Linda Gordon vividly illustrates in her discussion of the Voluntary Motherhood movement, not only took for granted the definition of women as primary child rearers but also drew on idealized images of motherhood as a basis for moral reform.

In contrast, contemporary feminists have challenged the definition of women by their reproductive status and have argued, as Juliet Mitchell has written, that when motherhood is used as a mystique, "it becomes an instrument of oppression."[28] The contemporary women's movement has worked to give women a choice *not* to mother—hence, struggles for birth control and abortion rights and for legitimation of forms of sexuality, including lesbianism, separated from reproduction. Feminists have emphasized the right of all women, whether or not they are mothers, to have access to activities beyond motherhood—hence, efforts to bring women into an equal position in the labor force and to diminish their ideological encapsulation by the family. Feminists have demystified motherhood by documenting examples of unfavorable conditions of childbirth as it has been organized by the predominantly male medical profession and by pointing to the darker, often unspoken experiences of motherhood: isolation and a degree of absorption in one's children that evokes excessive guilt and that may be damaging to mother and child. Feminists have challenged the division of labor that isolates mothers as full-time parents and separates fathers from children, and they have pressed for extensive reorganization of arrangements of child care through proposals for equal male involvement, flexible work hours, and widely accessible day care.

Recently, however, feminist discussions of motherhood have taken a new turn. In their essay, Nancy Chodorow and Susan Contratto discuss what seems to be a new stage in the feminist rethinking of motherhood. Feminists have turned from questions of choice and external conditions to the experience of motherhood itself. Chodorow and Contratto review an array of feminist writings about the experience of mothering—by Adrienne Rich, Shulamith Firestone, Dorothy Dinnerstein, Alice Rossi, Kate Millett, Jane Lazarre—and cull out underlying and shared assumptions. They argue that there is a startling convergence between the assumptions these feminists make about mothering and those made by more conservative writers like Selma Fraiberg. Both groups share an extreme, larger-than-life picture of mothers as all-powerful, with an omnipotence embodied either in perfection (or perfectability) or in destruction and death. Chodorow and Contratto trace the ideological roots of this picture and call for more realistic explorations of mothering, for an understanding that mothers have lives, needs, activities, and relationships apart from, interacting with, and sometimes contradicting the tasks of motherhood. They also observe that the actual voices of mothers are often missing in writings on motherhood.

Chodorow and Contratto's criticisms of recent writings on motherhood clear the way for Sara Ruddick's essay, "Maternal Thinking." Ruddick avoids the exaggerated portrayals of mothering that Chodorow and Contratto have criticized and starts instead with the daily practices of mothering. These practices are governed by an interest in preserving the life of the child, fostering the child's growth, and shaping a child who will be socially acceptable. Ruddick reflects upon the qualities of thought fostered by the daily practices of mothering. She is sensitive both to the positive sensibilities that emerge from "acting in the interests of preservation and growth" and the danger of opting for "inauthentic obedience to dominant patriarchal values," a danger that shows the need to transform maternal thought with feminist consciousness.

Relations Between the Sexes: The Tangle of Love and Domination

Women's and men's experiences of the family have been obscured not only by the glorification of motherhood but also by beliefs that relations between husbands and wives are mainly a matter of love and consensus. According to the functionalist account, with the development of industrialization, parents came to play a diminished role in selecting mates for their children, husbands lost much of the legal and material basis of their authority over their wives, and marriages increasingly were founded on love. Much of the sociological literature portrays contemporary marriage as an arrangement of love between equals, or near equals, using terms like "the companionate marriage," "egalitarian marriage," and "the symmetrical family."

Feminists, along with other critics of the family,[29] have put forth a different picture of relations between wives and husbands. Instead of love and companionship, they have emphasized patterns of inequality and conflict. Shulamith Firestone helped initiate this shift of vision; she argued that love is "the pivot of women's oppression today" because love between the sexes is "complicated, corrupted, or obstructed by an unequal balance of power."[30]

Men's greater power is evident in patterns of communication between husbands and wives,[31] in processes of family decision making,[32] and, in extreme form, in incidents of wife abuse. As William Goode has argued, the power of parents over children, and husbands over wives, is ultimately backed by force.[33] The least powerful members of families—children and women—are the most likely to be victims of violence. The women's movement has made wife abuse visible as a serious social problem; wife beating has been documented in all social classes and ethnic groups and is believed to be one of the most common and underreported of violent crimes.[34] That women, as well as men, physically abuse children also needs emphasis as one attempts to sort out complex patterns of dominance within families.

What is the source of men's power and women's subordination? This question, posed in general and in ways specific to the family, is the focus of considerable debate. Socialist feminists[35] emphasize men's control of women's labor within and outside the family—the personalized services women provide their husbands through housework and women's continuing economic dependence because of their sporadic patterns of employment, lower wages, and secondary position in the paid economy. Men's economic control of women persists, although earlier patterns have been undermined by the spread of individual wage labor under capitalism.[36]

While socialist feminists emphasize changing historical patterns in men's control of production and of women's labor, radical feminists[37] emphasize men's control of women's bodies as basic to "the patriarchy," a term they use to refer to male dominance throughout history.[38] The term is stark and blunt, and it focuses on the pervasive quality of men's power, enacted through the threat of violence and through control of women's sexuality and reproduction. Radical feminists have helped call attention to rape, wife battering, the sexual objectification of women, enforced sterilization, and men's control of women's access to birth control and abortion.

Women are not passive victims. They often resist men's control, developing their own forms of power and means of struggle. Like analyses of class and race domination, writings on sexual inequality often slide into portraying subordinates as victims instead of tracing the complexities of relations between the sexes. The complex dialectic of men's control and women's efforts to combat and circumvent it is revealed in a concrete way in Ann Whitehead's ethnography of cross-sex and same-sex relations in a rural working-class community in England.[39] The larger context of work, kinship, and friendship patterns provides fresh insight into conflict between husbands and wives.

In his essay, William Goode asks "why men resist" women's demands for equality. Observing that "we must never underestimate either the cunning or the staying power of those in charge," he compares the position of men with that of other dominant groups. Like whites or those of dominant social classes, men often "are not aware of how much the social structure yields advantages for them," and they "view small losses of deference, or advantages, or opportunities as large threats." The structural position of males is also different from that of groups that dominate on the basis of class or race. Because of heterosexual family arrangements, women and men are separated from their own sex-kind and develop mutual caring and shared stakes; whereas class and race groups are more spatially, materially, and emotionally separated from one another.

Goode observes that men's dominance over women, especially within the family, is intertwined with intimacy and mutual dependence. Feminists have helped specify the contradictions this entails, not only for struggles over power but also for experiences of intimacy and love. Firestone,[40] Chodorow,[41] and others have pointed to contradictions between men's and women's emotional needs. Chodorow argues that the fact that women do the primary parenting results in deep sex differences in personality. Men tend to have more rigid ego boundaries and to be more emotionally self-contained; women are more interdependent, defining themselves in relation to others. This leads the sexes to seek different kinds of love, to become entangled in what Chodorow calls "heterosexual knots." An understanding of gender divisions helps account for the difficult, often antagonistic relations between husbands and wives portrayed in studies of specific families.[42]

A Domestic Refuge for Whom? The Discovery of Housework

The ideologies of maternal and romantic love both suggest that the modern family, at its core, is defined by emotions. In the Parsonian version, the nuclear family, stripped of its productive functions, now specializes in socializing children and in the emotional sustenance of its members, with wives bearing the major burden for "socio-emotional" support. This is an updated version of a nineteenth-century ideology that portrayed the family as a refuge from a harsh outer world, a place of love rather than work.

Again differentiating the experiences of various family members, feminists have asked: For whom is the home a refuge, a nurturant haven? For men, who do far less housework than women, the home indeed may be experienced as a refuge, or at least as a place of leisure. But for almost all women, the home is a place of considerable work. Time budget studies [43] reveal a consistent pattern of women doing much more housework than men. Wives with full-time employment put in an additional 26 to 35 hours a week doing housework. Their husbands do the same or only slightly more housework—averaging between 10 and 14 hours a week— than men whose wives are full-time homemakers. Feminists cite these figures with a sense of injustice, arguing that there is a "politics of housework," [44] that the sexual division of labor, especially as more and more women enter the labor force, is fraught with male privilege, places an unfair burden on women, and should be changed.

The women's movement has helped establish housework as an important topic for research and for political action. Attention has been given to the nature of the work, which is often menial, repetitive, and done in isolation. Housework is less visible than paid work and yields little social status and no economic independence. In "Home Production for Use in a Market Economy," Clair Brown contrasts the small-scale, personalized home economy with the more efficient, large-scale, and impersonal market economy. In the last fifty years housework has declined in relative importance as a proportion of consumption activities undertaken by family members, leading to a further decline in the perceived value of housework and of the homemaker's bargaining power within her family. There has also been a decline in average household size and a subsequent loss of economies of scale, both in the time and the money needed to provide the essentials of setting up and running a household.

Housework has several guises, which have yet to be integrated into a coherent theory. As a form of labor, housework is connected with the organization of the larger economy. Under this guise, housework may be understood as a means by which the wage labor force is maintained and reproduced, to the benefit of capitalists (an argument Rayna Rapp reviews in her paper). Housework is also closely entwined with the internal emotional lives of families. As Clair Brown notes, housework is personalized and on-call, and much of it cannot be replaced by purchased goods. Housework involves a complex array of activities that sometimes conflict with one another: nurturing family members and personalized care in providing food, clothing, and shelter. Women are much more often the providers, and men and children the recipients, of these personalized services. Thus patterns of sexual inequality—men's privileges, and women's often unmet needs for nurturance and leisure time—are also central to the organization of housework.

Is the Family Isolated and Set Apart? The Question of Boundaries

The notion of the family as a domestic refuge presumes sharp boundaries between the family and the rest of society. As Brown demonstrates with historical data about changing household size, there *has* been a trend to smaller, more physically isolated household units. Feminists have emphasized the negative effects of this isolation on the mental state of housewives,[45] on relations between mothers and children,[46] and on the ability of women to develop shared consciousness as an oppressed group.

On the other hand, some feminists, especially socialist feminists, have joined those who argue that the private, self-supporting family is an ideology, a cultural ideal, that obscures variations by social class and continuing relations between families, the economy, and the state. In her essay, Rayna Rapp observes that nuclear families "are under cultural constraints to *appear* as autonomous and private." But the independence may be more a matter of appearance than reality because there are class-based differences in the abilities of households to realize the ideal of autonomy and self-support.

Rapp draws on empirical studies of contemporary families to demonstrate such differences. The black ghetto households described by Carol Stack[47] survive on welfare and through wide networks of exchange centered around female kin. They do not experience a split between "private" and "public." In the working-class families Lillian Rubin interviewed, households are more physically isolated and self-contained, and family members experience a sharp separation between private life and external wage labor that maintains the home.[48] There are, however, ongoing relations between home and paid work. Although the family is seen as an escape from production, men and women are bound to their jobs out of the family's need for economic survival, and in many ways—evident, for example, in power relations between husbands and wives and in their use of leisure time—the nature of paid work shapes the daily experience of families. Moreover, activities in the home (housework, consumption, child care), which are mostly done by women, serve to maintain and reproduce the labor force. Among middle-class corporate managers and professionals, the resource base of households is more stable; and when they need

exceptional economic resources, families can turn to nonfamilial institutions such as pension plans or bank credit. Wives provide unpaid support
services for their husbands' careers, for example, by entertaining or by
doing unpaid secretarial work for them at home.[49] Through community
activities and the work of consumption, middle-class wives contribute to
and display the family's social status.[50]

These social-class variations, which also entail differences in men's
and women's experiences of the family, challenge any simple understanding of the family as isolated and set apart from the rest of society. As Rapp
argues, families are in continuous interaction with other institutions, such
as work organizations, the welfare system, and schools.

In "The Place of the Family in the Origins of the Welfare State," Eli
Zaretsky argues against a widespread view that the modern welfare state
emerged by displacing the family as the main agent of social reproduction.
This linear view is held by functionalists such as Parsons, who theorize
about "modernization" and the increasing specialization of institutions,
and by Christopher Lasch, who defends the family against what he re-
gards as an historical "invasion" by the state. Zaretsky argues that this
view reifies both "the family" and "the state" and that the opposition
between state and family was established only with the emergence of
market capitalism in the early nineteenth century. Zaretsky demonstrates
the shifting and interactive—rather than linear—relationship of families
and the state through an analysis of state policies toward families. In
varying ways, state policies have continued to assume and even to
strengthen the family as a private economic unit. Thus Progressive era
reforms such as protective legislation for working women, child labor
legislation, and the family wage were designed to shore up the "normal"
self-supporting family, a family ideal that included a male breadwinner
and a woman whose main work was rearing children and maintaining the
home.

Nineteenth-century feminists took for granted a separation of the
spheres of family and paid work, of private and public life. Contemporary
feminists have challenged this dichotomy. By questioning the equation of
women and family, and by seeking to uncover women's—and men's—
experiences in their entirety,[51] feminists have moved beyond a bounded
understanding of women *and* of the family. With more and more women
in the paid labor force, for example, to understand women's lives is to
uncover relationships between family and paid work. I have already mentioned some of these relationships: Women's responsibility for mothering
and housework undermines their participation in paid labor, as does the
family ideology used to justify the sex segregation of the labor force and
women's subordinate economic position. This subordinated economic position, in turn, perpetuates women's dependence on men within families

and reinforces an unequal domestic division of labor. In tracing relationships of this kind, feminists have begun to develop analyses that transcend divisions like family and work or private and public.[52]

The Ambivalence Between Family and Market, Nurturance and Individualism

Although many feminists have begun to seek a more unitary understanding of gender relations, a sense of dualism remains basic to much feminist thinking about the family and other social institutions. The dualism touches on deep moral and emotional themes, on questions of judgment and value concerning the modern world. It is widely believed that relationships created and sustained in the family are different from those in the outer world, especially in the capitalist market. As Collier, Rosaldo, and Yanagisako phrase it, the family has come to represent nurturing, enduring, and noncontingent relations governed by feelings of morality. In contrast, market relations are characterized as impersonal, competitive, contractual, and temporary.[53] This division is often seen as one of gender: Women are equated with the family and defined as nurturers; men are associated with the market, with competition and impersonality.

As I have indicated, most feminists tend to emphasize the underside of this view of the family, calling attention to the oppression, conflict, and violence hidden behind a portrait of love and nurturance. Nurturance and altruism have been required more of women than of men, and women have paid a heavy price in being defined exclusively by motherhood and self-sacrifice. Feminists have claimed women's right to break from their embeddedness in the family, to seek full individualism and equality. In her essay, Renate Bridenthal observes that "feminists have opened a whole new vista by asking, *not what do women do for the family* (an older question), *but what does the family do for women?* What does it do *to* women?" This shift of consciousness, this demand for individualism and equality—an ideal derived from liberalism and the marketplace—is central to the women's movement.

There is another strand in feminist thinking, which Linda Gordon calls "the critique of the man-made society, the refusal to accept merely integration of female individuals into a competition whose rules we did not define and do not endorse. There is, in fact, a tradition of feminist criticism of capitalism itself, representing it as the opposite of the nurturing values of motherhood." This tradition was strong among "social housekeeping" feminists in the late nineteenth century who saw themselves spreading maternal nurturance into the larger world. An affirmation of women as intrinsically different from men, as more nurturant and mutually caring, is also central to the writings of contemporary radical feminists who, like Adrienne Rich,[54] affirm nurturant bonds among women as an alternative and challenge to patriarchal relations.

Several essays in this volume draw on women's connection to the family as a basis for criticizing market-based individualism while affirming women's right to full and equal access to the public world. Sara Ruddick argues that special qualities of thought, such as "attentive love," are developed through the practice of mothering and that such maternal thinking should be respected and—transformed by feminist consciousness—brought into the public world. Along similar lines, Clair Brown contrasts the home economy (based on the concept of mutual aid and service to others) with the market economy (a competitive economy rewarding the individual), and argues that the cooperative values of the family should be affirmed. David Spiegel also affirms the positive nature of the family as a bulwark against and a source of cure for—rather than solely a cause of—mental illness. And Susan Westerberg Prager discusses conflicts between individualistic and sharing principles in marital property law and argues for the value of family-based sharing.

This feminist affirmation of family-based "womanly qualities" involves a perplexing dilemma, as Eli Zaretsky eloquently notes: "It is a tragic paradox that the bases of love, dependence and altruism in human life and the historical oppression of women have been found in the same matrix." How can we, as feminists wanting to affirm values of equality, *and* of cooperation and concern for human needs, sort out this paradox, which lies at the heart of our efforts to create a better society?

Our efforts at rethinking and making social change can benefit from a close examination of contemporary "defenses of the family," which also vacillate between values of individualism and family-based nurturance. Unlike the feminist ambivalence, such defenses turn to the family as a retreat from, rather than a potential challenge of, the "heartless" world of the market. As Linda Gordon and Allen Hunter have suggested in a probing analysis of the New Right,[55] concern about the future of the family is often concern about the fate of care giving and nurturance, about values and needs denied and undermined by the fragmentation and impersonality fostered by capitalism. Rather than challenge capitalist and patriarchal arrangements in the public sphere, however, defenders of the family retreat to an idealized family with the nurturant mother as its symbolic core. They demand that the family, and women, make up for everything the indifferent and hostile outer world refuses to do.[56] The family that the New Right and Christopher Lasch defend is an idealized, middle-class, patriarchal family, a family predicated on male authority, heterosexuality, and romantic notions of motherhood. This family ideal denies women individualism, equality, and full access to economic and political resources.

Rather than defend "the family" as an unquestioned ideal, feminists seek a more realistic and complex understanding that is part of a larger program of social change. Our attention to the supportive and nurturant, as well as the oppressive, sides of families is not just an ambivalence; it points to a series of contradictions with which we are struggling in an effort to create a better society. I sometimes think of feminist contributions to rethinking the family, and other institutions, using the metaphor of a patterned piece of cloth. We have located a thread—the sex/gender system and patterns of sexual inequality—previously barely visible in the design. By pulling the thread, through feminist analysis and action, we have revealed that arrangements of gender and male dominance are a central part of the larger pattern. Once brought to view, that systematic thread alters the overall gestalt. But the pattern is complex, and we have yet to sort out adequately, for example, the relation of gender to age, social class, and race. We have yet to understand adequately the mix of domination and nurturance, conflict and supportiveness, within contemporary families, taken in all their variety. This complexity bears on the task ahead, as Linda Gordon notes, in arguing that we should keep the oppressive dimensions of modern families clearly in view and struggle against them, while also recognizing their supportive possibilities, which may point to a larger vision of human community. She concludes that the general task of feminism is "to defend all the gains of bourgeois individualism and liberal feminism, while transcending the capitalist-competitive aspects of individualism with a vision of loving, egalitarian communities."

Our rethinking of the family necessarily extends beyond a close consideration of what exists to careful thought and imagining about what might be. In envisioning and working to create a better world, we will necessarily have to transcend a separation between private and public, or family and society. The problems feminists have revealed in the family—women's subordination, conflicts between the sexes, the creation of sex-typed personalities in children—are also anchored in the organization of paid work, legal institutions, the schools. And the fragmentation and isolation that many call a "family crisis" is, in fact, a social crisis of much larger proportions whose solution will require changing the whole of social, economic, and political life.

Notes

1. The essays by Nancy Chodorow and Susan Contratto, Sara Ruddick, and Rayna Rapp were not part of the lecture series but were included to enhance the array of topics and perspectives in the book.

2. For example, Mark Poster, *Critical Theory of the Family* (New York: Seabury, 1978); D. H. J. Morgan, *Social Theory and the Family* (Boston: Routledge and Kegan Paul, 1975); and Arlene S. Skolnick and Jerome H. Skolnick, eds., *Family in Transition* (New York: Little, Brown, 1971).

3. Arguments such as the following can be found, in more complexity, in Juliet Mitchell, "Women: The Longest Revolution," *New Left Review* 40 (November/December 1966): 11–37; Jessie Bernard, *The Future of Marriage* (New York: Bantam, 1973); and Heidi Hartmann, "Capitalism, Patriarchy, and Job Segregation by Sex," *Signs: Journal of Women in Culture and Society* 1, no. 3, pt. 2. (Spring 1976): 137–70.

4. Data from U.S. Department of Commerce, Bureau of the Census, *Statistical Abstract of the United States* (Washington, D.C.: U.S. Government Printing Office, 1977).

5. The demystification of the monolithic family has helped bring attention to the variety of sexual, reproductive, and household arrangements not only in present U.S. society but also in other times and places. Partly because of domestic cycles and social and economic stratification, all societies contain multiple family forms. In *Women, Work, and Family* (New York: Holt, Rinehart and Winston, 1978), Louise Tilly and Joan Scott document and trace the implications of family variation for the lives of women of different ages and social classes in England and France in the last 250 years. Their study is an example of recent pathbreaking research on the family that has been inspired by feminist questions.

6. Nancy Chodorow, *The Reproduction of Mothering* (Berkeley, Calif.: University of California Press, 1978).

7. The nature of heterosexuality as a social institution rather than a biological given has also been opened for fresh analysis. A recent, insightful example of such rethinking is by Adrienne Rich, "Compulsory Heterosexuality and Lesbian Existence," *Signs: Journal of Women in Culture and Society* 5 (Spring 1980): 631–60. Rich challenges the assumption—widespread in feminist as well as other writing—that heterosexuality is "natural." She demonstrates the pressures and coercion toward heterosexuality built into the social and political organization of sexual ideologies (professional, pornographic), marriage, paid employment.

8. E. O. Wilson, *Sociobiology: The New Synthesis* (Cambridge, Mass.: Harvard University Press, 1975).

9. David Barash, *Sociobiology and Behavior* (New York: Elsevier, 1977).

10. For useful criticisms of sociobiology, see Arthur L. Caplan, ed., *The Sociobiology Debate* (New York: Harper & Row, 1978); and Ruth Hubbard and Marian Lowe, eds., *Genes and Gender: Pitfalls in Research on Sex and Gender*, vol. 2 (Staten Island, N.Y.: Gordian, 1979).

11. Marian Lowe, "Viewpoint: Sociobiology and Sex Differences," *Signs: Journal of Women in Culture and Society* 4, no. 1 (Autumn 1978): 119.

12. Talcott Parsons, *Social Structure and Personality* (New York: Free Press, 1970); and Talcott Parsons and Robert F. Bales, *Family, Socialization and Interaction Process* (New York: Free Press, 1955).

13. For more detailed criticisms of role theory as applied to analyses of gender, see Barrie Thorne, "Gender . . . How Is It Best Conceptualized?" in *Issues in Sex, Gender and Society*, eds. Laurel Richardson and Verta Taylor (Lexington, Mass.: D. C. Heath, 1981).

14. Ellen Ross, "Examining Family History: Women and Family," *Feminist Studies* 5, no. 1 (Spring 1979): 188.

15. Alice S. Rossi, "A Biosocial Perspective on Parenting," *Daedalus* 106, no. 2 (Spring 1979): 1–32.

16. On the basis of a vote of its membership, the American Sociological Association Research Section on Sex Roles recently changed its name to the Section on Sex and Gender.

17. Mitchell, "Women: The Longest Revolution," p. 20.

18. Gayle Rubin, "The Traffic in Women: Notes on the 'Political Economy' of Sex," in *Toward an Anthropology of Women*, ed. Rayna R. Reiter (New York: Monthly Review Press, 1975), pp. 157–210.

19. Ibid., p. 165.

20. Ibid., p. 172.

21. Dorothy Dinnerstein, *The Mermaid and the Minotaur* (New York: Harper & Row, 1976).

22. Ross, "Examining Family History," makes this criticism of the language used by demographers.

23. Colleen McGrath, "The Crisis of the Domestic Order," *Socialist Review* 43, no. 1 (1979): 17.

24. This criticism of Poster's book is beautifully developed in Ellen Ross, "Rethinking 'The Family,'" *Radical History Review* 20 (Spring/Summer 1979): 76–84.

25. Christopher Lasch, *Haven in a Heartless World* (New York: Basic, 1977).

26. For example, Max Horkheimer, "Authority and the Family," in *Critical Theory* (English ed.; New York: Herder and Herder, 1972).

27. See Ruth H. Bloch, "American Feminine Ideals in Transition: The Rise of the Moral Mother, 1785–1815," *Feminist Studies* 4, no. 2 (June 1978): 101–26.

28. Mitchell, "Women: The Longest Revolution," p. 28.

29. Lasch, *Haven in a Heartless World*, discusses sociological writings on the family dating back to the 1920s that *do* take account of conflict (e.g., the work of Willard Waller in the 1930s). Freud was certainly alert to family conflict, as were Horkheimer, Laing, and other family theorists. David Spiegel's paper reviews interpretations of the family as a cause of mental illness, which are found in the writings of Freud, Laing, Bateson, and others. I do not claim that recent feminists discovered that families are scenes of conflict and domination, but rather that feminists have emphasized that side of family life. Freud and Laing emphasize the domination of parents over children, while feminists are more sensitive to sexual inequality as a source of domination and conflict.

30. Shulamith Firestone, *The Dialectic of Sex* (New York: Morrow, 1970), p. 130.

31. Pamela Fishman, in "Interaction: The Work Women Do," *Social Problems* 25, no. 4 (1978): 397–406, provides a vivid study of male control and female deference in conversations of couples at home. She analyzed 52 hours of taped conversations of three couples and found that men controlled the conversation (i.e., which topics were pursued), while women did more of the "interaction work" of asking questions and providing verbal support. In *Body Politics: Power, Sex, and Nonverbal Communication* (Englewood Cliffs., N.J.: Prentice-Hall, 1977), Nancy Henley documents a general asymmetric pattern in men's and women's use of talk, touch, space, time, eye contact, and demeanor, a pattern that conveys men's dominance and women's subordination. Colin Bell and Howard Newby, in "Husbands and Wives: The Dynamics of the Deferential Dialectic," in *Dependence and Exploitation in Work and Marriage*, eds. Diana Leonard Barker and Sheila Allen (New York: Longman, 1976), pp. 152–68, write of the "deferential dialectic" between wives and husbands.

32. Research studies often measure marital power by the relative weight of each spouse in the making of decisions. This research tradition has many methodological and conceptual flaws, including the use of analytic frameworks that stress the individual and neglect structural bases of inequality. For a good overall critique, see Constantina Safilios-Rothschild, "The Study of Family Power Structure: A Review of 1960–1969," *Journal of Marriage and the Family* 32 (1970): 539–52. In a feminist reinterpretation of the literature on marital power, Dair Gillespie, in "Who Has the Power? The Marital Struggle," *Journal of Marriage and the Family* 33 (1971): 445–58, identifies the legal, economic, educational, and physical bases of greater male power.

33. William J. Goode, "Force and Violence in the Family," *Journal of Marriage and the Family* 33 (1971): 624–36.

34. McGrath, "The Crisis of the Domestic Order"; Del Martin, *Battered Wives* (San Francisco: Glide Publications, 1976).

35. For example, Hartmann, "Capitalism, Patriarchy, and Job Segregation by Sex"; and Barbara Easton, "Feminism and the Contemporary Family," *Socialist Review* 39, vol. 8, no. 3 (1978): 11–36.

36. Easton, ibid.; Linda Gordon and Allen Hunter, "Sex, Family and the New Right: Anti-Feminism as a Political Force," *Radical America* 11 and 12, nos. 6 and 1 (November 1977/February 1978 combined issue): 9–26.

37. For example, Mary Daly, *Gyn/Ecology: The Metaethics of Radical Feminism* (Boston: Beacon, 1978); Adrienne Rich, *Of Woman Born* (New York: Norton, 1976); and idem, *On Lies, Secrets, and Silence* (New York: Norton, 1979).

38. Joan Kelly, in "The Doubled Vision of Feminist Theory: A Postscript to the 'Women and Power' Conference," *Feminist Studies* 5, no. 1 (Spring 1979) 216–27, makes this summary distinction in clarifying the contributions of radical feminism and socialist feminism. She also urges the need for a more unified theory that can encompass both the "private" (sexual/reproductive) and "public" (socioeconomic) domains.

39. Ann Whitehead, "Sexual Antagonism in Herefordshire," in *Dependence and Exploitation in Work and Marriage*, eds. Diana Leonard Barker and Sheila Allen (New York: Longman, 1976), pp. 169–203.

40. Firestone, *The Dialectic of Sex.*

41. Nancy Chodorow, "Oedipal Asymmetries and Heterosexual Knots," *Social Problems* 28, no. 4 (1976): 454–68.

42. For example, Mirra Komarovsky, *Blue-Collar Marriage* (New York: Random House, 1962); Bernard, *The Future of Marriage;* Lillian Rubin, *Worlds of Pain: Life in the Working-Class Family* (New York: Basic, 1976); and Whitehead, "Sexual Antagonism in Herefordshire."

43. For example, Joann Vanek, "Time Spent in Housework," *Scientific American,* November 1974, pp. 116–20; and Joseph Pleck, "Men's Family Work: Three Perspectives and Some New Data," *Family Coordinator* 28 (1979): 481–88.

44. Pat Mainardi, "The Politics of Housework," in *Sisterhood Is Powerful,* ed. Robin Morgan (New York: Vintage, 1970), pp. 447–55.

45. For example, see Bernard, *The Future of Marriage.*

46. For example, see Chodorow, *The Reproduction of Mothering.*

47. Carol Stack, *All Our Kin: Strategies for Survival in a Black Community* (New York: Harper & Row, 1974).

48. Rubin, *Worlds of Pain.*

49. Rosabeth Moss Kanter, *Men and Women of the Corporation* (New York: Basic, 1977).

50. Hanna Papanek, "Family Status Production: The 'Work' and 'Non-Work' of Women," *Signs: Journal of Women in Culture and Society* 4, no. 4 (Summer 1979): 775–81.

51. Attention to the sex/gender system helps clarify the distinctive experiences of men as well as women. Close analysis of existing knowledge often reveals a paradox: Knowledge generalized as "universal" to some human group is often, implicitly, based more on men's than on women's lives and experiences. Knowledge specified by gender—much of it gathered within the last decade under the impetus of the women's movement—is more often about women than men. Men's experiences *as* men, in families, jobs, and other institutions, are being uncovered by researchers who are sensitive to gender divisions and relations (e.g., Goode in this volume; Rubin, *Worlds of Pain;* and Kanter, *Men and Women of the Corporation*).

52. See Kelly, "The Doubled Vision of Feminist Theory."

53. Unlike other authors in this book, who believe there are actual differences in the types of relationships found in the family and in the market, Collier, Rosaldo, and Yanagisako believe the dichotomy is best understood as a distorting ideology. This ideology obscures counterrealities (e.g., violence) within families, as well as sources of nurturance outside the family.

54. Rich, *On Lies, Secrets, and Silence.*

55. Gordon and Hunter, "Sex, Family and the New Right."

56. Analysis of romantic defenses of the family can also be found in Barbara Ehrenreich and Deirdre English, *For Her Own Good* (New York: Doubleday Anchor, 1979).

JANE COLLIER
MICHELLE Z. ROSALDO
SYLVIA YANAGISAKO

2

Is There a Family?
New Anthropological Views

This essay poses a rhetorical question in order to argue that most of our talk about families is clouded by unexplored notions of what families "really" are like. It is probably the case, universally, that people expect to have special connections with their geneaologically closest relations. But a knowledge of genealogy does not in itself promote understanding of what these special ties are about. The real importance of The Family in contemporary social life and belief has blinded us to its dynamics. Confusing ideal with reality, we fail to appreciate the deep significance of what are, cross-culturally, various ideologies of intimate relationship, and at the same time we fail to reckon with the complex human bonds and experiences all too comfortably sheltered by a faith in the "natural" source of a "nurture" we think is found in the home.

This essay is divided into three parts. The first examines what social scientists mean by The Family. It focuses on the work of Bronislaw Malinowski, the anthropologist who first convinced social scientists that The Family was a universal human institution. The second part also has social scientists as its focus, but it examines works by the nineteenth-century thinkers Malinowski refuted, for if—as we shall argue—Malinowski was wrong in viewing The Family as a universal human institution, it becomes important to explore the work of theorists who did not make Malinowski's mistakes. The final section then draws on the correct insights of nineteenth-century theorists to sketch some implications of viewing The Family, not as a concrete institution designed to fulfill universal human needs, but as an ideological construct associated with the modern state.

Malinowski's Concept of the Family

In 1913 Bronislaw Malinowski published a book called *The Family Among the Australian Aborigines* [1] in which he laid to rest earlier debates about whether all human societies had families. During the nineteenth century,

proponents of social evolution argued that primitives were sexually pro-
miscuous and therefore incapable of having families because children
would not recognize their fathers.[2] Malinowski refuted this notion by
showing that Australian aborigines, who were widely believed to practice
"primitive promiscuity," not only had rules regulating who might have
intercourse with whom during sexual orgies but also differentiated between legal marriages and casual unions. Malinowski thus "proved" that
Australian aborigines had marriage, and so proved that aboriginal children
had fathers, because each child's mother had but a single recognized husband.

Malinowski's book did not simply add data to one side of an ongoing
debate. It ended the debate altogether, for by distinguishing coitus from
conjugal relationships, Malinowski separated questions of sexual behavior
from questions of the family's universal existence. Evidence of sexual
promiscuity was henceforth irrelevant for deciding whether families
existed. Moreover, Malinowski argued that the conjugal relationship, and
therefore The Family, had to be universal because it fulfilled a universal
human need. As he wrote in a posthumously published book:

> The human infant needs parental protection for a much longer
> period than does the young of even the highest anthropoid apes.
> Hence, no culture could endure in which the act of repro-
> duction, that is, mating, pregnancy, and childbirth, was not
> linked up with the fact of legally-founded parenthood, that is, a
> relationship in which the father and mother have to look after the
> children for a long period, and, in turn, derive certain benefits
> from the care and trouble taken.[3]

In proving the existence of families among Australian aborigines,
Malinowski described three features of families that he believed flowed
from The Family's universal function of nurturing children. First, he
argued that families had to have clear boundaries, for if families were to
perform the vital function of nurturing young children, insiders had to be
distinguishable from outsiders so that everyone could know which adults
were responsible for the care of which children. Malinowski thus argued
that families formed bounded social units, and to prove that Australian
families formed such units, he demonstrated that aboriginal parents and
children recognized one another. Each aboriginal woman had a single
husband, even if some husbands had more than one wife and even if
husbands occasionally allowed wives to sleep with other men during tribal
ceremonies. Malinowski thus proved that each aboriginal child had a recognized mother and father, even if both parents occasionally engaged in
sexual relations with outsiders.

Second, Malinowski argued that families had to have a place where family members could be together and where the daily tasks associated with child rearing could be performed. He demonstrated, for example, that aboriginal parents and their immature children shared a single fire—a home and hearth where children were fed and nurtured—even though, among nomadic aborigines, the fire might be kindled in a different location each night.

Finally, Malinowski argued that family members felt affection for one another—that parents who invested long years in caring for children were rewarded by their own and their children's affections for one another. Malinowski felt that long and intimate association among family members fostered close emotional ties, particularly between parents and children, but also between spouses. Aboriginal parents and their children, for example, could be expected to feel the same emotions for one another as did English parents and children, and as proof of this point, Malinowski recounted touching stories of the efforts made by aboriginal parents to recover children lost during conflicts with other aborigines or with white settlers and efforts made by stolen aboriginal children to find their lost parents.

Malinowski's book on Australian aborigines thus gave social scientists a concept of The Family that consisted of a universal function, the nurturance of young children, mapped onto (1) a bounded set of people who recognized one another and who were distinguishable from other like groups; (2) a definite physical space, a hearth and home; and (3) a particular set of emotions, family love. This concept of The Family as an institution for nurturing young children has been enduring, probably because nurturing children is thought to be the primary function of families in modern industrial societies. The flaw in Malinowski's argument is the flaw common to all functionalist arguments: Because a social institution is observed to perform a necessary function does not mean either that the function would not be performed if the institution did not exist or that the function is responsible for the existence of the institution.

Later anthropologists have challenged Malinowski's idea that families always include fathers, but, ironically, they have kept all the other aspects of his definition. For example, later anthropologists have argued that the basic social unit is not the nuclear family including father but the unit composed of a mother and her children: "Whether or not a mate becomes attached to the mother on some more or less permanent basis is a variable matter."[4] In removing father from the family, however, later anthropologists have nevertheless retained Malinowski's concept of The Family as a functional unit, and so have retained all the features Malinowski took such pains to demonstrate. In the writings of modern anthropologists, the mother-child unit is described as performing the universally necessary function of nurturing young children. A mother and her children form a bounded group, distinguishable from other units of mothers and their children. A mother and her children share a place, a home and hearth. And, finally, a mother and her children share deep emotional bonds based on their prolonged and intimate contact.

Modern anthropologists may have removed father from The Family, but they did not modify the basic social science concept of The Family in which the function of child rearing is mapped onto a bounded set of people who share a place and who "love" one another. Yet it is exactly this concept of The Family that we, as feminist anthropologists, have found so difficult to apply. Although the biological facts of reproduction, when combined with a sufficiently elastic definition of marriage, make it possible for us, as social scientists, to find both mother-child units and Malinowski's conjugal-pairs-plus-children units in every human society, it is not at all clear that such Families necessarily exhibit the associated features Malinowski "proved" and modern anthropologists echo.

An outside observer, for example, may be able to delimit family boundaries in any and all societies by identifying the children of one woman and that woman's associated mate, but natives may not be interested in making such distinctions. In other words, natives may not be concerned to distinguish family members from outsiders, as Malinowski imagined natives should be when he argued that units of parents and children have to have clear boundaries in order for child-rearing responsibilities to be assigned efficiently. Many languages, for example, have no word to identify the unit of parents and children that English speakers call a "family." Among the Zinacantecos of southern Mexico, the basic social unit is identified as a "house," which may include from one to twenty people.[5] Zinacantecos have no difficulty talking about an individual's parents, children, or spouse; but Zinacantecos do not have a single word that identifies the unit of parents and children in such a way as to cut it off from other like units. In Zinacanteco society, the boundary between "houses" is linguistically marked, while the boundary between "family" units is not.

Just as some languages lack words for identifying units of parents and children, so some "families" lack places. Immature children in every society have to be fed and cared for, but parents and children do not necessarily eat and sleep together as a family in one place. Among the Mundurucu of tropical South America, for example, the men of a village traditionally lived in a men's house together with all the village boys over the age of thirteen; women lived with other women and young children in two or three houses grouped around the men's house.[6] In Mundurucu society, men and women ate and slept apart. Men ate in the men's house, sharing food the women had cooked and delivered to them; women ate with other women and children in their own houses. Married couples also slept apart, meeting only for sexual intercourse.

Finally, people around the world do not necessarily expect family members to "love" one another. People may expect husbands, wives, parents, and children to have strong feelings about one another, but they do not necessarily expect prolonged and intimate contact to breed the loving sentiments Malinowski imagined as universally rewarding parents for the care they invested in children. The mother-daughter relationship, for example, is not always pictured as warm and loving. In modern Zambia, girls are not expected to discuss personal problems with, or seek advice from, their mothers. Rather, Zambian girls are expected to seek out some older female relative to serve as confidante.[7] Similarly, among the Cheyenne Indians who lived on the American Great Plains during the last century, a mother was expected to have strained relations with her daughters.[8] Mothers are described as continually admonishing their daughters, leading the latter to seek affection from their fathers' sisters.

Of course, anthropologists have recognized that people everywhere do not share our deep faith in the loving, self-sacrificing mother, but in matters of family and motherhood, anthropologists, like all social scientists, have relied more on faith than evidence in constructing theoretical accounts. Because we *believe* mothers to be loving, anthropologists have proposed, for example, that a general explanation of the fact that men marry mother's brothers' daughters more frequently than they marry father's sisters' daughters is that men naturally seek affection (i.e., wives) where they have found affection in the past (i.e., from mothers and their kin).[9]

Looking Backward

The Malinowskian view of The Family as a universal institution—which maps the "function" of "nurturance" onto a collectivity of specific persons (presumably "nuclear" relations) associated with specific spaces ("the home") and specific affective bonds ("love")—corresponds, as we have seen, to that assumed by most contemporary writers on the subject. But a consideration of available ethnographic evidence suggests that the received view is a good deal more problematic than a naive observer might think. If Families in Malinowski's sense are *not* universal, then we must begin to ask about the biases that, in the past, have led us to misconstrue the ethnographic record. The issues here are too complex for thorough explication in this essay, but if we are to better understand the nature of "the family" in the present, it seems worthwhile to explore the question, first, of why so many social thinkers continue to believe in Capital-Letter Families as universal institutions, and second, whether anthropological tradition offers any alternatives to a "necessary and natural" view of what our families are. Only then will we be in a position to suggest "new anthropological perspectives" on the family today.

Our positive critique begins by moving backward. In the next few pages, we suggest that tentative answers to both questions posed above lie in the nineteenth-century intellectual trends that thinkers like Malinowski were at pains to reject. During the second half of the nineteenth century, a number of social and intellectual developments—among them, the evolutionary researches of Charles Darwin; the rise of "urban problems" in fast-growing cities; and the accumulation of data on non-Western peoples by missionaries and agents of the colonial states—contributed to what most of us would now recognize as the beginnings of modern social science. Alternately excited and perplexed by changes in a rapidly industrializing world, thinkers as diverse as socialist Frederick Engels[10] and bourgeois apologist Herbert Spencer[11]—to say nothing of a host of mythographers, historians of religion, and even feminists—attempted to identify the distinctive problems and potentials of their contemporary society by constructing *evolutionary* accounts of "how it all began." At base, a sense of "progress" gave direction to their thought, whether, like Spencer, they believed "man" had advanced from the love of violence to a more civilized love of peace or, like Engels, that humanity had moved from primitive promiscuity and incest toward monogamy and "individual sex love." Proud of their position in the modern world, some of these writers claimed that rules of force had been transcended by new rules of law,[12] while others thought that feminine "mysticism" in the past had been supplanted by a higher male "morality."[13]

At the same time, and whatever else they thought of capitalist social life (some of them criticized, but none wholly abhorred it), these writers also shared a sense of moral emptiness and a fear of instability and loss. Experience argued forcefully to them that moral order in their time did not rest on the unshakable hierarchy—from God to King to Father in the home—enjoyed by Europeans in the past.[14] Thus, whereas Malinowski's functionalism led him to stress the underlying continuities in all human social forms, his nineteenth-century predecessors were concerned to understand the facts and forces that set their experiential world apart. They were interested in comparative and, more narrowly, evolutionary accounts because their lives were torn between celebration and fear of change. For them, the family was important not because it had at all times been the same but because it was at once the moral precondition for, the triumph of, and the victim of developing capitalist society. Without the family and female spheres, thinkers like Ruskin feared we would fall victim to a market that destroys real human bonds.[15] Then again, while men like Engels could decry the impact of the market on familial life and love, he joined with more conservative counterparts to insist that our contemporary familial forms benefited from the individualist morality of modern life and reached to moral and romantic heights unknown before.

Given this purpose and the limited data with which they had to work, it is hardly surprising that the vast majority of what these nineteenth-century writers said is easily dismissed today. They argued that in simpler days such things as incest were the norm; they thought that women ruled in "matriarchal" and peace-loving states or, alternatively, that brute force determined the primitive right and wrong. None of these visions of a more natural, more feminine, more sexy, or more violent primitive world squares with contemporary evidence about what, in technological and organizational terms, might be reckoned relatively "primitive" or "simple" social forms. We would suggest, however, that whatever their mistakes, these nineteenth-century thinkers *can* help us rethink the family today, at least in part because we are (unfortunately) their heirs, in the area of prejudice, and partly because their concern to characterize difference and change gave rise to insights much more promising than their functionalist critics may have thought.

To begin, although nineteenth-century evolutionary theorists did not believe The Family to be universal, the roots of modern assumptions can be seen in their belief that women are, and have at all times been, defined by nurturant, connective, and reproductive roles that *do not change* through time. Most nineteenth-century thinkers imaged social development as a process of differentiation from a relatively confused (and thus incestuous) and indiscriminate female-oriented state to one in which men fight, destroy their "natural" social bonds, and then forge public and political ties to create a human "order." For some, it seemed reasonable to assume that women dominated, as matriarchs, in the undifferentiated early state, but even these theorists believed that women everywhere were "mothers" first, defined by "nurturant" concerns and thus excluded from the business competition, cooperation, social ordering, and social change propelled and dominated by their male counterparts. And so, while nineteenth-century writers differed in their evaluations of such things as "women's status," they all believed that female reproductive roles made women different from and complementary to men and guaranteed both the relative passivity of women in human history and the relative continuity of "feminine" domains and functions in human societies. Social change consisted in the acts of men, who left their mothers behind in shrinking homes. And women's nurturant sphere was recognized as a complementary and necessary corrective to the more competitive pursuits of men, not because these thinkers recognized women as political actors who influence the world, but because they feared the unchecked and morally questionable growth of a male-dominated capitalist market.

For nineteenth-century evolutionists, women were associated, in short, with an unchanging biological role and a romanticized community of the past, while men were imaged as the agents of all social process. And though contemporary thinkers have been ready to dismiss manifold aspects of their now-dated school of thought, on this point we remain, perhaps unwittingly, their heirs. Victorian assumptions about gender and the relationship between competitive male markets and peace-loving female homes were not abandoned in later functionalist schools of thought at least in part because pervasive sexist biases make it easy to forget that women, like men, are important actors in *all* social worlds. Even more, the functionalists, themselves concerned to understand all human social forms in terms of biological "needs," turned out to strengthen earlier beliefs associating action, change, and interest with the deeds of men because they thought of kinship in terms of biologically given ties, of "families" as units geared to reproductive needs, and finally, of women as mere "reproducers" whose contribution to society was essentially defined by the requirements of their homes.

If most modern social scientists have inherited Victorian biases that tend ultimately to support a view uniting women and The Family to an apparently unchanging set of biologically given needs, we have at the same time failed to reckon with the one small area in which Victorian evolutionists were right. They understood, as we do not today, that families—like religions, economies, governments, or courts of law—are *not* unchanging but the product of various social forms, that the relationships of spouses and parents to their young are apt to be different things in different social orders. More particularly, although nineteenth-century writers had primitive society all wrong, they were correct in insisting that *family* in the modern sense—a unit bounded, biologically as well as legally defined, associated with property, self-sufficiency, with affect and a space "inside" the home—is something that emerges not in Stone Age caves but in complex state-governed social forms. Tribal peoples may speak readily of lineages, households, and clans, but—as we have seen—they rarely have a word denoting Family as a particular and limited group of kin; they rarely worry about differences between legitimate and illegitimate heirs or find themselves concerned (as we so often are today) that what children and/or parents do reflects on their family's public image and self-esteem. Political influence in tribal groups in fact consists in adding children to one's home and, far from distinguishing Smith from Jones, encouraging one's neighbors to join one's household as if kin. By contrast, modern bounded Families try to keep their neighbors out. Clearly their character, ideology, and functions are not given for all times. Instead, to borrow the Victorian phrase, The Family is a "moral" unit, a way of organizing and thinking about human relationships in a world in which the domestic is perceived to be in opposition to a politics shaped outside the home, and individuals find themselves dependent on a set of relatively noncontingent ties in order to survive the dictates of an impersonal market and external political order.

In short, what the Victorians recognized and we have tended to forget is, first, that human social life has varied in its "moral"—we might say its "cultural" or "ideological"—forms, and so it takes more than making babies to make Families. And having seen The Family as something more than a response to omnipresent, biologically given needs, they realized too that Families do not everywhere exist; rather, The Family (thought to be universal by most social scientists today) is a moral and ideological unit that appears, not universally, but in particular social orders. The Family as we know it is not a "natural" group created by the claims of "blood" but a sphere of human relationships shaped by a state that recognizes Families as units that hold property, provide for care and welfare, and attend particularly to the young—a sphere conceptualized as a realm of love and intimacy *in opposition* to the more "impersonal" norms that dominate modern economies and politics. One can, in nonstate social forms, find groups of genealogically related people who interact daily and share material resources, but the contents of their daily ties, the ways they think about their bonds and their conception of the relationship between immediate "familial" links and other kinds of sociality, are apt to be different from the ideas and feelings we think rightfully belong to families we know. Stated otherwise, because our notions of The Family are rooted in a contrast between "public" and "private" spheres, we will not find that Families like ours exist in a society where public and political life is radically different from our own.

Victorian thinkers rightly understood the link between the bounded modern Family and the modern state, although they thought the two related by a necessary teleology of moral progress. Our point resembles theirs not in the *explanations* we would seek but in our feeling that if we, today, are interested in change, we must begin to probe and understand change in the families of the past. Here the Victorians, not the functionalists, are our rightful guides because the former recognized that *all* human social ties have "cultural" or "moral" shapes, and more specifically, that the particular "morality" of contemporary familial forms is rooted in a set of processes that link our intimate experiences and bonds to public politics.

Toward a Rethinking

Our perspective on families therefore compels us to listen carefully to what the natives in other societies say about their relationships with genealogically close kin. The same is true of the natives in our own society. Our understanding of families in contemporary American society can be only as rich as our understanding of what The Family represents symbolically to Americans. A complete cultural analysis of The Family as an American ideological construct, of course, is beyond the scope of this essay. But we can indicate some of the directions such an analysis would take and how it would deepen our knowledge of American families.

One of the central notions in the modern American construct of The Family is that of nurturance. When antifeminists attack the Equal Rights Amendment, for example, much of their rhetoric plays on the anticipated loss of the nurturant, intimate bonds we associate with The Family. Likewise, when pro-life forces decry abortion, they cast it as the ultimate denial of nurturance. In a sense, these arguments are variations of a functionalist view that weds families to specific functions. The logic of the argument is that because people need nurturance, and people get nurtured in The Family, then people need The Family. Yet if we adopt the perspective that The Family is an ideological unit rather than merely a functional unit, we are encouraged to subject this syllogism to closer scrutiny. We can ask, first, What do people mean by nurturance? Obviously, they mean more than mere nourishment—that is, the provision of food, clothing, and shelter required for biological survival. What is evoked by the word nurturance is a certain kind of relationship: a relationship that entails affection and love, that is based on cooperation as opposed to competition, that is enduring rather than temporary, that is noncontingent rather than contingent upon performance, and that is governed by feeling and morality instead of law and contract.

The reason we have stated these attributes of The Family in terms of oppositions is because in a symbolic system the meanings of concepts are often best illuminated by explicating their opposites. Hence, to understand our American construct of The Family, we first have to map the larger system of constructs of which it is only a part. When we undertake such analysis of The Family in our society, we discover that what gives shape to much of our conception of The Family is its symbolic opposition to work and business, in other words, to the market relations of capitalism. For it is in the market, where we sell our labor and negotiate contract relations of business, that we associate with competitive, temporary, contingent relations that must be buttressed by law and legal sanctions.

The symbolic opposition between The Family and market relations renders our strong attachment to The Family understandable, but it also discloses the particularity of our construct of The Family. We can hardly be speaking of a universal notion of The Family shared by people everywhere and for all time because people everywhere and for all time have not participated in market relations out of which they have constructed a contrastive notion of the family.

The realization that our idea of The Family is part of a set of symbolic oppositions through which we interpret our experience in a particular society compels us to ask to what extent this set of oppositions reflects real relations between people and to what extent it also shapes them. We do not adhere to a model of culture in which ideology is isolated from people's experience. On the other hand, neither do we construe the connection between people's constructs and people's experience to be a simple one of epiphenomenal reflection. Rather, we are interested in understanding how people come to summarize their experience in folk constructs that gloss over the diversity, complexity, and contradictions in their relationships. If, for example, we consider the second premise of the aforementioned syllogism—the idea that people get "nurtured" in families—we can ask how people reconcile this premise with the fact that relationships in families are not always this simple or altruistic. We need not resort to the evidence offered by social historians (e.g., Philippe Aries [16] and Lawrence Stone [17]) of the harsh treatment and neglect of children and spouses in the history of the Western family, for we need only read our local newspaper to learn of similar abuses among contemporary families. And we can point to other studies, such as Young and Willmott's *Family and Kinship in East London*, [18] that reveal how people often find more intimacy and emotional support in relationships with individuals and groups outside The Family than they do in their relationships with family members.

The point is not that our ancestors or our contemporaries have been uniformly mean and nonnurturant to family members but that we have all been both nice and mean, both generous and ungenerous, to them. In like manner, our actions toward family members are not always motivated by selfless altruism but are also motivated by instrumental self-interest. What is significant is that, despite the fact that our complex relationships are the result of complex motivations, we ideologize relations within The Family as nurturant while casting relationships outside The Family—particularly in the sphere of work and business—as just the opposite.

We must be wary of oversimplifying matters by explaining away those disparities between our notion of the nurturant Family and our real actions toward family members as the predictable failing of imperfect beings. For there is more here than the mere disjunction of the ideal and the real. The American construct of The Family, after all, is complex enough to comprise some key contradictions. The Family is seen as representing not only the antithesis of the market relations of capitalism; it is also sacralized in our minds as the last stronghold against The State, as the symbolic refuge from the intrusions of a public domain that constantly threatens our sense of privacy and self-determination. Consequently, we can hardly be surprised to find that the punishments imposed on people who commit physical violence are lighter when their victims are their own family members.[19] Indeed, the American sense of the privacy of the things that go on inside families is so strong that a smaller percentage of homicides involving family members are prosecuted than those involving strangers.[20] We are faced with the irony that in our society the place where nurturance and noncontingent affection are supposed to be located is simultaneously the place where violence is most tolerated.

There are other dilemmas about The Family that an examination of its ideological nature can help us better understand. For example, the hypothesis that in England and the United States marriages among lower-income ("working-class") groups are characterized by a greater degree of "conjugal role segregation" than are marriages among middle-income groups has generated considerable confusion. Since Bott observed that working-class couples in her study of London families exhibited more "segregated" conjugal roles than "middle-class" couples, who tended toward more "joint" conjugal roles,[21] researchers have come forth with a range of diverse and confusing findings. On the one hand, some researchers have found that working-class couples indeed report more segregated conjugal role-relationships—in other words, clearly differentiated male and female tasks, as well as interests and activities—than do middle-class couples.[22] Other researchers, however, have raised critical methodological questions about how one goes about defining a joint activity and hence measuring the degree of "jointness" in a conjugal relationship.[23] Platt's finding that couples who reported "jointness" in one activity were not particularly likely to report "jointness" in another activity is significant because it demonstrates that "jointness" is not a general characteristic of a relationship that manifests itself uniformly over a range of domains. Couples carry out some activities and tasks together or do them separately but equally; they also have other activities in which they do not both participate. The measurement of the "jointness" of conjugal relationships becomes even more problematic when we recognize that what one individual or couple may label a "joint activity," another individual or couple may consider a "separate activity." In Bott's study, for example, some couples felt that all activities carried out by husband and wife in each other's presence were

> similar in kind regardless of whether the activities were
> complementary (e.g. sexual intercourse, though no one talked

about this directly in the home interview), independent (e.g. husband repairing book while the wife read or knitted), or shared (e.g. washing up together, entertaining friends, going to the pictures together). It was not even necessary that husband and wife should actually be together. As long as they were both at home it was felt that their activities partook of some special, shared, family quality.[24]

In other words, the distinction Bott drew among "joint," "differentiated," and "autonomic" (independent) relationships summarized the way people thought and felt about their activities rather than what they were observed to actually do. Again, it is not simply that there is a disjunction between what people say they do and what they in fact do. The more cogent point is that the meaning people attach to action, whether they view it as coordinated and therefore shared or in some other way, is an integral component of that action and cannot be divorced from it in our analysis. When we compare the conjugal relationships of middle-income and low-income people, or any of the family relationships among different class, age, ethnic, and regional sectors of American society, we must recognize that our comparisons rest on differences and similarities in ideological and moral meanings as well as on differences and similarities in action.

Finally, the awareness that The Family is not a concrete "thing" that fulfills concrete "needs" but an ideological construct with moral implications can lead to a more refined analysis of historical change in the American or Western family than has devolved upon us from our functionalist ancestors. The functionalist view of industrialization, urbanization, and family change depicts The Family as responding to alterations in economic and social conditions in rather mechanistic ways. As production gets removed from the family's domain, there is less need for strict rules and clear authority structures in the family to accomplish productive work. At the same time, individuals who now must work for wages in impersonal settings need a haven where they can obtain emotional support and gratification. Hence, The Family becomes more concerned with "expressive" functions, and what emerges is the modern "companionate family." In short, in the functionalist narrative The Family and its constituent members "adapt" to fulfill functional requirements created for it by the industrialization of production. Once we begin to view The Family as an ideological unit and pay due respect to it as a moral statement, however, we can begin to unravel the more complex, dialectical process through which family relationships and The Family as a construct were mutually transformed. We can examine, for one, the ways in which people and state institutions acted, rather than merely reacted, to assign certain functions to groupings of kin by making them legally responsible for these functions. We can investigate, as Eli Zaretsky does in his essay in this volume, the manner in which the increasing limitations placed on agents of the community and the state with regard to negotiating the relationships between family members enhanced the independence of The Family. We can begin to understand the consequences of social reforms and wage policies for the age and sex inequalities in families. And we can elucidate the interplay between these social changes and the cultural transformations that assigned new meanings and modified old ones to make The Family what we think it to be today.

Ultimately, this sort of rethinking will lead to a questioning of the somewhat contradictory modern views that families are things we need (the more "impersonal" the public world, the more we need them) and at the same time that loving families are disappearing. In a variety of ways, individuals today *do* look to families for a "love" that money cannot buy and find; our contemporary world makes "love" more fragile than most of us hope and "nurturance" more self-interested than we believe.[25] But what we fail to recognize is that familial nurturance and the social forces that turn our ideal families into mere fleeting dreams are *equally* creations of the world we know *today*. Rather than think of the ideal family as a world we lost (or, like the Victorians, as a world just recently achieved), it is important for us to recognize that while families symbolize deep and salient modern themes, contemporary families are unlikely to fulfill our equally modern nurturant needs.

We probably have no cause to fear (or hope) that The Family will dissolve. What we can begin to ask is what we *want* our families to do. Then, distinguishing our hopes from what we have, we can begin to analyze the social forces that enhance or undermine the realization of the kinds of human bonds we need.

Notes

1. Bronislaw Malinowski, *The Family Among the Australian Aborigines* (London: University of London Press, 1913).

2. Lewis Henry Morgan, *Ancient Society* (New York: Holt, 1877).

3. Bronislaw Malinowski, *A Scientific Theory of Culture* (Chapel Hill: University of North Carolina Press, 1944), p. 99.

4. Robin Fox, *Kinship and Marriage* (London: Penguin, 1967), p. 39.

5. Evon Z. Vogt, *Zinacantan: A Maya Community in the Highlands of Chiapas* (Cambridge, Mass.: Harvard University Press, 1969).

6. Yolanda and Robert Murphy, *Women of the Forest* (New York: Columbia University Press, 1974).

7. Ilsa Schuster, *New Women of Lusaka* (Palo Alto: Mayfield, 1979).

8. E. Adamson Hoebel, *The Cheyennes: Indians of the Great Plains* (New York: Holt, Rinehart and Winston, 1978).

9. George C. Homans and David M. Schneider, *Marriage, Authority, and Final Causes* (Glencoe, Ill.: Free Press, 1955).

10. Frederick Engels, *The Origin of the Family, Private Property and the State*, in *Karl Marx and Frederick Engels: Selected Works*, vol. 2 (Moscow: Foreign Language Publishing House, 1955).

11. Herbert Spencer, *The Principles of Sociology*, vol. 1, *Domestic Institutions* (New York: Appleton, 1973).

12. John Stuart Mill, *The Subjection of Women* (London: Longmans, Green, Reader and Dyer, 1869).

13. J. J. Bachofen, *Das Mutterrecht* (Stuttgart, 1861).

14. Elizabeth Fee, "The Sexual Politics of Victorian Social Anthropology," in *Clio's Banner Raised*, ed. M. Hartman and L. Banner (New York: Harper & Row, 1974).

15. John Ruskin, "Of Queen's Gardens," in *Sesame and Lilies* (London: J. M. Dent, 1907).

16. Philippe Aries, *Centuries of Childhood*, trans. Robert Baldick (New York: Vintage, 1962).

17. Lawrence Stone, *The Family, Sex, and Marriage in England 1500–1800* (London: Weidenfeld and Nicholson, 1977).

18. Michael Young and Peter Willmott, *Family and Kinship in East London* (London: Routledge and Kegal Paul, 1957).

19. Henry P. Lundsgaarde, *Murder in Space City: A Cultural Analysis of Houston Homicide Patterns* (New York: Oxford University Press, 1977).

20. Ibid.

21. Elizabeth Bott, *Family and Social Network: Roles, Norms, and External Relationships in Ordinary Urban Families* (London: Tavistock, 1957).

22. Herbert J. Gans, *The Urban Villagers* (New York: Free Press, 1962); C. Rosser and C. Harris, *The Family and Social Change* (London: Routledge and Kegan Paul, 1965).

23. John Platt, "Some Problems in Measuring the Jointness of Conjugal Role-Relationships," *Sociology* 3 (1969): 287–97; Christopher Turner, "Conjugal Roles and Social Networks: A Re-examination of an Hypothesis," *Human Relations* 20 (1967): 121–30; and Morris Zelditch, Jr., "Family, Marriage and Kinship," in *A Handbook of Modern Sociology*, ed. R. E. L. Faris (Chicago: Rand McNally, 1964), pp. 680–707.

24. Bott, *Family and Social Network*, p. 240.

25. Rayna Rapp, "Family and Class in Contemporary America: Notes Toward an Understanding of Ideology," *Science and Society* 42 (Fall 1978): 278–300, republished in this volume.

3

LINDA GORDON

Why Nineteenth-Century Feminists Did Not Support "Birth Control" and Twentieth-Century Feminists Do: Feminism, Reproduction, and the Family

The question of *changes* in feminist attitudes toward reproductive control has been understandably neglected in the face of today's beleaguered but relatively unified feminist position in support of women's reproductive rights. Still, changes in the feminist position over time and conflicts within the feminist tradition are important. This historical overview provides some insights into the contemporary controversy over reproductive rights and the more inclusive controversy over the family norms our society should have.

In this essay I narrate a complex historical story very briefly,[1] offering only the minimum of information required to answer the title question in a rudimentary way. In addition, the narrative sheds light on several related issues: (1) the relation between technology and social change, as exemplified in the development of birth-control technology; (2) the poverty of generalizations about the family that do not specifically focus on the sex/gender system;[2] (3) certain political and ideological contradictions within the feminist tradition; and (4) some sources of the revival of the right-wing, particularly the Moral Majority, in the United States.

No existing social theory, religious or materialist, has satisfactorily explained why and how societies regulate reproduction as they do. This lack of explanation is even more odd when one bears in mind that all

40

societies regulate reproduction, and there are many differences among these sets of social rules.

One reason for the absence of satisfactory theorizing is that human reproduction involves a relation between two sexes and therefore two genders. No social theory prior to modern feminism tried to use gender as a fundamental category of social analysis. To some extent, this blind spot has been reinforced in the last century, despite the existence of feminist theory as a new vision. In the nineteenth century, Marxism began to remove the blinders and examine the material origins and perpetuation of male supremacy; more recently, the dominant Marxism became vulgarized into a productionist determinism that once again ignored the gender system.

The popularity of technological explanations, and technological determinism, further reinforced the blinders. By technological determinism I mean the view that inventions, the product of human inventiveness, shape basic social alternatives. In the field of birth control this view has constructed the following picture: Once there were no effective means of birth control, and therefore the birthrate was controlled only by natural variables such as women's health and physiological fertility, or people's sexual drive; the development of contraception in this century has revolutionized the birthrate, family size, and women's life options. These changes, of course, were conditioned by other technological advances that reduced mortality rates.[3] This technological explanation is wrong, however. Technological changes have been influential, but in themselves they do not provide an explanation for the history and continuity of the birth-control controversy.

Neither will so-called family-history explanations, which usually employ the assumptions of "modernization theory." This approach to birth control argues that urbanization and industrialization created an economic preference for smaller families along with a character structure more secular and more oriented to pleasure.[4] Ignoring class and sexual conflicts within these "modernizing" societies, the modernization theorists cannot explain the controversy about reproductive control.

And this controversy badly needs explanation. The abortion struggle today is in part an updated version of a birth-control struggle at least 150 years old. No issue of women's liberation has ever been as hotly contested; no conflict in industrial society, with the exception of the social relations of labor itself, has been as bitter; and there may be no social issue that is more passionately debated.

Let me introduce a brief historical summary. Between earliest recorded history, and even as far back as some prehistoric archeological evidence, until the 1870s, there were no significant technological advances in birth control whatever. All the basic forms of birth control—abortions, douches, condoms, and devices to cover the cervix—are ancient. The social regulation of the use of these techniques changed in various historical eras and places in the context of power relations and economic needs. By and large, birth control was uncontroversial and widely practiced in preagricultural societies; by contrast, in peasant societies large families were an asset, continuing high infant mortality necessitated many pregnancies, and birth control was suppressed.

Let us proceed now to the early-nineteenth-century United States. At that time there were two developments: (1) a falling birthrate and an increased use of birth control and (2) the first political movements for reproductive control. At this time, urbanization and industrialization began to create living conditions in which large families were no longer economical. In 1810 the birthrate in the United States started to fall and has been falling ever since. In the early nineteenth century, in a society with a strong element of prudery, it was difficult to get evidence of private use of contraception, and at first puzzled observers thought that there was a physiological decline in fertility! But by the 1840s new evidence appeared: a rise in abortions.[5] The demand for birth control had outstripped the availability of contraceptive techniques. Moreover, the average abortion client was no longer a single girl in trouble but a married woman who already had children.

Also from the 1840s there appeared the first American birth-control movement within the women's rights movement, in the form of a demand for "voluntary motherhood." The meaning of that phrase should be evident. It had no antimotherhood implications; in fact, Voluntary Motherhood advocates argued that willing mothers would be better mothers.

In their line of argument we can see that motherhood had broader connotations for them than for us today. A century ago, feminists and nonfeminists alike assumed (at least I have found no exception) that women were naturally those who should not only give birth to children but should also do primary child raising, as well as perform the nurturing functions for the whole society: maintaining friendship networks, cultural institutions, and rituals; creating beautiful environments; and nurturing husbands, relatives, and other women. Their feminism manipulated the cult of domesticity, translating it into what was later called "social housekeeping," spreading the virtues of an idealized home throughout the society.[6] Thus, in the nineteenth century the overall demand for women's rights was frequently couched in terms of a greater respect for motherhood.

Voluntary Motherhood was a campaign exclusively focused on women. It must be distinguished from two other, separate streams in the historical movement for contraception. The first was neo-Malthusianism, or population control, a plan to ameliorate social problems by reducing the size of populations on a large scale. This ideology says nothing about women's rights; a satisfactory solution in an overcrowded country might be to sterilize half the women and let the other half have all the children they wanted. Neo-Malthusianism came late to the United States because in this country underpopulation, not overpopulation, was the dominant fear until World War II.

The second movement, eugenics, was really a subcategory of neo-Malthusianism, an effort to apply population control differentially and thus to reduce the size of certain unwanted human "types." Eugenical thought originally was primarily directed at the elimination of idiocy, criminality, and drunkenness, on the misguided theory that such undesirable qualities were hereditary. After the Civil War, however, with social stratification deepening, eugenics took on a different orientation. The upper-class WASP elite of the industrial North became increasingly aware of its own small-family pattern, in contrast to the continuing large-family preferences of immigrants and the rural poor. From as early as the 1860s, the fear of so-called race suicide emerged. In that phrase, race was used ambiguously: to equate the "human race" with WASPs. Out of fears of a loss of political (and social and economic) dominance to an expanding population of "inferiors" grew a plan for reestablishing social stability through differential breeding: The superior should have more children, the inferior fewer. (In the twentieth century blacks and the welfare poor replaced immigrants and sharecroppers as the primary targets of eugenical policies. But that is getting ahead of our story.)

By the end of the century, then, there were three separate reproduction control movements—Voluntary Motherhood, population control, and eugenics. All three were to some extent responses to the fact that birth control *was* being widely used. And all three to some extent required better reproductive-control techniques. Yet on another, crucial dimension there was a sharp difference among them: The eugenists and population controllers supported the legalization of contraception, but the Voluntary Motherhood advocates opposed it. For birth control, they proposed abstinence—either periodic, based on an incorrect rhythm method, or long-term, allowing for intercourse only when a conception was desired. Their position was the more odd since they were the ones most blamed for the rise in birth-control use. Antifeminists of the mid-nineteenth century, just as today, charged feminism with destroying motherhood and the family and encouraging sexual licentiousness. In a way, their opponents were (and are) right, and the feminists wrong. Despite their denials, the feminists, by raising women's self-respect and aspirations, did lend implicit support to birth-control use.

Furthermore, the backlash was able, in the nineteenth century, to ride its antifeminist rhetoric to several important victories. First, a physicians' campaign to outlaw abortion got most states to legislate against it for the first time; before this, abortion in the early months was legal. Second, in the mid-nineteenth century, the Catholic church also banned abortion for the first time, having previously accepted it in the early months. Third, in 1873, the Comstock law, named after a notorious prude who was postmaster-general, made it a federal crime to send obscene material through the mails, and listed birth control as an obscene subject. Most opponents of birth control at this time did not distinguish contraception from abortion; they called it all murder and immorality. Nevertheless, the repression did not work. Then, as now, birth-control use continued to rise and the birthrate continued to fall.

It bears repeating that this struggle took place *with no new technological inventions.* The only nineteenth-century contribution to birth-control technology—the vulcanization of rubber, which permitted the manufacture of better condoms and diaphragms—had no impact in this country until this century. What, then, caused the decline in the birthrate, the rise of pro-birth-control movements, and the backlash against birth control?

In the late nineteenth century a debate raged about this question. One side blamed feminism, arguing that women, stirred up by licentious propaganda, were rejecting their duties to society and seeking selfish gratification. The other side blamed the industrial economy, showing that children were no longer respectful nor economically profitable toward their parents. In fact, these two explanations were both correct and were fundamentally the same. Feminism was a response to the industrial economy that had robbed women of their traditional productive labor and turned them—at least those of the prosperous classes, who were most likely to become feminists—into unpaid, disrespected housekeepers. Feminism was also, ideologically, a response to the liberal individualism that was once the revolutionary credo of the bourgeoisie and later became the justifying ideology of capitalism. The convergence between feminism and a new economic setup can be seen further in the fact that decisions about birth control and family size have in the main not been controversial within families; new class aspirations shared by husbands and wives included new views of the place of women as well as of family size. The birthrate drop started first among the professional and managerial strata, who cared most about educating their children well (which is expensive), and who contributed most feminists to the movement. From here the small-family tendency moved both upward to the capitalist class and downward to the working class, just as women's rights ideas moved both up and down from their middle-class origins. The biggest differential in family size was not primarily class, defined in a static way, but urbanization. By and large, migrants, both foreigners and southern blacks, coming from peasant societies, slowly relinquished their large-family preferences, settled for fewer children, and adopted positive attitudes toward birth control.

Why, then, did nineteenth-century feminists cling so hard to such a backward position as their condemnation of contraception? (And they were tenacious. As late as the 1920s, feminists of the earlier generations were lined up against Margaret Sanger and other birth-control pioneers.) There are two reasons I want to advance. The first is that they wanted Voluntary Motherhood not as a single-issue reform but as part of a broad movement for the empowerment of women, and some possible reforms within the spectrum of women's needs contradicted each other, creating a double bind for the feminists. A second reason lies in a great intellectual and cultural ambivalence within feminism: It represented both the highest development of liberal individualism and also a critique of liberal individualism. Let me discuss these reasons briefly.

The Voluntary Motherhood advocates, as I have said, were part of a general women's rights movement; they were also working for suffrage, property rights, employment opportunities, and some of the more daring for divorce rights. Their concern for all the needs of women, even to some extent their attempt to grasp the larger problems of working-class women, led them to recognize a number of contradictions. First, they realized that while women needed freedom from excessive childbearing, they also needed the respect and self-respect motherhood brought. By and large, motherhood then was the only challenging, dignified, and rewarding work that women could get (it still is, for the majority of women). Second, they understood that while women needed freedom from pregnancy, they also needed freedom from male sexual tyranny, especially in a society that had almost completely suppressed accurate information about female sexuality and replaced it with information and attitudes so false as to virtually guarantee that women would not enjoy sex. Abstinence as a form of birth control may well have been the solution that made most sense in the particular historical circumstance. Abstinence helped women strengthen their ability to say no to their husbands' sexual demands, for example, while contraception and abortion would have weakened it. Nineteenth-century feminists have often been considered prudish, and indeed they were reluctant, for example, to name the sexual parts of the body; but they were not reluctant to speak of marital rape, which traditionalists found even more shocking. A few feminists even began discussing the possibility of forms of sexual contact other than intercourse as a means of nonprocreative sex, thus opening a challenge to phallic sexual norms that was continued a century later. In other words, some women had figured out that it was not sex they disliked so much as the particular sexual activity they had experienced.

The Voluntary Motherhood advocates faced a second set of contradictions in their ambivalent attitude toward individualism. The essence of their feminism was their anger at the suppression of the capabilities and aspirations of individual women. They envisaged a public sphere of adults equal in rights, though unequal in native abilities, each individual guaranteed maximum opportunity for self-development. At the same time they were firmly committed to the family. They did not challenge gender, or even "sex roles." They did not challenge heterosexual marriage based on a firm sexual division of labor (man the chief breadwinner, woman the mother in that expanded sense described above), even though this family form condemned women to remaining primarily out of the public sphere. Many of them could see the problems with this arrangement, but all of them felt sure that the family was an absolutely essential institution for the maintenance of civilization. At moments, some of their rhetoric suggests that they glimpsed the possibility of the further individualization and atomization of people the wage labor system could bring, and they feared it. Fear of that individualism reverberates in many socialists and among feminists today; a world in which self-improvement, competition, and isolation dominate human energies is not appealing. Indeed, what civilization *meant* to nineteenth-century feminists was the tempering of the individual struggle for survival by greater social values and aspirations that, they believed, women supported through their nurturing role in the division of labor. And yet their very movement was increasing the number of women who joined that atomized world of the labor market. Their historic compromise must be seen sympathetically in that context: They argued that more respect for women should be used to reinforce motherhood, to give it more freedom, respect, and self-respect. Hence their reluctance to accept a form of birth control that could exempt women from motherhood.

Feminists changed their minds about contraception in the early twentieth century. Again, no new techniques affected them; rather, after they changed their minds, they took the initiative in finding the technology they needed. Two leaders, Emma Goldman and Margaret Sanger, separately traveled to Europe where rubber diaphragms were being prescribed in labor and trade-union-funded health clinics. The women personally imported these devices into the United States. In America, as in Europe, these new pro-birth-control feminists were mainly in and around the Socialist Party. It is logical, I think, that socialist feminists were the first to take a pro-contraception position. Concerned as they were with the working class, they realized the consequences and hardships of a massive employment of women; attempting as they were to build a working-class movement, they saw the weakness of a movement in which women were politically immobilized by sexism and exclusive responsibilities for large families; having rejected religion and viewing traditional morality as a form of social control beneficial to the capitalist class, they saw liberating possibilities in a freer sexual life.

All along, feminists had been responding to family change and trying to direct and even initiate it. The trajectory of change that formed the primary experience of most nineteenth-century feminists was a decline of patriarchy [7] that produced increased independence for grown children without enhancing very much the autonomy of women (with one exception, educated single women). In that context it was reasonable for women to cling to their work as mothers as the basis for their social status and desired political power. By the early twentieth century, the further development of industrial capitalism had begun to allow a vision of greater independence for women. Not only prosperous women but also working-class women in the World War I era were experiencing the effects of public education, mass employment of women, the transformation of virtually the entire male population into a wage labor force, and extensive commodity production replacing most household production. These changes created both negative and positive consequences for women. Negatively, the separation of productive from reproductive labor, in the context of a capitalist culture, demeaned the social status of motherhood. Positively, the devaluing of domestic work allowed a vision of a public role for women, in work and politics, that for the first time in the history of feminism made women want equality. (Early feminists did not dream of full equality between the sexes.) And equality for women absolutely required reproductive self-control.

When socialist feminists first adopted pro-birth-control positions in the early twentieth century, nonfeminist socialists had divided reactions. The majority of the U.S. Socialist Party, for example, believed that, at best, birth control was a dangerous distraction from the class struggle. Some responded even more negatively, out of a traditional anti-neo-Malthusian appraisal that the major purpose of reproductive control was to reduce the numbers and hence the strength of the working class. Some Socialists, however, supported the birth-control movement, if weakly, because they believed it could reduce women's domestic burdens and free them for greater political activity in support of their class interests.

By contrast, black radicals in the United States in the 1910s tended to support birth control far more frequently. They saw it as a tool for the self-determination of black Americans. In the 1920s and afterward, however, birth control was increasingly absorbed into programs aimed not at self-determination but at social control by the elite. Eugenics became a dominant motif in the effort to legalize contraception and sterilization, and even birth controllers from the socialist-feminist tradition, such as Margaret Sanger, made accommodations with the eugenists. These policies cost the birth controllers most of their black support—and many of their white radical supporters as well.

Sanger and other spokespeople used racist rhetoric, urging reduction of the birthrates of the "undesirables"; private birth-control clinics in the 1910s and '20s experimented with evaluating the eugenic worth of their clients and advising them on the desirability of their reproductive intentions. The first publicly funded birth-control clinics appeared in the South in the 1930s, sold to southern state public health services on the grounds that they would lower the black birthrate. Throughout the country during the Great Depression, birth control was touted as a means of lowering welfare costs. In these developments were premonitions of the involuntary and coercive sterilizations performed today. (A 1979 study shows that 70 percent of hospitals fail to comply with DHEW sterilization guidelines.) [8]

Thus the cry of genocide that began to be raised against reproductive-control campaigns in the 1930s, and continues today, is not wrong. It is only too simple. It arises from at least three sources. First, the tensions between white feminism and black liberation movements that arose in the struggle over the Fourteenth Amendment underlie this problem and have virtually blotted out the contribution of black feminists (not only today but historically). So convoluted are these tensions that antiabortionists have manipulated the fear of genocide in a racist way—suggesting, for example, that black and working-class women do not need or want reproductive self-determination, that they are satisfied with their status, that aspirations for independence and prestige exist only among privileged white women.[9]

Second, beyond this general distrust is the actual racism of the white-dominated women's movement, which was clearly manifested in the birth-control movement as much by socialist as by liberal feminists. Its pattern resembled that of the white-dominated labor movement. Elizabeth Cady Stanton's appeal for giving the vote to educated women in preference to ignorant men is of a piece with trade-union denunciation of blacks as scabs even as they excluded them from their unions.

Third, and most pertinent, is the dominance of the relatively conservative population-control and eugenics programs over the feminist birth-control program. Planned Parenthood's use of small-family ideology and its international emphasis on sterilization rather than safe and controllable contraception have far overshadowed its feminist program for women's self-determination. Most Americans do not distinguish between birth control as a program of individual rights and population control as social policy. Moreover, many scholars continue this ideological confusion and fail to make this essential analytic distinction. The tendency to fetishize reproduction-control technology, as if the diaphragm or the pill, rather than the social relations that promote their use, were the news, further legitimates this analytic mush.

The distinctions started to reappear in the 1960s with the emergence of abortion as the key reproductive-control issue. In the early twentieth century, most feminists did not support abortion for several reasons: reluctance to take on too much of a backlash at once; their own conviction that sex belonged primarily in marriage, where contraceptive use was more likely to be systematic and where an unplanned child was not usually the total disaster it might be for an unmarried woman; and the fact that most poor women still had no access to decent medical care. The contemporary drive for abortion rights was a response to several factors that developed gradually in the 1920–60 period. First, there was a great increase in teen-age sexual activity without contraceptive use—in other words, it was not technology that increased sexual activity but the behavior that increased the demand. Second, there was a great increase in the number of families absolutely dependent on two incomes and an increase in women-headed families, thus making it no longer possible for mothers to stay home with an unplanned baby; this spurred the demand for abortion among married women for whom contraception had failed. The third and perhaps more surprising factor behind the movement for abortion rights was the relative underdevelopment of contraception. In this factor we see yet another flaw in the technological-determinist explanation of birth control. Far from being an area of great progress, the field of contraception today lags far behind our need for it. Women must still do almost all the contracepting, and they are forced to choose among unwieldy, dangerous, or irreversible methods.

The changes in the dominant feminist positions about birth control should now be clearer. For feminists, the issue of reproductive control is a part of an overall calculus of how to improve women's situation. The birth-control campaign of the late 1960s and '70s was not a single-issue reform campaign, such as that of the population controllers and eugenists who had dominated in the 1920s through '50s. Feminists always have to balance the gains and losses from contraception and abortion against the other problems women face, such as unequal employment opportunity, unequal wealth, unequal education, and unequal domestic responsibilities. Thus a position appropriate to one historical era was not appropriate in another when the balance of women's needs and possibilities had changed.

Contemporary feminist positions about birth control are still ambivalent. Within the reproductive rights rubric, groups have primarily emphasized single issues: abortion, sterilization abuse, vaginal self-examination. Few have addressed the issues of sex and motherhood overall, and their contemporary meanings for women of different classes. These two questions, about the proper role of sex and motherhood in women's lives, are publicly asked now mainly by the New Right, because of the "crisis" in the family. This crisis of the family is not new—indeed it was the foundation of the rise of feminism, the crack in the social structure that made feminism possible. It is hardly a criticism of contemporary feminism that it has not been able to produce a definitive program for liberated sex and parenthood—these failings are part of what propels the women's movement, just as they propel the new right-wing antifeminist movement. Still, it is important to call attention to the centrality of the family crisis to contemporary politics and to the need for further development of feminist theory about sex, reproduction and the family.

In thinking about the family, contemporary feminism, like feminism a century ago, contains an ambivalence between individualism and its critique. The individualism has reached a much higher development with the challenge to gender definitions. Few modern feminists would argue that women are innately suited to domestic activity and unsuited to public activity. The rejection of gender is an ultimate commitment to the right of all individuals to develop to their highest potential. Unfortunately, the most visible heroines of such struggles immediately suggest some of the problems with this uncritical individualism; for example, a new image of the liberated woman, complete with briefcase, career, sex partners, and silk blouse, but absolutely without nurturing responsibilities. Of course, this liberated woman is primarily a creature of the capitalist economy, not feminism. Moreover, she is a creature of the media, for there are few such women in reality. But parts of the feminist movement identify with this ideal. Those parts of the movement have deemphasized the other side of the feminist tradition: the critique of the man-made society, the refusal to accept merely integration of female individuals into a competition whose rules we did not define and do not endorse. There is, in fact, a tradition of feminist criticism of capitalism itself, representing it as the opposite of the nurturing values of motherhood.[10] Without weakening our support of the rights of individual women to seek achievement, it is important to keep both sides of this ambivalence in view. Feminists have conducted a close scrutiny of the family in the last years and have seen how oppressive it can be for women. But undermining the family has costs, for women as well as men, in the form of isolation and the further deterioration of child raising, general unhappiness, social distrust and, solipsism; and sensitivity to these problems is also part of the feminist heritage.

The feminist critique of individualism should give us some insight into the opposition. What are the abortion opponents afraid of? I do not think it is the loss of fetuses, for most. For example, I doubt there would have been such a big backlash had the legalization of abortion occurred under the auspices of the population controllers rather than in the context of a powerful women's liberation movement. The abortion opponents today, like those of a hundred years ago, are afraid of a loss of mothering, in the symbolic sense.[11] They fear a completely individualized society with all services based on cash nexus relationships, without the influence of nurturing women counteracting the completely egoistic principles of the economy, and without any forms in which children can learn about lasting human commitments to other people. Many feminists have the same fears. The overlap is minimal, of course. Most abortion opponents are right-wingers, involved in a deeply antidemocratic, anti-civil libertarian, violent, and sexist philosophy. Still, their fear of unchecked individualism is not without substance.

The problem is to develop a feminist program and philosophy that defends individual rights and also builds constructive bonds between individuals. This raises anew the question of the family. The truth is that feminism has undermined the family as it once existed faster than it has been able to substitute more egalitarian communities. This is not a criticism of the women's movement. Perhaps families held together by domination, fear, violence, squelched talents, and resignation should not survive. Furthermore, the women's movement has already done a great deal toward building supportive institutions that prefigure a better society: day-care centers, shelters, women's centers, communes, gay bars and bars where women feel comfortable, publications, women's studies programs, and health clinics. The movement has done even more in creating a new consciousness that pervades the entire culture. There has been a veritable explosion of feminist cultural work, a new definition of what is political and of what is a social problem, a new concept—sexism—that is widely understood. Even the mass media reflect a new respect for relations between women; a strong lesbian liberation movement has arisen; and, perhaps one of the best indices of the status of women in the whole society, a more respectful attitude toward single women has developed.

These very successes have created problems. Clearly the successes created a backlash. More complicated, the successes in consciousness changing outstripped successes in community and institution building. The nuclear, male-dominated family remains for the vast majority the only experience of permanent, noninstrumental personal commitments. Within the family, motherhood still is—and may forever be—one of the most challenging and rewarding emotional and work experiences people can have. The feminist reproductive rights movement faces the task of finding a program that equally defends women's individual rights to freedom, including sexual freedom, *and* the dignity of women's need and capacity for nurturance and being nurtured, with or without biological motherhood. This is but the application to one issue—reproduction—of the general task of feminism: to defend all the gains of bourgeois individualism and liberal feminism while transcending the capitalist- competitive aspects of individualism with a vision of loving, egalitarian communities.

Notes

1. I have told this story more fully in my book *Woman's Body, Woman's Right: A Social History of Birth Control in America* (New York: Viking Penguin, 1977). In the interpretation offered here, I am indebted to ideas garnered in my discussions with many feminist scholars, and particularly the work of Ellen Dubois and Allen Hunter.

2. The phrase "sex-gender system," was first used by Gayle Rubin in her essay "The Traffic in Women," in *Toward an Anthropology of Women*, ed. Rayna R. Reiter (New York: Monthly Review, 1975), and I am indebted to her theoretical conception. What I mean in using the phrase here, and elsewhere in this essay, is that sexual differences, which are biological, are everywhere in human society accompanied by socially constructed concepts of feminine and masculine gender. Gender includes the sexual division of labor, personality attributes, self-conception. Gender is much deeper than the popular sociological concept "sex roles," but is nevertheless culturally, not biologically, determined. An example of the difference is that female pregnancy and childbirth are biologically determined; while breast feeding and mothering are assigned to women by social regulation. (In this context it is worth noting that sex is a biological dichotomy only loosely and that there are many exceptions—infertile men and women, people whose chromosomal and anatomical construction is neither exclusively male nor female, among others.)

3. My characterization of the technological-determinist view of birth-control history is a composite picture and therefore schematic and slightly exaggerated. Some recent examples of such an interpretation can be found in James Reed's *From Private Vice to Public Virtue* (New York: Basic, 1978).

4. An example of this use of modernization theory is Edward Shorter's *The Making of the Modern Family* (New York: Basic, 1975).

5. See Gordon, *Woman's Body, Woman's Right*, chap. 3. For corroboration in a more recent historical study, see James Mohr's *Abortion in America* (New York: Oxford University Press, 1978), chaps. 2 and 3.

6. This view of feminism was offered by the nineteenth-century suffragists

themselves; it can be found argued well in several general surveys of the women's rights movement, including Aileen Kraditor's *Ideas of the Woman Suffrage Movement* (New York: Columbia University Press, 1965).

7. Today many feminists use the term "patriarchy" as a general synonym for male supremacy; in that sense it would be questionable to assert that patriarchy had declined. I use "patriarchy" in a specific historical sense: referring to a system of family production in which the male head of the family (hence patriarchy, meaning rule of the *father*) controls the wealth and labor power of all family members. In a patriarchal system, for example, unmarried and childless men lacked the power of fathers since they often lacked labor power; by comparison, it would be hard to argue that today unmarried or childless men were weaker than fathers. The development of industrial production (incidentally, in its "socialist" as well as capitalist varieties) tended to weaken patriarchy by providing opportunities for economic and social independence for children and women. Thus, notice that patriarchy is a system of generational as well as gender relations.

8. R. Bogue and D. W. Sigelman, *Sterilization Report Number 3: Continuing Violations of Federal Sterilization Guidelines by Teaching Hospitals in 1979* (Washington, D.C.: Public Citizen Health Research Group, 1979), as summarized in *Family Planning Perspectives* 11, no. 6 (November/December 1979): 366–67.

9. For example, Elizabeth Moore, in *In These Times*, 28 February 1979.

10. These ideas are argued more fully and supported in my "Individualism and the Critique of Individualism in the History of Feminist Theory" (paper given at the Simone de Beauvoir Commemorative Conference, 1979).

11. See Linda Gordon and Allen Hunter, "Sex, Family, and the New Right: Anti-feminism as a Political Force," *Radical America*, November 1977–February 1978; reprinted as a pamphlet by the New England Free Press, 60 Union Square, Somerville, Mass. 02143. Throughout this paper I am indebted to Hunter's work on the New Right.

4

The Fantasy
of the Perfect Mother

In the late 1960s and early '70s, feminists raised initial questions and developed a consensus of sorts about mothering. We pointed to the pervasive pronatalism of our culture; argued for safe, available abortions and birth control; criticized the health-care system; and advocated maternity and paternity benefits and leaves as well as accessible and subsidized parent- and community-controlled day care, innovative work-time arrangements, shared parenting, and other nontraditional child-rearing and household arrangements. These consensual positions among feminists all centered on the argument that women's lives should not be totally constrained by child care or childbearing. Women should be free to choose not to bear children; should have easy access to safe contraception and abortion; should be able to continue their other work if mothers; and should have available to them good day care. In contrast, recent feminist writing on motherhood focuses more on the experience of mothering: If a woman wants to be a mother, what is or should be her experience? Given that parenting is necessary in any society, who should parent and how should the parenting be done? Feminist writing now recognizes that many women, including many feminists, want to have children and experience mothering as a rich and complex endeavor.

The new feminist writing has turned to mothering even while insisting on women's right to choose not to mother or to do other things in addition to mothering. Feminists often wish to speak to nonfeminist or

© 1980 by Nancy Chodorow and Susan Contratto.

We are enormously indebted to Linda Gordon, Arlie Hochschild, Sara Ruddick, Judith Stacey, Catharine Stimpson, and Barrie Thorne for their very careful reading of an earlier version of this essay. We also benefited greatly from discussions with Sherry Ortner and Norma Wikler. Although these people did not always agree with our positions, their ideas aided our ongoing explorations of the issues we examine. NIMH Training Grant MH 15 122-03 provided support for Susan Contratto during the writing of the essay.

antifeminist mothers about mothering without succumbing to heterosexism or promaternalism. The assumption that women have the right to mother, as well as not to mother, and the recognition that mothering, though it may be conflictual and oppressive, is also emotionally central and gratifying in some women's lives, has created a level of tension and ambivalence in recent writing that was missing in the earlier discussion.

This essay examines certain recurrent psychological themes in recent feminist writing on motherhood.[1] These themes include a sense that mothers are totally responsible for the outcomes of their mothering, even if their behavior is in turn shaped by male-dominant society. Belief in the all-powerful mother spawns a recurrent tendency to blame the mother on the one hand, and a fantasy of maternal perfectibility on the other. The writings also elaborate maternal sexuality or asexuality, aggression and omnipotence in the mother-child relationship, and the isolation of the mother-child dyad. This isolation provides the supercharged environment in which aggression and, to a lesser degree, sexuality become problematic, and the context in which a fantasy of the perfect mother can also be played out.

We point to, and are concerned with, two features of these understandings of motherhood. They have an unprocessed quality; it is as if notions that the personal is political have been interpreted to mean that almost primal fantasies constitute feminist politics or theory. Further, we think there is a striking continuity between these feminist treatments of motherhood and themes found in the culture at large, even among antifeminists. Feminists differ about the meaning of motherhood and women's mothering, but each of these themes finds its complement in nonfeminist or antifeminist writing. Both these features of the writings we discuss are problematic for feminist theory and politics.

The All-Powerful Mother: Blame and Idealization

Feminist writing on motherhood assumes an all-powerful mother who, because she is totally responsible for how her children turn out, is blamed for everything from her daughter's limitations to the crisis of human existence. Nancy Friday's *My Mother/My Self* exemplifies this genre at its most extreme.[2] The book's central argument is that mothers are noxious to daughters, and that a daughter's subsequent unhappinesses and failings stem from this initial relationship. Friday follows the daughter through the life cycle and shows at each stage how mothers forcefully, intentionally, and often viciously constrain and control daughters, keep them from individuating, and, especially, deny daughters their sexuality and keep them from men.[3] Mothers make daughters in their image: As the mother, in becoming a mother, has denied her own sexuality, so she must deny sexuality to her daughter. Friday even seems to blame mothers for the act of toilet training their daughters.[4]

Even when Friday points to other causes of a daughter's problems, it is still the mother's fault: Sexual information learned in school or from friends doesn't alter a mother's impact; women are ultimately responsible even for obstetrical atrocities performed by men in the interests of male power. Friday relates Seymour Fisher's finding that good female relationships with men depend on the belief that a daughter's father will not desert her, but then she asks, "But who put on the sexual brakes to begin with?"[5] Friday makes occasional disclaimers; for example, blaming mother is not taking responsibility for oneself.[6] But these disclaimers are buried in 460 pages of the opposite message. They are certainly not the message we remember from the book.

It is not clear whether Friday considers herself a feminist (though she certainly claims to be a woman's advocate and many see her as a feminist). In any event, she reflects in extreme form a widespread feminist position, one that also argues that mothers are the agents of their daughters' oppression and also pays lip service (or more) to the fact that mothers themselves are oppressed and are therefore not responsible. Judith Arcana's *Our Mothers' Daughters*,[7] for instance, written out of explicit feminist commitment and concern, gives us an account almost exactly like Friday's. The only difference from Friday is that Arcana claims that maternal behavior is a product of mothers' entrapment within patriarchy rather than a product of their evil intentions.

While Friday and Arcana condemn mothers for what they do to their daughters, Dorothy Dinnerstein in *The Mermaid and the Minotaur* discusses the disastrous impact of maternal caretaking on sons, daughters, and society as a whole.[8] Dinnerstein claims that, as a result of "mother-dominated infancy," adult men and women are "semi-human, monstrous"—grown-up children acting out a species-suicidal pathology.[9] In Dinnerstein's account the mother is an object of children's fury and desperation, and children will put up with and create anything to escape her evil influence: "The deepest root of our acquiescence to the maiming and mutual imprisonment of men and women lies in the monolithic fact of human childhood: under the arrangements that now prevail, a woman is the parental person who is every infant's first love, first witness, and first boss, the person who presides over the infant's first encounters with the natural surroundings and who exists for the infant as the first representative of the flesh."[10]

Dinnerstein's account, like Friday's and Arcana's, confuses infantile fantasy with the actuality of maternal behavior. Thus, even as Dinnerstein describes the infantile fantasies that emerge from female-dominated child care, she also asserts that mothers are in fact all-powerful, fearsome creatures. She emphasizes the *"absolute power"* of the *"mother's life-and-death control over helpless infancy: an intimately carnal control"* whose *"wrath is all-potent"* and whose *"intentionality is so formidable—so terrifying and . . . so alluring."* [11] This potency engages with the infant's totally helpless need and dependence; it humiliates, controls, and dominates as it seduces, succors, and saves. As a result, according to Dinnerstein, the mother (or whoever would care for the child) is inevitably the child's adversary.

Dinnerstein says that women's exclusive mothering affects the child's relationship to mother and father, attitudes toward the body, and adult erotic capacities. It shapes the later ambivalence toward nature and nature's resources, creates an unhealthy split between love and work, produces adults who parent differently according to sex, fosters particular kinds of destructive power and ensures patriarchal control of that power, and forms the nature of our history-making impulse. [12] In short, women's all-powerful mothering shapes the child's entire psychological, social, and political experience and is responsible for a species life that "is cancerous, out of control." [13]

The other side of blaming the mother is idealization of her and her possibilities: If only the mother wouldn't do what she is doing, she would be perfect. Friday's perfect mother is self-sacrificing and giving (though ultimately in the interest of her own deferred emotional rewards): "The truly loving mother is one whose interest and happiness is in seeing her daughter as a person, not just a possession. It is a process of being so generous and loving that she will forego some of her own pleasure and security to add to her daughter's development. If she does this in a genuine way, she really does end up with that Love Insurance Policy." "It is a noble role that mother must play here." [14] Friday, the new woman's advocate, sounds like the most traditional traditionalist.

Most feminist writing does not expect mothers to change on their own. As feminists locate blame, they also focus on the conditions—those of patriarchy—in which bad mothering takes place, in which mothers are victims and powerless in the perpetuation of evil. But this implies that if only we could remove these patriarchal constraints, mothering could be perfect. Arcana, in pointing to women who have broken out of the traditional mold, wants to turn these women into perfect mothers: "Such women may mother us all." [15]

These writings suggest not only that mothers can be perfect but also that the child's needs (e.g., those of the daughters in the books by Friday and Arcana) are necessarily legitimate and must be met. Such an implication persists in the most subtle and sophisticated feminist accounts. Jane Flax, for instance, offers an analysis of the psychodynamics of the mother-daughter relationship in which she writes of the difficulties of being a mother in a male-dominant society and of the psychological conflicts that setting generates.[16] She offers perceptive insights into the contradictory needs that emerge from being mothered by a woman. But her article still implies that mothers can be perfect and that the child's felt desires are absolute needs: "As a result of all these conflicts, it is more difficult for the mother to be as emotionally available as her infant daughter needs her to be."[17] The "needs" to which she refers are those of women patients talking about their mothers, and Flax accepts their accounts. She does not suggest that a child's "needs" might be unrealistic or unreasonable.

We find the idealization of maternal possibility not only in those accounts that blame the mother but also in another strain of feminist writing on motherhood, one that begins from identification with the mother rather than with the daughter. Adrienne Rich and Alice Rossi also premise their investigations of motherhood on the assumption that a maternal ideal or perfection could emerge with the overthrow of patriarchy.[18] Both discuss mothering as it has been affected by patriarchy and describe how patriarchy has controlled—as Rich observes, even killed—mothers and children. Mothers are not powerful, but powerless under patriarchy.

Rich provides a moving account of maternal love and concern and a vision of the potential power of women's maternal bodies, which could enable women to be intellectually, spiritually, and sexually transformative, and which could forge nurturant, sexual, and spiritual linkages among women:

> The repossession by women of our bodies will bring far more
> essential change to human society than the seizing of the means
> of production by workers. . . . We need to imagine a world in
> which every woman is the presiding genius of her own body. In
> such a world, women will truly create new life, bringing forth
> not only children (if and as we choose), but the visions and the
> thinking necessary to sustain, console and alter human
> existence—a new relationship to the universe. Sexuality, politics
> intelligence, position, motherhood, work, community, intimacy
> will develop new meanings; thinking itself will be transformed.
> This is where we have to begin.[19]

Rossi, like Rich, turns to women's maternalism, but she focuses less on the global social and cultural implications of the freeing of motherhood from patriarchal technological constraints and more on the possibilities of the mothering experience. Rossi argues that women have a "biological edge" in parental capacities and implies that children will do best with their natural mothers if these mothers can reclaim their bodies and come in touch with their innate mothering potential, and if their experience can be removed from male-dominant social organization. Rossi stresses the natural and untutored quality of some of women's intuitive responses to infants and the potential interconnection of sexual and maternal gratification. All these qualities could be enhanced if their expression were not distorted or destroyed by doctor-centered obstetric management, by industrial threats to fetuses and pregnant women, by too-close spacing of children, by women mothering according to a male life script (i.e., self-involved instead of nurturant). The return to a more natural mothering relationship would also sustain and further connections among women, the "women's culture" that the feminist movement has emphasized. Like Rich, Rossi implies that mothering could be wonderful if women could recognize and take pleasure in their procreative and maternal capacities and if these were not taken over by institutional constraints and alienated understandings of mothering.

Sexuality

Contradictory fantasies and expectations about maternity/mothering and sexuality also emerge in the new feminist literature. In the *Dialectic of Sex*, an influential early feminist book, Shulamith Firestone argued that biological sex is the basic social category and contradiction.[20] The reproductive difference between the sexes—that women bear children—leads to a sexual division of labor that is the root of all women's oppression by men, as well as oppressions of class and race. Since the fact of their biological childbearing capacities causes women's oppression, women must be freed from this biology. According to Firestone, the solution would be a technology that eliminates biological reproduction, untied to anyone's procreative body. This would end both biological and social motherhood.

In place of a male-dominant society based on women's biology and the biological family, Firestone envisions a society with total sexual liberation and a positively valued polymorphous perversity. By implication, freeing women from their reproductive biology leads to, and is a prerequisite of, sexual liberation. According to Firestone, pregnant bodies are ugly, and motherhood and sexuality are incompatible. In the new society, people would have individual freedom to move in and out of relationships, children could live where and with whom they want, and there would be no parental relationships as we know them. "Down with childhood" is the other side of "down with mothers." Firestone argues that the only alternative to the inequities of the family is no family at all, no long-term commitments of anyone to anyone; everyone must be an individual without ties. Thus, for Firestone, individualism goes along with a liberated sexuality, and both are inherently opposed to motherhood. For Nancy Friday, also, women's goal in life is to attain sexual individuality, which is the opposite of being a mother. Womanhood is nonmaternal (hetero)sexuality. Relationships between mother and daughter—and between women generally—are entirely negative. From early childhood, little girls try to do one another in. Sexual relationships with men offer the only positive direction and the best thing a mother can do for her daughter is to promote her heterosexuality.

One strand of feminism, then, is represented by Shulamith Firestone, who would wipe out women's procreative capacities altogether, and by Nancy Friday, who poses a choice for women between exercising their procreative capacities and expressing their sexuality. Both imply a radical split between sexuality and maternity and opt for sexuality, either in its polymorphous perverse or its genital heterosexual form.

We find an opposing strand in Rossi and Rich, who identify motherhood with sexuality and would locate one foundation of women's liberation and fulfillment in the repossession (in the broadest sense) of their maternal bodies. Rich and Rossi imply that patriarchal institutions have distorted a natural maternal essence and potential for the mother-child bond. Rossi points to the inherent sexual pleasures of the mothering experience, and Rich suggests a connection between the physical pleasures of the mother-infant (especially mother-daughter) relationship and sexual bonds between women.

Aggression and Death

If having a child makes a mother all-powerful or totally powerless, if women's maternal potential requires the desexing of women or enables fully embodied power, then the child who evokes this arrangement must also be all-powerful. The child's existence or potential existence can dominate the mother's. This leads to a fourth theme that emerges in recent feminist writing on motherhood, a theme that grows out of the writer's identification as a mother or potential mother: an almost primal aggression in the mother-child relationship, an aggression that goes from mother to child, from child to mother, from mother-as-child to her own mother. Cemented by maternal and infantile rage, motherhood becomes linked to destruction and death. Rich, for instance, introduces and concludes her account of mothering within patriarchy with the story of a depressed suburban housewife and mother who decapitated her two youngest children.

Feminist Studies, one of the major scholarly feminist journals, published a special issue, "Toward a Feminist Theory of Motherhood," on this theme.[21] With four exceptions, the issue is about motherhood, horror, and death. We read articles, poems, and autobiographical accounts about maternal death, children's deaths, the blood of childbirth, spontaneous abortions, stillbirths, the inability to conceive, childbirth as an experience of death, nineteenth-century obstetric torture techniques, unmothered monsters, child murder, and incest. Some of these articles, poems, and accounts are beautifully written, finely constructed, powerful, and persuasive. They illuminate women's fantasies and fears and guide us insightfully to themes and preoccupations we had not previously considered. Yet, the whole obliterates the parts: We are left, not with memories of these individual creations, but with impressions of an inextricable linkage of motherhood, blood, gore, destruction, and death.

Rachel Blau DuPlessis, the issue editor, points out that the contributions to the issue, in stressing the intertwining of birth, life, and death, react to cultural images of the mother as idealized nurturer. DuPlessis points out that there is, as yet, no synthesis,[22] but she also does not seem to want to create one. On the contrary, polarities are writ large; an almost satanic imagery of blood, guts, and destruction and subjective expostulation substitutes for cultural idealization. There is little attempt to investigate reality in its complex subjective and objective breadth.

Kate Millett's recent book, *The Basement: Meditations on a Human Sacrifice*, further extends the linkage of motherhood, violence, and death.[23] The book is a true account of a woman, her seven children, and their torture-murder of a sixteen-year-old girl who was left in the woman's charge by her parents. Millet portrays the torturer-protagonist as society's victim: The squalor and poverty that surround her and her abandonment by men are not of her making. Therefore, her craziness is inevitable and understandable. Motherhood contributes to the violence she feels: She is supposed to be the "responsible" adult with her children, in a situation where she has little power, and she visits her rage and frustration on one of them. The victim-mother creates a victim-child.

Jane Lazarre's feminist and autobiographical book, *The Mother Knot*, certainly less absolute and bleak than *The Basement*, also tells a story of maternal anger and victimization, and of the link between mother as victim and child as victim.[24] Lazarre sets out to tell the story of maternal ambivalence—the only "eternal and natural" feature of motherhood. Motherhood turns the woman's love relationship into the formal role pattern of Husband and Wife and brings her to the brink of madness. The protagonist's ambivalence is her profoundest reality. She desperately loves and resents her child, feels tenderness and rage at her husband. Hate and love, fury and overwhelming joy, remain unfused and unresolved, experienced only in their pure and alternating forms.[25]

In these accounts, a fantasied omnipotence, played out in the realm of aggression and anger, oscillates between mother and child. On the one hand, we have an all-powerful mother and a powerless child. On the other hand, we have the child who identifies with the all-powerful mother and whose very being casts its mother into the role of total victim or angel. Thus, in the *Feminist Studies* special issue, in Millett's story, and in Rich's account of the woman who murders her children, we find the notion that having a child is enough to kill a woman or make a woman into a murderer. Being a mother is a matter of life and death; having a child destroys the mother or the child. If antifeminists have tended more than feminists to blame the mother, feminists tend to blame the child, or the having of children.

Why? There is, of course, historical and psychological truth here. Women's lives change radically when they have children, and caring for children in our society is difficult. The institution of motherhood, as Rich shows, is indeed oppressive to mothers and to those who are not mothers. Moreover, millions of women have died in childbirth throughout history, often as a direct result of obstetrical interference. In the past, infant mortality was often as likely as infant survival. Even today, the United States ranks high in infant mortality rates when compared with other industrialized nations. Moreover, surviving a child, or experiencing one's infant's death, in an age when we expect orderly generational progression, is a tragedy that can leave a permanent scar.

And yet death and destruction are by no means the whole experience or institution of motherhood. Rich and Millett suggest that the continuity of violence from men to women and women to children accounts for the link of motherhood and death, and we feel this is partly correct. The *Feminist Studies* issue seems to suggest an even deeper, more inevitable link. The writer is the mother whose individuality and separateness are threatened by the child and whose fantasy therefore kills it; and she is the child who is both the destroyer of the mother and the object of destruction. In this rendition, mother and child seem caught in a fantasied exclusive and exclusionary dyad where aggression, frustration, and rage hold sway. These writers merge fantasies of maternal omnipotence into the totalizing quality of the experience of the mother-child relationship.

Maternal Isolation

Another assumption apparent in recent feminist literature is that mother and child are an isolated dyad. Mother and child are seen as both physically and psychologically apart from the world, existing within a magic (or cursed) circle. Sometimes, as in Millett's work, the isolation has a physical boundary to it. The woman's home is her castle, in which she is isolated and all-powerful in motherhood. The children's fathers have left her. Her neighbors, hearing the screams from her basement, choose to leave her alone; they say it is her right and responsibility to discipline her children, and besides, they do not want to get involved. Other adults—social workers, the school personnel, the minister—are also loath to tread on a mother's space.

More often, the isolation is psychological. Rich talks of the isolation that comes from responsibility, that of the single adult woman who, though physically surrounded by others, bears the total task of mothering. The successes, failures, and day-to-day burdens of child care are particularly hers. Lazarre chillingly describes the isolation of responsibility she faces (and creates). And she shows how that isolation helps lead to her desolation, rage, and destructiveness. Dinnerstein sees the isolation from the point of view of the child's development and describes how it magnifies the relation to the mother and creates in the child a desperate need to escape.

At the same time, some feminist writing wishes to maintain a form of isolated mother-child relationship but to make it unique and special in a positive way. The protagonist of *The Mother Knot* sets herself off from others and wishes to retreat into the perfect unit of infant and mother. Rich and Rossi wish conditions to change so that mothers receive the community support that would enable the specialness of the mothering relation to emerge.

In these accounts, this isolation, in which mother and child live in a unique and potent relationship, explains and even justifies the effects of mothering. It explains why mothers (even in their oppression by patriarchy) are so all-powerful in relation to their children, and why the mother-child relation is likely to be so bound up with powerful feelings. Mother and child are on a psychological desert island. Having only each other, each is continually impinging and intruding on the other, and there is no possibility of escape. As a result, the other becomes the object of aggressive fantasies and behaviors, and mothering becomes linked to extremist expectations about sexuality.

Cultural and Psychological Roots of Feminist Interpretations of Mothering

We have discussed four interrelated psychological themes that emerge from recent feminist work on mothering: (1) blaming and idealizing the mother, assuming that mothers are or can be all-powerful and perfect and that mothering either destroys the world or generates world perfection; (2) extreme expectations of maternal sexuality, asserting the incompatibility of motherhood and sexuality or romanticizing maternal sexuality; (3) a link between motherhood and aggression or death; and (4) an emphasis on the isolation of mother and child. All these themes share common characteristics: their continuity with dominant cultural understandings of mothering and their rootedness in unprocessed, infantile fantasies about mothers.

Our cultural understandings of mothering have a long history, but reached a peak in the nineteenth century. That century witnessed the growth of a sexual division of spheres that materially grounded mother-child isolation and bequeathed us a picture of the ideal mother who would guarantee both morally perfect children and a morally desirable world.[26] At a time when everyone's life was being affected by the frenzied growth of developing industrial capitalism, somehow mothers were seen as having total control and unlimited power in the creation of their children.

Post-Freudian psychology assumes the mother-child isolated unit that nineteenth-century industrial development produced and elaborates the notion that the early mother-infant relationship is central to later psychological development and to the psychological, emotional, and relational life of the child. As a result of this assumption, virtually all developmental research of the last thirty-five years has been directed to this early period. This has further reinforced and seemed to substantiate the popular view that the relationship of mother and infant has extraordinary significance. The assumption has also often led to a psychological determinism and reductionism that argues that what happens in the earliest mother-infant relationship determines the whole of history, society, and culture.[27]

Both nineteenth-century cultural ideology about motherhood and post-Freudian psychological theory blame mothers for any failings in their children and idealize possible maternal perfection. Blaming the mother, a major outcome of these theories and a major theme in feminist writings, has a long social history. David Levy's *Maternal Overprotection*, the Momism of Wylie and Erikson, literature on the schizophrenogenic mother, Rheingold's analysis of maternal aggression as the primary pathogenic influence on the child, Slater's discussion of the oedipally titillating, overwhelming mother, and Lasch's account of the mother "impos[ing] her madness on everyone else," all suggest the terrible outcome of the omnipotent mother.[28] With the exception of Slater, they ignore any conditions that determine or foster maternal behavior in the first place and accept a completely deterministic view of child development.[29]

More recently, as women have entered the paid labor force and some have chosen not to become mothers, mothers have been blamed more for what is called "maternal deprivation" than for "maternal overprotection." Selma Fraiberg's recent *Every Child's Birthright: In Defense of Mothering* is a good example.[30] Describing herself as the child's advocate, Fraiberg has no sympathy for women who choose to work. Her message is clear: A good mother does not use regular substitute child care before the age of three.

Thus, feminists' tendency to blame the mother (the perspective of feminist-as-child) fits into cultural patterning. Feminists simply add on to this picture the notion that conditions other than the mother's incompetence or intentional malevolence create this maternal behavior. But feminists do not question the accuracy of this characterization of maternal behavior, nor its effects.

As we suggested, idealization and blaming the mother are two sides of the same belief in the all-powerful mother. In the nineteenth century, the bourgeois mother received moral training and guidance to enhance her motherly performance, guidance that, if followed, would lead children and the world to moral perfection. In contemporary child-rearing manuals, the good mother knows naturally how to mother if she will only follow her instincts,[31] or can be perfect if she will only stay home full-time,[32] or can provide proper stimulation and gentle teaching to her child.[33] Feminists take issue with the notion that a mother can be perfect in the here and now, given male dominance, lack of equality in marriage, and inadequate resources and support, but the fantasy of the perfect mother remains: If current limitations on mothers were eliminated, mothers would know naturally how to be good.

Blame and idealization of mothers have become our cultural ideology. This ideology, however, gains meaning from and is partially produced by infantile fantasies that are themselves the outcome of being mothered exclusively by one woman. If mothers have exclusive responsibility for infants who are totally dependent, then to the infant they are the source of all good and evil.[34] Times of closeness, oneness, and joy are the quintessence of perfect understanding; times of distress, frustration, discomfort, and too great separation are entirely the mother's fault. For the infant, the mother is not someone with her own life, wants, needs, history, other social relationships, work. She is known only in her capacity as mother. Growing up means learning that she, like other people in one's life, has and wants a life of her own, and that loving her means recognizing her subjectivity and appreciating her separateness. But people have trouble doing this and continue, condoned and supported by the ideology about mothers they subsequently learn, to experience mothers solely as people who did or did not live up to their child's expectations. This creates the quality of rage we find in "blame-the-mother" literature and the unrealistic expectation that perfection would result if only a mother would devote her life completely to her child and all impediments to doing so were removed. Psyche and culture merge here and reflexively create one another.

Originally, idealization of mothers is an infantile fantasy: No human being can be perfect. Thus, although the idealization of maternal life found in both Rich's and Rossi's writing is more from the perspective of mothers, their accounts are also informed by some identification with the stance of the child, who *needs* certain things in order to develop. One focus of Rossi's argument is the biological tie of infant to mother. Rich also claims that the child has powerful, strong feelings for the mother, "authentic" need—"a need vaster than any single human being could satisfy, except by loving continuously, unconditionally, from dawn to dark, and often in the middle of the night."[35] This need is evoked by the sense of uniqueness of the mother, by her singularity. This leads us to ask: What will happen to these "authentic" needs, and who will fulfill them? Does Rich think these intense feelings will disappear in a non-male-dominant world? Or are they inherent in mothering and, therefore, unavoidable? To what degree are they a product of the institution of motherhood under patriarchy and the experience of mothering it generates? And once there are "needs" and feelings like this, won't we start evaluating and idealizing mothers who do and do not meet them, and do and do not feel them?[36]

Fantasy and cultural ideology also meet in themes about maternal sexuality. An assumed incompatibility between sexuality and motherhood is largely a product of our nineteenth-century heritage, and some women psychoanalysts have helped perpetuate this cultural and psychological belief. In the *Psychology of Women*, Helene Deutsch claims clinical and literary support for the view that there is a natural and desirable psychological split between motherliness and erotic feelings.[37] Therese Benedek suggests that "mature" (i.e., motherly) women are simply less sexual than "immature" women.[38]

Ambivalence about maternal bodies, especially around sexuality, is present in the experience of many women, both as mothers and as daughters/children or would-be mothers. The trend, ideologically and for individual women, has been to opt for asexual motherhood. Rossi and Rich argue strongly against the view that motherhood and sexuality are incompatible; other feminists, like Firestone and Friday, accept the traditional view of incompatibility yet, unlike the analysts, argue in favor of sexuality.[39]

The understandings of motherhood we have been describing are larger than life and seen only in extremes. For Dinnerstein, women's mothering generates conditions that threaten to destroy human existence. For DuPlessis, a feminist theory of motherhood must begin with the inextricable link of motherhood and death; motherhood, she says, relates to heaven and hell, and to speech and silence; the overcoming of the institution of motherhood will be the end of dualism. For Friday, we must choose to be sexual or maternal. For Firestone, we must either accept inequality or give up our reproductive biology.

Rage is an inevitable outcome of this extremism. Psychological theory and cultural ideology have focused on the harm that mothers can do to their children, and some feminists continue to focus on this harm. We magnify the impact of one individual, the mother, and when the child in us suffers the inevitable frustrations of living, we blame our mothers. *My*

Mother/My Self has been extraordinarily popular. It speaks to the daughter in all women and tells them that their problems are not political, social, personal, or, heaven forbid, caused by men; their problems are caused solely by their mothers. We are all prone to mother-hating, for we live in a society that says that mothers can and should do all for their children. Moreover, we were all mothered, and our psyches retain the imprint of these origins.

Other feminists move beyond this position. They describe aggression done to women first by men and then by children, which leads to mothers' rageful fantasies and behaviors. Children's aggression in this model is expectation as much as actuality. Starting from the belief that "perfect" mothering is both centrally important and possible, if only a mother is totally devoted and attentive, as these feminists become mothers, or imagine being mothers, they fear the experience as all-consuming and come unconsciously and consciously to resent, fear, and feel devoured by their children. The outcome is the powerful aggressive feelings and behaviors and preoccupation with death we described above. The outcome also is to experience a total and overwhelming isolation of self with child.

Thus we can see a progressive logic to feminist themes about motherhood, a logic that moves a woman from an identification as daughter or child to identification as mother. Drawing from and reflecting a cultural ideology and infantile sense of infantile need and maternal responsibility for the outcomes of child rearing, feminists begin by identifying with the child and blaming the mother, or by expecting her to be more than perfect. Cultural ideology and fantasy can also lead to idealization of maternal life from the point of view of the mother, as in the writing of Rossi and Rich. More often, the belief in total infantile need and maternal responsiblity, and identification with the angry child, lead to a maternal identification that is in its turn full of rage and fear, and a sense that the conditions of patriarchy totally oppress mothers and isolate them with their child.

Feminism and Mothering: Moving Beyond a Politics of Primary Process

Where does this analysis lead us? In our identities as women, theoretically and programmatically, feminists need to move beyond the extremist assumptions and fantasies we have described. Insofar as we treat mothers as larger than life, omnipotent, all-powerful, or all-powerless, and motherhood as intimately connected to death, we deny mothers the complexity of their lives, their selfhood, their agency in creating from institutional context and experienced feelings. We deny them their place in a two-way relationship with their children, manifold relationships with the rest of the world; and we deny ourselves as mothers. But insofar as mothers are women, this involves a denial of all women as active subjects and a denial and split in our self-identities as children/daughters and people as well. This reflexively self-denying split of self from mother who is a fantasy partially accounts for the ambivalence and anger found in much of this writing.

As political beings, we must also question our involvement in child-centered assumptions about mothers. As individuals we can lament the past, wish we had gotten more than we had, wish we had been "better" mothered, and so forth. Although this stance may provide some temporary catharsis, it does not in itself help us to understand what we might do, personally or politically, in the present. We may think "our mothers" got us into this situation, but this knowledge alone can never tell us how to get out of it. Catharsis and rage may be a first step to political activity or working to change one's situation, but by themselves they lead nowhere. Rather, they trap us in our private psychical reality, and they dissipate energy.

In particular, feminists need to be especially self-conscious about the way they draw upon fantasy to inform theory and politics. Much of the feminist writing we have considered puts forth fantasy, or primary process thinking as the whole of reality or as a self-evident basis for theory and politics.[40] Fantasies are obviously fundamental experiences, and we must take them into account in creating a feminism that speaks to women's lives, but they cannot in themselves constitute theory or justify political choices. We need to analyze and reflect upon them, to allow secondary process thinking to mediate and interpret primary process reality. Moreover, it is not enough simply to claim that a particular fantasy, feeling, or behavior is a product of patriarchy, or women's oppression, and that therefore it cannot be further evaluated.

A striking instance of the problem created by accepting fantasy as the self-evident basis of theory or politics—of believing that it is enough to know that a woman's feeling or behavior is a product of her oppression—is a peculiar preoccupation with and moral paralysis around acts of maternal violence in some of the accounts discussed. In the case of violence against women, feminists have been outraged. We have focused on the fact of this violence and have worked to protect women from the wife beater, rapist, and assaulter. We have been properly angered by research and policies whose goal is to understand the individual motivations and causes of this violence rather than to eliminate it and protect its victims. By contrast, when we read Rich on maternal violence, Millett on maternal torture-murder, and the rampant aggression conveyed in the *Feminist Studies* issue, we find that maternal violence is described but not opposed. These writings focus on the cause and motivation of maternal violence—"patriarchy"—to the exclusion of the fact of the violence.

The preoccupation with fantasies and their sources in oppression has embroiled us in violence, has allowed us to understand but not to condemn it, as we do in the case of violence against women. This preoccupation does not allow for the necessary political and moral argument that people, even within oppressive systems, can choose among a variety of actions; that although unreflected-upon feeling may determine action, it need not.

These accounts thus reflect the assumption that any act motivated by an internal emotional state, if that state reacts to women's oppression, is by definition political. Further, they lead to the conclusion that all acts motivated in this way are equally correct as political actions. But it is inadequate to imply that women's fantasies are automatically an extension of the personal that is political. Consider, for example, an abused wife who has murderous fantasies toward an abusive husband and kills him. We might call her act political, and we would in many circumstances defend her in the courts. But most of us would have preferred that she had left him and started a new life with the aid of a support group or shelter for battered wives. We would consider this a better individual and political strategy. That the personal is political, that we can understand motherhood as experience and institution, implies that fantasies and feelings inform but do not directly determine our thoughtful, analyzed political decisions and judgments. The feminist accounts of mothering we discussed do not take that step. They do not move beyond seeing personal experience (feeling) and political institution (patriarchy) as absolute.

Recent feminist writing on motherhood has moved us forward in many areas. Adrienne Rich has transformed our ability to locate the many facets of motherhood as institution and has written powerfully of the complexity of maternal feeling and experience. Other feminists have called attention to the constraints, if not horrors, of mothering in a male-dominant society that devalues mothering, a society in which many mothers have no economic, communal, familial, or medical resources. Dorothy Dinnerstein persuaded many feminists of the serious consequences of exclusively female mothering. The *Feminist Studies* special issue, Nancy Friday, and Jane Lazarre have all revealed how overwhelmed women may feel as mothers or as children (daughters) of mothers. Rich, Rossi, and Lazarre have begun to articulate for us, sometimes in idealized ways (or ways that threaten to maintain the equation of woman and mother), what a nonpatriarchal motherhood or nurturance might be.

But all this writing has been limited in a particular way: Feminist theories of motherhood have not been able to move further because, as we have suggested, they are trapped in the dominant cultural assumptions and fantasies about mothering, *which in turn* rest on fantasied and unexamined notions of child development. Feminists have analyzed assumptions and biases in various disciplines, and feminism early on led us to notice cultural assumptions about gender (e.g., about sexual orientation) in society. But feminists have been trying to build a theory of mothering without examining or noticing that a theory of mothering requires a theory of childhood and child development as well.

Instead of developing this theory, feminists have built their theories of mothering on the dominant cultural and psychological assumptions about childhood. Drawing on psychoanalysis, these assumptions include an idealization of early infancy, in which development is seen exclusively as a painful process. The baby is most peaceful in utero, and birth is the first trauma and fraught with inevitable anxiety. There is now a trend toward trying to take the edge off this experience by nonviolent birth. After initial bonding to a primary caretaker—a process both fragile and portentous—the infant begins the slow and often reluctant process of individuation, separation, and growth. Infantile rage, frustration, anxiety, loss, and fear spur emotional and cognitive development. Total dependency gives way to ambivalent independence, insatiable needs are grudgingly put aside when faced with reality, and impulses are tamed and controlled.

In this account children inevitably grow up with a residue of rage against those who frustrate their needs, even though they can grow up only if their needs are frustrated. In this model of development, mother and child are adversaries. The good mother helps the child grow up for his or her own good, and we expect and therefore allow children to be furious with their mothers for doing so. Rich's discussion of children's needs suggests such a model, as does Jane Flax's lack of differentiation between needs and wants. Dinnerstein's argument is based on the inevitable adversary relationship of parent and child. Her recommendation for shared parenting stems from her wish that the inevitable rage toward caretakers be shared between women and men.

A second set of assumptions in some feminist work draws from a simple role-learning theory of development. In the writings of Friday, Firestone, and Arcana we find the notion that children (daughters) are victims and recipients of pressures from their mothers in particular and from the culture in general. Mothers and the culture expect the repression of sexuality, feminine passivity and dependence, and docile role acceptance; and daughters passively conform to these expectations.

These models of child development seriously constrain feminist accounts of mothering. We would suggest that feminists draw upon and work to develop theories of child development that are interactive and that accord the infant and child agency and intentionality, rather than characterize it as a passive reactor to drives or environmental pressures. We need to build theories that recognize collaboration and compromise as well as conflict. We should look to theories that stress relational capacities and experiences instead of insatiable, insistent drives; to theories in which needs do not equal wants; in which separation is not equivalent to deprivation, and in which autonomy is different from abandonment; in which the child is thought to have some interest in growth and development. We need to separate what we take to be the infant's or child's subjective feelings from a more inclusive appraisal of the state of the infant or child. And we need theories that examine how the tie to primary caretakers develops and changes for both caretakers and child, and that examine the rewards of noninfantile modes of relating and cognizing. We must begin to look at times other than infancy in the developmental life span and relationships over time to people other than the mother to get a more accurate picture of what growing up is about.[41]

In the feminist writing we have discussed, there is an extraordinary current of energy and searching. To the extent that these accounts speak to shared feelings, they communicate with other women. The fantasy of the perfect mother, however, has led to the cultural oppression of women in the interest of a child whose needs are also fantasied. Although feminists did not invent this vision of motherhood and childhood, they have borrowed it. Feminist views of mothering, as mother and as daughter, have united infantile fantasies and a culturally child-centered perspective with a myth of maternal omnipotence, creating a totalistic, extreme, yet fragmented view of mothering and the mother-child relation in which both mother and child are paradoxically victim yet omnipotent. To begin to transform the relations of parenting and the relations of gender, to begin to transform women's lives, we must move beyond the myths and misconceptions embodied in the fantasy of the perfect mother.

Notes

1. The authors we discuss are all white and (broadly) professional/middle class. Thus they do not necessarily represent the whole feminist spectrum. We are focusing on certain dominant *themes* in several major feminist analyses of motherhood, but do not claim to discuss all aspects of these works nor all feminist writing on motherhood. Although we are often critical of the work we discuss, we have also learned from and been moved by some of this writing.

2. Nancy Friday, *My Mother/My Self* (New York: Delacorte, 1977).

3. Ibid., p. 105.

4. Ibid., pp. 133, 145.

5. Ibid., pp. 147, 157.

6. Ibid., p. 83.

7. Judith Arcana, *Our Mothers' Daughters* (Berkeley: Shameless Hussy Press, 1979).

8. Dorothy Dinnerstein, *The Mermaid and the Minotaur* (New York: Harper & Row, 1976).

9. Ibid., pp. 83, 85.

10. Ibid., p. 28.

11. Ibid., pp. 161, 164.

12. Ibid., p. 81.

13. Ibid., p. 253. Nancy Chodorow's *The Reproduction of Mothering* (Berkeley: University of California Press, 1978) has some important similarities with Dinnerstein's argument. Both books focus on the psychological meanings and consequences of women's mothering, and both argue that male and female parenting is essential for social change. Further, both take the stand that the conflicts typically found in relationships between adult men and women in our culture are grounded in the fact that both sexes are mothered by women. We are not considering Chodorow's argument here because we believe it is significantly different in ways that make it not relevant to our argument. Although Chodorow argues that women's mothering is perhaps the central feature in the reproduction of gender inequality, she also specifies the outcome of mothering in a way that leaves some autonomy to other aspects of cultural and social life. She does not take the extremist, portentous position of Dinnerstein and, in fact, has been criticized unfavorably on that score. As part of our argument holds that extremism in the analysis of mothering hurts feminist understanding and politics, we are more comfortable with this less apocalyptic approach.

14. Friday, *My Mother/My Self*, pp. 69, 113.

15. Arcana, *Our Mothers' Daughters*, p. 37.

16. Jane Flax, "The Conflict Between Nurturance and Autonomy in Mother-Daughter Relationships and Within Feminism," *Feminist Studies* 2 (June 1978): 171–89.

17. Ibid., p. 175.

18. Adrienne Rich, *Of Woman Born* (New York: Norton, 1976); Alice S.

Rossi, "Maternalism, Sexuality and the New Feminism," in *Contemporary Sexual Behavior*, ed. Joseph Zubin and John Money (Baltimore: Johns Hopkins University Press, 1973); idem, "A Biosocial Perspective on Parenting," *Daedalus* 106, no. 2 (1977): 1–31; and idem, "Considering 'A Biosocial Perspective on Parenting': Reply by Alice Rossi," *Signs* 4 no. 4 (Summer 1979): 712–17. Rich has been lauded and idealized by many feminists, whereas Rossi, also a feminist, has been criticized for making antifeminist arguments. Rossi's work, put forth in several articles, is not nearly as theoretically complete or comprehensive as Rich's, but we cite them together because their accounts are remarkably similar in their fundamentals. Both decry the patriarchal alienation of women from their maternal bodies and mothering experiences; both link motherhood and sexuality (see below); both advocate compensatory training for men even while suggesting that women's maternal nature is in some way unique.

19. Rich, *Of Woman Born*, p. 292.

20. Shulamith Firestone, *The Dialectic of Sex* (New York: Morrow, 1970).

21. *Feminist Studies*, "Special Issue: Toward a Feminist Theory of Motherhood," 2 (June 1978).

22. Rachel Blau DuPlessis, "Washing Blood," *Feminist Studies* 2 (June 1978): 1–12.

23. Kate Millett, *The Basement: Meditations on a Human Sacrifice* (New York: Simon and Schuster, 1979).

24. Jane Lazarre, *The Mother Knot* (New York: Dell, 1976).

25. Phyllis Chesler's recent *With Child: A Diary of Motherhood* (New York: Crowell, 1979) echoes many of these themes in a more straightforward autobiographical manner.

26. Ruth H. Bloch, "American Feminine Ideals in Transition: The Rise of the Moral Mother, 1785–1815," *Feminist Studies* 2 (June 1978): 100–126.

27. See, for instance, Dinnerstein, *Mermaid and the Minotaur;* Norman O. Brown, *Life Against Death* (Middletown, Conn.: Wesleyan University Press, 1959); and Lloyd de Mause, ed., *The History of Childhood* (New York: Psychohistory Press, 1974).

28. David Levy, *Maternal Overprotection* (New York: GColumbia University Press, 1943); Philip Wylie, *Generation of Vipers* (New York: Farrar, Rinehart, 1942); Erik Erikson, *Childhood and Society* (New York: Norton, 1950); Theodore Lidz, Stephen Fleck, and Alice R. Cornelison, *Schizophrenia and the Family* (New York: International Universities Press, 1965); Joseph C. Rheingold, *The Fear of Being a Woman: A Theory of Maternal Destructiveness* (New York: Grune and Stratton, 1964); Philip E. Slater, *The Pursuit of Loneliness* (Boston: Beacon, 1970); Philip E. Slater, *Earthwalk* (New York: Bantam, 1974); and Christopher Lasch, *Haven in a Heartless World: The Family Besieged* (New York: Basic, 1977), p. 153.

29. For a more extended discussion of the issue of maternal blame in the psychological literature, see Susan Contratto Weisskopf, "Maternal Guilt and Mental Health Professionals: A Reconfirming Interaction," Michigan Occasional Paper, no. 5 (Ann Arbor: University of Michigan Women's Studies Program, 1978).

30. Selma Fraiberg, *Every Child's Birthright: In Defense of Mothering* (New York: Basic, 1977).

31. Benjamin Spock, *The Pocket Book of Baby and Child Care* (New York: Pocket, 1945, 1946, 1957, 1968); and D. W. Winnicott, *The Child, the Family, and the Outside World* (New York: Penguin, 1964).

32. Fraiberg, *Every Child's Birthright;* and T. Berry Brazelton, *Infants and Mothers: Differences in Development* (New York: Delacorte, 1969).

33. Frank Caplan, *The First Twelve Months of Life* (New York: Bantam, 1971); and Penelope Leach, *Your Baby and Child from Birth to Age Five* (New York: Knopf, 1978).

34. We are assuming in this argument that infants are at a stage of cognitive and ego development where they use concrete categories that are grossly affectively laden. With maturity, these categories become more elaborated, complicated, and subtle. See Jean Piaget, *The Construction of Reality in the Child* (New York: Basic, 1954); idem, *The Language and Thought of the Child* (New York: Humanities, 1959); W. R. D. Fairbairn, *An Object-Relations Theory of the Personality* (New York: Basic, 1952); Otto Kernberg, *Borderline Conditions and Pathological Narcissism* (New York: Jason Aronson, 1975); and idem, *Object Relations Theory and Clinical Psychoanalysis* (New York: Jason Aronson, 1976).

35. Rich, *Of Woman Born*, p. 4.

36. Rich's passionate, wide-ranging work has been the inspiration for much subsequent feminist writing on motherhood (see Ruddick, this volume; *Feminist Studies* Special Issue, June 1978; and *Frontiers* 3, "Special Issue: Mothers and Daughters" (Summer 1978). We also see her work as a magnificent contribution. In some ways we feel that in criticizing it and expecting it to be even more perfect, we are reproducing the fantasy of the perfect mother. Nevertheless, we continue to think that it is problematic to look to the uniqueness and potential of women's maternal bodies and relationships, however broadly defined, for the perfectibility of women and society, and we are critical of theories of motherhood that begin from notions of need (see below).

37. Helen Deutsch, *The Psychology of Women*, vols. 1 and 2 (New York: Grune and Stratton, 1944, 1945).

38. Therese Benedek, Untitled "Discussion of Sherfey's Paper on Female Sexuality," *Journal of the American Psychoanalytic Association* 3 (1968): 424–48; and idem, "On the Psychobiology of Gender Identity," *Annual of Psychoanalysis* (New York: International Universities Press, 1976), 4:117–62.

39. See Susan (Contratto) Weisskopf, "Maternal Sexuality and Asexual Motherhood," *Signs* 5 (Summer 1980): 766–82, for a more detailed discussion of these issues. We suspect that infantile fantasies are also part of the root of notions of asexual motherhood.

40. Jessica Benjamin has suggested that we make this ideological and political work sound too easy. We do not mean to minimize the psychological processes involved in genuinely overcoming extreme feelings about mothers and mothering, the difficult struggle and growth involved in giving up infantile idealization and rage and learning to tolerate ambivalence. This process, Benjamin suggests, is something like forgiving and mourning one's should-be-perfect mother and one's should-have-been-perfect childhood. Our point here is that even if this difficult psychological work has not been accomplished, another struggle must go on: that against allowing these feelings to become the basis of theory or politics.

As we have argued, this lack of mediation or self-censorship, this putting forth of fantasy as final truth, is certainly not unique to feminist writing on motherhood. Writing and thinking about motherhood across the spectrum is rife with unexamined assumptions about maternal perfection, overwhelming rage, and so forth. We stress here that such thinking is particularly problematic for feminists.

41. Psychoanalytic object-relations theory stresses the relational affective development we have in mind. For feminist uses of this tradition, see Jessica Benjamin, "The Ends of Internalization: Adorno's Social Psychology," *Telos* 32 (Summer 1977): 42–64; idem, "Authority and the Family Revisited: or, a World Without Fathers?" *New German Critique* 13 (Winter 1978): 35–57; Chodorow, *Reproduction of Mothering;* Nancy Chodorow, "Feminism and Difference: Gender, Relation, and Difference in Psychoanalytic Perspective," *Socialist Review* 46 (1979): 51–69; and Evelyn Fox Keller, "Gender and Science," *Psychoanalysis and Contemporary Thought* 1 (1978): 409–33. Cognitive developmental psychology in the Piagetian tradition gives the child agency in making something of its environment and an interest in development and change. For a feminist use of this tradition, see Carol Gilligan, "In a Different Voice: Women's Conceptions of the Self and of Morality," *Harvard Educational Review* 47 (November 1977): 481–517; idem, "Woman's Place in Man's Life Cycle," *Harvard Educational Review* 49 (Spring 1979): 431–446.

5

SARA RUDDICK

Maternal Thinking

We are familiar with Victorian renditions of Ideal Maternal Love. My own favorite, like so many of these poems, was written by a son.

> There was a young man loved a maid
> Who taunted him, "Are you afraid,"
> She asked, "to bring me today
> Your mother's head upon a tray?"
>
> He went and slew his mother dead,
> Tore from her breast her heart so red,
> Then towards his lady love he raced,
> But tripped and fell in all his haste.
>
> As the heart rolled on the ground
> It gave forth a plaintive sound.
> And it spoke, in accents mild:
> "Did you hurt yourself, my child?" [1]

Though many of the story's wishes and fantasies are familiar, there is an unfamiliar twist to the poem. The maid asked for the mother's head, the son brought her heart. The maid feared and respected thoughts; the son believed only feelings are powerful. Again we are not surprised. The passions of maternity are so sudden, intense, and confusing that we often remain ignorant of the perspective, the *thought* that has developed from mothering. Lacking pride, we have failed to deepen or articulate that thought. This is a paper about the head of the mother.

A longer version of this paper appeared in *Feminist Studies* 6, no. 3 (Summer 1980): 343–67. Used by permission of *Feminist Studies*, % Women's Studies Program, University of Maryland, College Park, Md. 20742.

I would like especially to thank Sandra Bartky, Gail Bragg, Bell Chevigny, Nancy Chodorow, Margaret Comstock, Mary Felstiner, Berenice Fisher, Marilyn Frye, Susan Harding, Evelyn Fox Keller, Jane Lilienfield, Jane Marcus, Adrienne Rich, Amelie Rorty, William Ruddick, Barrie Thorne, Marilyn Blatt Young, readers for *Feminist Studies*, and Rayna Rapp.

I speak about a mother's *thought*—the intellectual capacities she develops, the judgments she makes, the metaphysical attitudes she assumes, the values she affirms. A mother engages in a discipline. That is, she asks certain questions rather than others; she establishes criteria for the truth, adequacy, and relevance of proposed answers; and she cares about the findings she makes and can act on. Like any discipline, hers has *characteristic* errors, temptations, and goals. The discipline of maternal thought consists in establishing criteria for determining failure and success, in setting the priorities, and in identifying the virtues and liabilities the criteria presume. To describe the capacities, judgments, metaphysical attitudes, and values of maternal thought does not presume maternal achievement. It is to describe a *conception* of achievement, the end to which maternal efforts are directed, conceptions and ends that are different from dominant public ones.[2]

In stating my claims about maternal thinking, I use a vocabulary developed in formulating theories about the general nature of thought.[3] According to these theories, *all* thought arises out of social practice. In their practices, people respond to a reality that appears to them as given, as presenting certain *demands*. The response to demands is shaped by *interests* that are generally interests in preserving, reproducing, directing, and understanding individual and group life.

These four interests are general in the sense that they arise out of the conditions of humans-in-nature and characterize us as a species. In addition, particular practices are characterized by specific interests in meeting the demands that some reality imposes on its participants. Religious, scientific, historical, mathematical, or any other thinking constitutes a disciplined response to a reality that appears to be "given." Socially organized thinkers name, elaborate, and test the particular realities to which they respond.

Maternal practice responds to the historical reality of a biological child in a particular social world. The agents of maternal practice, acting in response to the demands of their children, acquire a conceptual scheme—a vocabulary and logic of connections—through which they order and express the facts and values of their practice. In judgments and self-reflection, they refine and concretize this scheme. Intellectual activities are distinguishable but not separable from disciplines of feeling. There is a unity of reflection, judgment, and emotion. This unity I call "maternal thinking." Although I will not digress to argue the point here, it is important that maternal thinking is no more interest-governed, no more emotional, and no more relative to a particular reality (the growing child) than the thinking that arises from scientific, religious, or any other practice.

The demands of children and the interests in meeting those demands are always and only expressed by people in particular cultures and classes of their culture, living in specific geographical, technological, and historical settings. Some features of the mothering experience are invariant and nearly unchangeable; others, though changeable, are nearly universal.[4] It is therefore possible to identify interests that seem to govern maternal practice throughout the species. However, it is impossible even to begin to specify these interests without importing features specific to the class, ethnic group, and particular sex-gender system in which the interests are realized. In this essay I draw upon my knowledge of the institutions of motherhood in middle-class, white, Protestant, capitalist, patriarchal America, for these have expressed themselves in the heterosexual nuclear family in which I mother and was mothered. Although I have tried to compensate for the limits of my particular social and sexual history, I principally depend on others to correct my interpretations and translate across cultures.[5]

Interests Governing Maternal Practice

Children "demand" that their lives be preserved and their growth fostered. Their social group "demands" that their growth be shaped in a way acceptable to the next generation. Maternal practice is governed by (at least) three interests in satisfying these demands for preservation, growth, and acceptability. Preservation is the most invariant and primary of the three. Because a caretaking mother typically bears her own children, preservation begins when conception is recognized and accepted. Although the form of preservation depends on widely variant beliefs about the fragility and care of the fetus, women have always had a lore in which they recorded their concerns for the baby they "carried." Once born, a child is physically vulnerable for many years. Even when she lives with the father of her child or other female adults, even when she has money to purchase or finds available supportive health and welfare services, a mother typically considers herself, and is considered by others, to be responsible for the maintenance of the life of her child.

Interest in fostering the physical, emotional, and intellectual growth of her child soon supplements a mother's interest in its preservation. The human child is typically capable of complicated emotional and intellectual development; the human adult is radically different in kind from the child it once was. A woman who mothers may be aided or assaulted by the help and advice of fathers, teachers, doctors, moralists, therapists, and others who have an interest in fostering and shaping the growth of her child. Although rarely given primary credit, a mother typically holds herself, and is held by others, responsible for the *malfunction* of the growth process.

From early on, certainly by the middle years of childhood, a mother is governed by a third interest: She must shape natural growth in such a way that her child becomes the sort of adult that she can appreciate and others can accept. Mothers will vary enormously, individually and socially, in the traits and lives they will appreciate in their children. Nevertheless, a mother typically takes as the criterion of her success the production of a young adult acceptable to her group.

The three interests in preservation, growth, and acceptability of the child govern maternal practices in general. Not all mothers are, as individuals, governed by these interests, however. Some mothers are incapable of interested participation in the practices of mothering because of emotional, intellectual, or physical disability. Severe poverty may make interested maternal practice and therefore maternal thinking nearly impossible. Then, of course, mothers engage in practices other than, and often conflicting with, mothering. Some mothers, aware of the derogation and confinement of women in maternal practice, may be disaffected. In short, actual mothers have the same relation to maternal practice as actual scientists have to scientific practice or actual believers have to religious practices. As mothers, they are governed by the interests of their respective practices. But the style, skill, commitment, and integrity with which they engage in these practices differ widely from individual to individual.

Interests in the preservation, growth, and acceptability of the child are frequently and unavoidably in conflict. A mother who watches a child eagerly push a friend aside as she or he climbs a tree is torn between preserving the child from danger, encouraging the child's physical skills and courage, and shaping a child according to moral restraints, which might, for example, inhibit the child's joy in competitive climbing. Although some mothers deny or are insensitive to the conflict, and others are clear about which interest should take precedence, mothers typically know that they cannot secure each interest, they know that goods conflict, and they know that unqualified success in realizing interests is an illusion. This unavoidable conflict of basic interests is one objective basis for the maternal humility that I will shortly describe.

The Interest in Preserving the Life of the Child

A mother, acting in the interest of preserving and maintaining life, is in a peculiar relation to "nature." As childbearer, she often takes herself, and is taken by others, to be an especially "natural" member of her culture. As child tender, she must respect nature's limits and court its favor with foresightful actions ranging from immunizations to caps on household poisons to magical imprecation, warnings, and prayers. "Nature" with its unpredictable varieties of dirt and disease is her enemy as much as her ally. Her children are natural creatures, often unable to understand or abet her efforts to protect them. Because they frequently find her necessary direction constraining, a mother can experience her children's own liveliness as another enemy of the life she is preserving.

No wonder, then, that as she engages in preservation, a mother is liable to the temptations of fearfulness and excessive control. If she is alone with two or more young children as she tries to carry out her responsibilities, then control of herself, her children, and her physical environment is her only option, however rigid or excessive she looks to outsiders. Though necessarily controlling their acts, *reflecting* mothers themselves identify rigid or excessive control as the likely defects of the virtues they are required to practice. The identification of liability as such, with its implication of the will to overcome, characterizes this aspect of maternal thought. The epithet "controlling mother" is often unsympathetic, even matraphobic. On the other hand, it may, in line with the insights of maternal thought, remind us of what maternal thinking *counts as* failure.

To a mother, "life" may well seem "terrible, hostile, and quick to pounce on you if you give it a chance." [6] In response, she develops a metaphysical attitude toward "Being as such," an attitude I call "holding," an attitude governed by the priority of keeping over acquiring, of conserving the fragile, of maintaining whatever is at hand and necessary to the child's life. It is an attitude elicited by the work of "world-*protection*, world-*preservation*, world-*repair* . . . the invisible weaving of a frayed and threadbare family life." [7]

The priority of holding over acquiring distinguishes maternal thinking from scientific thinking and from the instrumentalism of technocracy. To be sure, under the pressures of consumerism, holding may become frantic accumulating and storing. More seriously, a parent may feel compelled to preserve her *own* children, whatever befalls most other children. The more competitive and hierarchical the society, the more thwarted a mother's individual, autonomous pursuits, the more likely that preservation will become egocentric, frantic, and cruel. Mothers recognize these dangers and fight them.

Holding, preserving mothers have distinctive ways of seeing and being in the world that are worth considering. For example, faced with the fragility of the lives it seeks to preserve, maternal thinking recognizes humility and resilient cheerfulness as virtues of its practice. In so doing it takes issue with popular moralities of assertiveness and much contemporary moral theory. [8]

Humility is a metaphysical attitude one takes toward a world beyond one's control. One might conceive of the world as governed by necessity and change (as I do) or by supernatural forces that cannot be comprehended. In either case, humility implies a profound sense of the limits of one's actions and of the unpredictability of the consequences of one's work. As the philosopher Iris Murdoch puts it: "Every natural thing, including one's own mind, is subject to chance. . . . One might say that chance is a subdivision of death. . . . We cannot dominate the world." [9] Humility that emerges from maternal practices accepts not only the facts of damage and death but also the facts of the independent and uncontrollable, developing and increasingly separate existences of the lives it seeks to preserve. "Humility is not a peculiar habit of self-effacement, rather like having an inaudible voice, it is selfless respect for reality and one of the most difficult and central of virtues." [10]

If in the face of danger, disappointment, and unpredictability, mothers are liable to melancholy, they are also aware that a kind, resilient good humor is a virtue. This good humor must not be confused with the cheery denial that is both a liability and, unfortunately, a characteristic of maternal practice. Mothers are tempted to denial simply by the insupportable difficulty of passionately loving a fragile creature in a physically threatening, socially violent, pervasively uncaring and competitive world. Defensive denial is exacerbated as it is officially encouraged, when we must defend against perceptions of our own subordination. Our cheery denials are cruel to our children and demoralizing to ourselves.

Clear-sighted cheerfulness is the virtue of which denial is the degenerative form. It is clear-sighted cheerfulness that Spinoza must have had in mind when he said: "Cheerfulness is always a good thing and never excessive"; it "increases and assists the power of action." [11] Denying cheeriness drains intellectual energy and befuddles the will; the cheerfulness honored in maternal thought increases and assists the power of maternal action.

In a daily way, cheerfulness is a matter-of-fact willingness to continue, to give birth and to accept having given birth, to welcome life despite its conditions. Resilient good humor is a style of mothering "in the deepest sense of 'style' in which to discover the right style is to discover what you are really trying to do." [12]

Because in the dominant society "humility" and "cheerfulness" name virtues of subordinates, and because these virtues have in fact developed in conditions of subordination, it is difficult to credit them and easy to confuse them with the self-effacement and cheery denial that are their degenerative forms. Again and again, in attempting to articulate maternal thought, language is sicklied o'er by the pale cast of sentimentality and thought itself takes on a greeting-card quality. Yet literature shows us many mothers who in their "holding" actions value the humility and resilient good humor I have described. One can meet such mothers, recognize their thought, any day one learns to listen. One can appreciate the effects of their disciplined perseverance in the unnecessarily beautiful artifacts of the culture they created. "I made my quilt to keep my family warm. I made it beautiful so my heart would not break." [13]

The Interest in Fostering the Child's Growth

Mothers must not only preserve fragile life. They must also foster growth and welcome change. If the "being" preserved seems always to be endangered, undone, slipping away, the "being" that changes is always developing, building, purposively moving away. The "holding," preserving mother must, in response to change, be simultaneously a changing mother. Her conceptual scheme in terms of which she makes sense of herself, her child, and their common world will be more the Aristotelian biologist's than the Platonic mathematician's. Innovation takes precedence over permanence, disclosure and responsiveness over clarity and certainty. The idea of "objective reality" itself "undergoes important modification when it is to be understood, not in relation to the world described by science, but in relation to the progressing life of a person." [14]

Women are said to value open over closed structure, to eschew the clear-cut and unambiguous, to refuse a sharp division between inner and outer or self and other. They also are said to depend on and prize the private inner lives of the mind. [15] If these facets of the "female mind" are elicited by maternal practices, they may well be interwoven responses to the changeability of a growing child. A child is itself an "open structure" whose acts are irregular, unpredictable, often mysterious. A mother, in order to understand her child, must assume the existence of a conscious continuing person whose acts make sense in terms of perceptions and responses to a meaning-filled world. She knows that her child's fantasies and thoughts are connected not only to the child's power to act but often are the only basis for her understanding of the child and for the child's self-understanding.

A mother, in short, is committed to two philosophical positions: She is a mentalist rather than a behaviorist, and she assumes the priority of personhood over action. Moreover, if her "mentalism" is to enable her to understand and love, she must be realistic about the psyche whose growth she fosters. *All* psyches are moved by fear, lust, anger, pride, and defenses against them; by what Simone Weil called "*natural* movements of the soul" and likened to laws of physical gravity. [16] This is not to deny that the soul is also blessed by "grace," "light," and erotic hungering for goodness. [17] However, mothers cannot take grace for granted, nor can they force or deny the less flattering aggrandizing and consolatory operations of childhood psychic life.

Her realistic appreciation of a person's continuous mental life allows a mother to expect change, to change with change. As psychologist Jean

Baker Miller puts it: "In a very immediate and day to day way women *live* for change." [18] Change requires a kind of learning in which what one learns cannot be applied exactly, often not even by analogy, to a new situation. If science agrees to take as real the reliable results of *repeatable* experiments,[19] its learning will be different in kind from maternal learning. Miller is hopeful that if we attend to maternal practices, we can develop new ways of studying learning appropriate to the changing natures of all people and communities, for it is not only children who change, grow, and need help in growing. Most obviously those who care for children must change in response to changing reality. And we all might grow—as opposed to aging—if we could learn how. For everyone's benefit, "women must now face the task of putting their vast unrecognized experience with change into a new and broader level of operation." [20]

Miller writes of achievement, of women who have learned to change and respond to change. But she admits: "Tragically in our society, women are prevented from fully enjoying these pleasures (of growth) themselves by being made to feel that fostering them in others is the only valid role for all women and by the loneliness, drudgery and isolated non-cooperative household setting in which they work." [21]

Similarly, in delineating maternal thought, I do not claim that mothers realize, in themselves, the capacities and virtues we learn to value as we care for others. Rather, mothers develop *conceptions* of abilities and virtues, according to which they measure themselves and interpret their actions. It is no great sorrow that some mothers never acquire humility, resilient good humor, realism, respect for persons, and responsiveness to growth—that all of us fail often in many ways. What is a great sorrow is to find the task itself misdescribed, sentimentalized, and devalued.

The Interest in Shaping an Acceptable Child

The third demand that governs maternal practice is the demand, at once social and personal, that the child's growth be shaped in a manner that makes life acceptable. "Acceptability" is defined in terms of the values of the mother's social group—whatever of its values she has internalized as her own plus values of group members whom she feels she must please or is fearful of displeasing. Society demands that a mother produce an adult acceptable to the next generation. Mothers, roughly half of society, have an interest in meeting that demand. They are also governed by a more stringent form of acceptability. They want the child they produce to be a person that they themselves, and those closest to them, can appreciate. The demand of appreciability gives an urgency, sometimes exhilarating, sometimes anguishing, to maternal practice.

The task of producing an appreciable child gives a mother a unique opportunity to explore, create, and insist on her own values; to train her children for strength and virtue; and ultimately to develop openness and reciprocity in regard to her child's most threatening differences from her, namely, moral ones. As a mother thinks upon the appreciability of her child, her maternal work becomes a self-conscious, reflective expression of a disciplined conscience.

In response to the demand of acceptability, maternal thinking becomes contradictory—that is, it betrays its own interest in the growth of children. Almost everywhere, the practices of mothering take place in societies in which women of all classes are less powerful than men of their class to determine the conditions under which their children grow. Throughout history, most women have mothered in conditions of military and social violence and often of extreme poverty. They have been governed by men, and increasingly by managers and experts of both sexes, whose policies mothers neither shape nor control. Out of maternal powerlessness, in response to a society whose values it does not determine, maternal thinking has often and largely opted for inauthenticity and "good" of others.

By "inauthenticity" I designate a double willingness—first, a willingness to *travailler pour l'armée*,[22] to accept the uses to which others put one's children; and second, a willingness to remain blind to the implications of those uses for the actual lives of women and children. Maternal thought embodies inauthenticity by taking on the values of the dominant culture. Like the "holding" of preservation, "inauthenticity" is a mostly nonconscious response to Being as Such. Only this attitude is not a caretaker's response to the natural exigencies of child tending but a subordinate's reaction to a social reality essentially characterized by the domination and subordination of persons. Inauthenticity constructs and then assumes a world in which one's own values do not count. It is allied to fatalism and to some religious thought—some versions of Christianity, for example. As inauthenticity is lived out in maternal practice, it gives rise to the values of obedience and "being good"; that is, it is taken as an achievement to fulfill the values of the dominant culture. Obedience is related to humility in the face of the limits of one's powers. But, unlike humility, which respects indifferent nature, the incomprehensible supernatural, and human fallibility, obedience respects the actual control and preferences of dominant people.

Individual mothers, living out maternal thought, take on the values of the subcultures to which they belong and the men with whom they are allied. Because some groups and many men are vibrantly moral, these values are not necessarily inadequate. Nevertheless, even moral groups and men almost always accept the relative subordination of women, whatever other ideals of equality and autonomy they may hold. A "good" mother may well be praised for colluding in her own subordination, with destructive consequences to herself and her children. Moreover, most groups and men impose at least some values that are psychologically and physically damaging to children. Yet, to be "good," a mother may be expected to endorse these inimical values. She is the person principally responsible for training her children in the ways and desires of obedience. This may mean training her daughters for powerlessness, her sons for war, and both for crippling work in dehumanizing factories, businesses, and professions. It may mean training both daughters and sons for defensive or arrogant power over others in sexual, economic, or political life. A mother who trains either for powerlessness or abusive power over others betrays the life she has preserved, whose growth she has fostered. She denies her children even the possibility of being strong and good.

The strain of colluding in one's own powerlessness, coupled with the frequent and much greater strain of betraying the children one has tended, would be insupportable if conscious. A mother under strain may internalize as her own some values that are clearly inimical to her children. She has, after all, usually been rewarded for such protective albeit destructive internalization. Additionally, she may blind herself to the implications of her obedience, a blindness excused and exacerbated by the cheeriness of denial. For precariously but deeply protected mothers, feminist accounts of power relations and their cost call into question the worthiness of maternal work and the genuineness of maternal love. Such women, understandably, fight insight as others fight bodily assault, revealing in their struggles a commitment to their own sufferings that may look "neurotic" but is in fact, given their options, realistic.

When I described maternal thought arising out of the interests in growth and preservation, I was not speaking of the actual achievement of mothers, but of a conception of achievement. Similarly, in describing the thought arising out of the interest in acceptability, I am not speaking of actual mothers' adherence to dominant values, but of a conception of their relations to those values in which obedience and "being good" is considered an achievement. Many individual mothers "fail," that is, they insist on their own values and will not remain blind to the implications of dominant values for the lives of their children. Moreover, given the damaging effects of prevailing sexual arrangements and social hierarchies on maternal lives, it is clearly outrageous to blame mothers for their (our) obedience.

Obedience is largely a function of social powerlessness. Maternal work is done according to the Law of the Symbolic Father and under His Watchful Eye, as well as, typically, according to the desires, even whims, of the father's house. "This is my Father's world / Oh let me ne'er forget / that though the wrong be oft so strong, / He is the ruler yet." In these conditions of work, inauthentic obedience to dominant patriarchal values is as plausible a maternal response as respect for the results of experiment is in scientific work.

As I have said, the work of mothering can become a rewarding, disciplined expression of conscience. In order for this opportunity to be realized, either collectively or by individual mothers, maternal thought will have to be transformed by feminist consciousness.

> Coming to have a feminist consciousness is the experience of coming to know the truth about oneself and one's society. . . . The very *meaning* of what the feminist apprehends is illuminated by the light of what ought to be. . . . The feminist apprehends certain features of social reality *as* intolerable, as to be rejected in behalf of a transforming project for the future. . . . Social reality is revealed as deceptive. . . . What is really happening is quite different from what appears to be happening.[23]

Feminist consciousness will first transform inauthentic obedience into wariness, uncertain reflection, and at times, anguished confusion. The feminist becomes "marked by the experience of moral ambiguity" as she learns new ways of living without betraying her women's past, without denying her obligations to others. "She no longer knows what sort of person she ought to be, and therefore she does not know what she ought to do. One moral paradigm is called into question by the laborious and often obscure emergence of another."[24]

Out of confusion will arise new voices, recognized not so much by the content of the truths they enunciate as by the honesty and courage of enunciation. They will be at once familiar and original, these voices arising out of maternal practice, affirming its own criteria of acceptability, insisting that the dominant values are unacceptable and need not be accepted.

The Capacity for Attentive Love

Finally, I would like to discuss a capacity, attention, and a virtue, love, that are central to the conception of achievement that maternal thought as a whole articulates. This capacity and virtue, when realized, invigorate preservation and enable growth. Attention and love again and again undermine a mother's inauthentic obedience as she perceives and endorses a child's experience though society finds it intolerable. The identification of the capacity of attention and the virtue of love is at once the foundation and the corrective of maternal thought.

The notion of "attention" is central to the philosophy of Simone Weil and is developed, along with the related notion of "love," by Iris Murdoch, who was profoundly influenced by Weil. Attention and love are fundamental to the construction of "objective reality" understood "in relation to the progressing life of a person," a "reality which is revealed to the patient eye of love." [25] Attention is an *intellectual* capacity connected even by definition with love, a special "knowledge of the individual." [26] "The name of this intense, pure, disinterested, gratuitous, generous attention is love." [27] Weil thinks that the capacity for attention is a "miracle." Murdoch ties it more closely to familiar achievement: "The task of attention goes on all the time and at apparently empty and everyday moments we are 'looking,' making those little peering efforts of imagination which have such important cumulative results." [28]

For Weil and Murdoch, the enemy of attention is what they call "fantasy," defined not as rich imaginative play, which does have a central role in maternal thinking, but as the "proliferation of blinding self-centered aims and images." [29] Fantasy, according to their original conception, is intellectual and imaginative activity in the service of consolation, domination, anxiety, and aggrandizement. It is reverie designed to protect the psyche from pain, self-induced blindness designed to protect it from insight. Fantasy, so defined, works in the service of inauthenticity. "The difficulty is to keep the attention fixed on the real situation" [30]—or, as I would say, on the real children. Attention to real children, children seen by the "patient eye of love," "teaches us how real things [real children] can be looked at and loved without being seized and used, without being appropriated into the greedy organism of the self." [31]

Much in maternal practices works against attentive love: intensity of identification, vicarious living through a child, daily wear of maternal work, harassment and indignities of an indifferent social order, and the clamor of children themselves. Although attention is elicited by the very reality it reveals—the reality of a growing person—it is a discipline that requires effort and self-training. Love, the love of children at any rate, is not only the most intense of attachments but it is also a detachment, a giving up, a letting grow. To love a child without seizing or using it, to see the child's reality with the patient, loving eye of attention—such loving and attending might well describe the separation of mother and child from the mother's point of view. Of course, many mothers fail much of the time in attentive love and loving attention. Many mothers also train themselves in the looking, self-restraining, and empathy that is loving attention. They can be heard doing so in any playground or coffee klatch.

I am not saying that mothers, individually or collectively, are (or are not) especially wonderful people. My point is that out of maternal practices distinctive ways of conceptualizing, ordering, and valuing arise. We *think* differently about what it *means* and what it takes to be "wonderful," to be a person, to be real.

Murdoch and Weil, neither mothers themselves nor especially concerned with mothers, are clear about the absolute value of attentive love and the reality it reveals. Weil writes:

> In the first legend of the Grail, it is said that the Grail . . . belongs to the first comer who asks the guardian of the vessel, a king three quarters paralyzed by the most painful wound, "What are you going through?"
>
> The love of our neighbor in all its fullness simply means being able to say to him: "What are you going through?" . . . Only he who is capable of attention can do this.[32]

I do not claim absolute value but only that attentive love, the training to ask, "What are you going through?" is central to maternal practices. If I am right about its place in maternal thought, and if Weil and Murdoch are right about its absolute value, the self-conscious inclusion of maternal thought in the dominant culture will be of general intellectual and moral benefit.

Some Social and Political Implications

I have described a "thought" arising out of maternal practices organized by the interests of preservation, growth, and acceptability. Although in some respects the thought is "contradictory" (i.e., it betrays its own values and must be transformed by feminist consciousness), the thought as a whole, with its fulcrum and correction in attentive love, is worthy of being expressed and respected. This thought has emerged out of maternal practices that are oppressive to women and children. I believe that it has emerged largely in response to the relatively invariable requirements of children and despite oppressive circumstances. As in all women's thought, some worthy aspects of maternal thought may arise out of identification with the powerless and excluded. However, oppression is largely responsible for the defects rather than the strengths of maternal thought, as in the obedient goodness to which mothers find themselves "naturally" subscribing. When the oppressiveness of gender arrangements is combined with the oppression of race, poverty, or the multiple injuries of class, it is a miracle that maternal thought can arise at all. On the other hand, that it does indeed arise, miraculously, is clear both from literature (Alice Walker, Tillie Olsen, Maya Angelou, Agness Smedley, Lucille Clifton, Louisa May Alcott, Audre Lorde, Marilyn French, Grace Paley, and countless others) and from daily experience. Maternal thought *identifies* priorities, attitudes, and virtues; *conceives* of achievement. The more oppressive the institutions of motherhood, the greater the pain and struggle in living out the worthy and transforming the damaging aspects of thought.

Maternal thinking is only one aspect of "womanly" thinking.[33] In articulating and respecting the maternal, I do not underwrite the still current, false, and pernicious identification of womanhood with biological or adoptive mothering of particular children in families. For me, "maternal" is a social category. Although maternal thinking arises out of actual child-caring practices, biological parenting is neither necessary nor sufficient. Many women and some men express maternal thinking in various kinds of working and caring with others. And some biological mothers, especially in misogynistic societies, take a fearful, defensive distance from their own mothering and the maternal lives of any women.

Maternal thought does, I believe, exist for all women in a radically different way than for men. It is because we are *daughters*, nurtured and trained by women, that we early receive maternal love with special attention to its implications for our bodies, our passions, and our ambitions. We are alert to the values and costs of maternal practices whether we are determined to engage in them or avoid them.

It is now argued that the most revolutionary change we can make in the institution of motherhood is to include men equally in every aspect of child care. When men and women are living together with children, it seems not only fair but deeply moral that they share in every aspect of child care. To prevent or excuse men from maternal practice is to encourage them to separate public action from private affection, the privilege of parenthood from its cares. Moreover, even when men are absent from the nursery, their dominance in every other public and private room shapes a child's earliest conceptions of power. To familiarize children with "natural" domination at their earliest age in a context of primitive love, assertion, and sexual passion is to prepare them to find equally "natural" and exhaustive the division between exploiter and exploited that pervades the world. Although daughter and son alike may internalize "natural" domination, neither typically can live with it easily. Identifying with and imitating exploiters, we are overcome with self-hate; aligning ourselves with the exploited, we are fearful and manipulative. Again and again, family power dramas are repeated in psychic, interpersonal, and professional dramas, while they are institutionalized in economic, political, and international life. Radically recasting the power-gender roles in those dramas just might revolutionize social conscience.[34]

Assimilating men into child care both inside and outside the home would also be conducive to serious social reform. Responsible, equal child caring would require men to relinquish power and their own favorable position in the division between intellectual/professional and service labor as that division expresses itself domestically. Loss of preferred status at home might make socially privileged men more suspicious of unnecessary divisions of labor and damaging hierarchies in the public world.

Moreover, if men were emotionally and practically committed to child care, they would reform the work world in parents' interests. Once no one "else" was minding the child, there would be good day-care centers with flexible hours, day-care centers to which parents could trust their children from infancy on. These day-care centers, like the workweek itself, would be managed "flexibly," in response to human needs as well as "productivity," with an eye to growth rather than measurable "profit." Such moral reforms of economic life would probably begin with professions and managers servicing themselves. Even in nonsocialist countries, however, their benefits could be unpredictably extensive.

I would not argue that the assimilation of men into child care is the primary social goal for mothers. Rather, we must work to bring a *transformed* maternal thought into the public realm, to make the preservation and growth of *all* children a work of public conscience and legislation. This will not be easy. Mothers are no less corrupted than anyone else by concerns of status and class. Often our misguided efforts on behalf of the success and purity of our children frighten them and everyone else around them. As we increase and enjoy our public effectiveness, we will have less reason to live vicariously through our children. We may then begin to learn to sustain a creative tension between our inevitable and fierce desire to foster our own children and the less compulsive desire that all children grow and flourish.

Nonetheless, it would be foolish to believe that mothers, just because they are mothers, can transcend class interest and implement principles of justice. All feminists must join in articulating a theory of justice shaped by and incorporating maternal thinking. Moreover, the generalization of attentive love to *all* children requires politics. The most enlightened thought is not enough.

Closer to home again, we must refashion our domestic life in the hope that the personal will in fact betoken the political. We must begin by resisting the temptation to construe "home" simplemindedly, as a matter of justice between mothers and fathers. Single parents, lesbian mothers, and coparenting women remind us that many ways to provide children with examples of caring do not incorporate sexual inequalities of power and privilege. Those of us who live with the fathers of our children will eagerly welcome shared parenthood—for overwhelming practical as well as ideological reasons. But in our eagerness, we must not forget that so long as a mother is not effective publicly and self-respecting privately, male presence can be harmful as well as beneficial. It does a woman no good to have the power of the Symbolic Father brought right into the nursery, often despite the deep, affectionate egalitarianism of an individual man. It takes a strong mother and father to resist temptations to domination and subordination for which they have been trained and are socially rewarded. And whatever the hard-won equality and mutual respect an individual couple may achieve, as long as a mother—even if she is no more parent than father—is derogated and subordinate outside the home, children will feel angry, confused, and "wildly unmothered." [35]

Despite these reservations, I look forward to the day when men are willing and able to share equally and actively in transformed maternal practices. When that day comes, will we still identify some thought as maternal rather than merely parental? Might we echo the cry of some feminists—there shall be no more "women"—with our own—there shall be no more "mothers," only people engaging in child care? To keep matters clear I would put the point differently. On that day there will be no more "fathers," no more people of either sex who have power over their children's lives and moral authority in their children's world, though they do not do the work of attentive love. There will be mothers of both sexes who live out a transformed maternal thought in communities that share parental care—practically, emotionally, economically, and socially. Such communities will have learned from their mothers how to value children's lives.

Notes

1. From J. Echergray, "Severed Heart," quoted by Jessie Bernard in *The Future of Motherhood* (New York: Dial, 1974), p. 4.

2. Nothing I say about maternal thought suggests that the women who engage in it cannot engage in other intellectual discourse. A materal thinker may also be an experimental psychologist, a poet, a mathematician, an architect, a physicist. I believe that because most thinkers have been men, most disciplines are partly shaped by "male" concepts, values, styles, and strategies. Unless we have identified "male" and "female" aspects of thought, however, the claim of gender bias is an empty one. I do not doubt that disciplines are also shaped by transgender interests, values, and concepts, which women, whether or not they engage in maternal practices, may fully share. To the extent that the disciplines are shaped by "male" thought, mothers and other women may feel alienated by the practices and thinking of their own discipline. Correlatively, when thinkers are as apt to be women as men, thought itself may change. On these and related points see Evelyn Keller, "Gender and Science," *Psychoanalysis and Contemporary Thought* 1, no. 3 (1978): 409–53; and idem, "He, She and Id in Scientific Discourse" (manuscript, 1980).

3. I derive the vocabulary most specifically from Jurgen Habermas, *Knowledge and Human Interests* (Boston: Beacon, 1971). I have been equally influenced by other philosophical relativists, most notably by Peter Winch, Ludwig Wittgenstein, and Suzanne Kessler and Wendy McKenna. See Winch, "Understanding a Primitive Society" and other papers, in *Ethics and Action* (London: Routledge & Kegan Paul, 1972); Wittgenstein, *Philosophical Investigations, Remarks on the Foundations of Mathematics, Zettel,* and *On Certainty* (Oxford: Blackwell, 1953, 1956, 1967, 1969); and Kessler and McKenna, *Gender* (New York: Wiley, 1978).

4. Examples of the invariant and *nearly* unchangeable include long gestation inside the mother's body; prolonged infant and childhood dependence; physical fragility of infancy; radical qualitative and quantitative change ("growth") in emotional and intellectual capacities from infancy to adulthood; long development and psychological complexity of human sexual desire, of memory and other cognitive capacities, and of "object relations." Features that are *nearly* universal and certainly changeable include the identification of childbearing and child caring, the consequent delegation of child care to biological mothers and other women, and the relative subordination of women in any social class to men of that class.

5. To see the universal in particulars, to assimilate differences and extend kinship, is a legacy of the ecumenical Protestantism in which I was raised. I am well aware that even nonviolent, well-meaning Protestant assimilations can be obtuse and cruel for others. Therefore I am dependent on others, morally as well as intellectually, for the statement of differences, the assessment of their effects on every aspect of maternal lives, and finally for radical correction as well as for expansion of any general theory I would offer. However, I do not *believe* that the thinking I describe is limited only to "privileged white women," as one reader put it. I first came to the notion of "maternal thinking" and the virtues of maternal practices through personal exchange with Tillie Olsen and then through reading her fiction. Similarly, I believe that "Man Child: A Black Lesbian Feminist's Response" by Audre Lorde, *Conditions,* no. 4 (1979): 30–36, is an excellent example of what I call "maternal thinking transformed by feminist consciousness." My "assimilation" of Olsen's and Lorde's work in no way denies differences that separate us nor the biases those differences may introduce into my account. These are only two of many examples of writers in different social circumstances who express what I take to be "maternal thinking."

6. The words are Mrs. Ramsay's in Virginia Woolf's *To the Lighthouse* (New York: Harcourt, Brace and World, 1927), p. 92.

7. Adrienne Rich, "Conditions for Work: The Common World of Women," in *Working It Out,* ed. Sara Ruddick and Pamela Daniels (New York: Pantheon, 1977). Italics mine.

8. For the comparison, see Iris Murdoch, *The Sovereignty of Good* (New York: Shocken, 1971). Popular moralities as well as contemporary moral theory tend to emphasize decision, assertion, happiness, authenticity, and justification by principle.

9. Ibid. p. 99.

10. Ibid., p. 95.

11. Spinoza, *Ethics,* Book 3, Proposition 42, demonstration. See also Proposition 40, Note and Proposition 45, both in Book 3.

12. Bernard Williams, *Morality* (New York: Harper Torchbooks, 1972), p. 11.

13. The words are a Texas farmwoman's who quilted as she huddled with her family in a shelter as, above them, a tornado destroyed their home. The story was told to me by Miriam Schapiro.

14. Murdoch, *Sovereignty of Good*, p. 26.

15. These are differences often attributed to women both by themselves and by psychologists. For a critical review of the literature, see Eleanor Maccoby and Carol Jacklin, *The Psychology of Sex Differences* (Stanford, Calif.: Stanford University Press, 1974). For a plausible account of women's valuing of inner life, see Patricia Meyer Spacks, *The Female Imagination* (New York: Knopf, 1975). Maccoby and Jacklin are critical both of the findings I mentioned and of adequacy of the psychological experiments they survey for testing or discovering these differences. I make little use of psychology, more of literature, in thinking about the cognitive sex differences I discuss. Psychologists are not, so far as I know, talking about women who have empathically identified with and assimilated maternal practices, either by engaging in them or by identifying with their own or other mothers. It would be hard to identify such a subgroup of women without circularity. But even if one could make the identification, tests would have to be devised that did not measure achievement but conception of achievement. Mothers, to take one example, may well prize the inner life, but they have so little time for it or are so self-protectively defended against their own insights that they gradually lose the capacity for inner life. Or again, a mother may not maintain sharp boundaries between herself and her child or between her child's "outer" action and inner life. However, she *must* maintain some boundaries. We value what we are in danger of losing (e.g., inner life); we identify virtues because we recognize temptations to vice (e.g., openness because we are tempted to rigid control); we refuse what we fear giving way to (e.g., either pathological symbiotic identification *or* an unworkable division between our own and our children's interests). It is difficult to imagine tests sophisticated and sensitive enough to measure such conceptions, priorities, and values. I have found psychoanalytic theory the most useful of psychologies and Nancy Chodorow's *The Reproduction of Mothering* (Berkeley: University of California Press, 1978) the most helpful in applying psychoanalytic theory to maternal practices.

16. Simone Weil, "Gravity and Grace," in *Gravity and Grace* (London: Routledge & Kegan Paul, 1952; first French ed., 1947), passim.

17. Ibid., and other essays in *Gravity and Grace*. Both the language and concepts are indebted to Plato.

18. Jean Baker Miller, *Toward a New Psychology for Women* (Boston: Beacon, 1973), p. 54.

19. As Habermas argues, *Knowledge and Human Interest*.

20. Miller, *Toward a New Psychology for Women*, p. 56.

21. Ibid., p. 40.

22. I am indebted to Adrienne Rich, *Of Woman Born* (New York: Norton, 1976), especially chap. 8, both for this phrase and for the working out of the idea of inauthenticity. My debt to this book as a whole is pervasive.

23. Sandra Lee Bartky, "Toward a Phenomenology of Feminist Conscious-

ness," in *Feminism and Philosophy*, ed. Mary Vetterling-Braggin, Frederick A. Elliston, and Jane English (Totowa, N.J.: Littlefield, Adams, 1977), pp. 22–37. Quotes from pp. 33, 25, 28, 29.

24. Bartky, "Phenomenology of Feminist Consciousness," p. 31. On the riskiness of authenticity, the courage it requires of women, see also Miller, *Toward a New Psychology for Women*, chap. 9.

25. Murdoch, *Sovereignty of Good*, p. 40.

26. Ibid., p. 28.

27. Simone Weil, "Human Personality," in *Collected Essays*, chosen and translated by Richard Rees (London: Oxford University Press, 1962). Also *Simone Weil Reader*, ed. George A. Panichas (New York: McKay, 1977), p. 333.

28. Murdoch, *Sovereignty of Good*, p. 43.

29. Ibid., p. 67.

30. Ibid., p. 91.

31. Ibid., p. 65.

32. Simone Weil, "Reflections of the Right Use of School Studies with a View to the Love of God," in *Waiting for God* (New York: Putnam's, 1951), p. 115.

33. Among other possible aspects of women's thought are those that might arise from our sexual lives, from our "homemaking," from the special conflict women feel between allegiance on the one hand to women and their world and on the other hand to all people of their kin and culture. Any identifiable aspect of women's thought will be interrelated to all the others. Since women almost everywhere are relatively powerless in relation to men of their class, all aspects of women's thought will be affected by powerlessness. Whether we are discussing the thought arising from women's bodily, sexual, maternal, homemaking, linguistic, or any other experience, we are faced with a confluence of powerlessness and the "womanly," whatever that might be.

34. These points have been made by many feminists, most provocatively and thoroughly by Dorothy Dinnerstein, *The Mermaid and the Minotaur* (New York: Harper & Row, 1976).

35. Rich, *Of Woman Born*, p. 225.

6

DAVID SPIEGEL, M.D.

Mothering, Fathering, and Mental Illness

The relationship of families to mental illness is important from a feminist perspective because *family* is a code word for *mother*. According to the traditional view, the father is the proactive parent, the one who deals with the outside world and provides food, housing, and money. The mother is seen as responsible for the family environment, for the psychological well-being of her children, and for the emotional atmosphere in the home. To whatever extent we have believed that mothers do something special for their children, we have been more than willing to believe that failures in mothering do something devastating to children. In line with this conventional—and distorted—view, perceived or real defects in the emotional environment of the family or the child's psychological development have usually been attributed to some failure in the mother rather than the father. Most family explanations for serious mental illness focus on problems in the mother-child, not the father-child interaction.

Paradoxically, the developmental argument for a causative relationship between the extreme forms of mental illness and malicious mothering is the weakest. It would truly be amazing if the quality of relatedness to both mother and father in the first ten years of life did not have a profound influence on our character and the quality of relationships with others. But can it cause psychotic episodes complete with delusions, hallucinations, and overwhelming anxiety? This archetypal form of mental illness has been used to scapegoat mothers, yet its occurrence is probably the least related to the quality of mothering among the variety of mental illnesses. Schizophrenia usually begins in the late teens and early twenties, and the person so affected experiences a profound disorganization of personality

I wish to express my appreciation to Natalie Shainess, M.D., Barrie Thorne, and Marilyn Yalom for their advice and critical review of the manuscript.

characterized by disruption of thought processes, idiosyncratic beliefs such as delusions of persecution, an appearance of emotional emptiness masking pervasive anxiety, and at times hallucinated voices. This illness, which afflicts one percent of the population, has been for centuries a battleground for conflicting theories about mind, body, and soul.

In this essay I first examine several explanatory systems for mental illness developed over the centuries in Western thinking, focusing especially on those comparatively recent theories that link family structure and especially mothering to severe mental illness. Then I review some contemporary developments in psychiatric thought that are consistent with a more equitable distribution of responsibility between both parents in shaping the mental health of their children.

Western Conceptions of Madness

The patterns of definition and treatment of madness from the Middle Ages to the twentieth century follow a surprisingly simple but interesting course that is quite relevant to the role of the family in mental illness. In essence, the attribution of the causes of madness come closer and closer to home, starting with the devil or a variety of outside animal forces, passing through the body, and moving on to the individual's will and psyche, making the individual's psychological and family environment especially important. In the fifteenth century, when possession by outside animal forces was given as a principal explanation, the mad were sent away from their communities, literally deported in the proverbial ship of fools destined nowhere. Metaphorically these people were sending madness back whence it came, that is, elsewhere.

In the ensuing several centuries, the derangement of mind was more closely associated with a derangement of the body, with such explanations as animal spirits in the channels of the nerves or the presence of black bile producing melancholia. Mental illness was defined as *delirium*, literally meaning "out of the furrow," implying that as the result of a disease of the body the mind has left the path of reason. As Foucault notes, this became an inversion of the ancient Greek notion in that madness was seen as a derivative of the dream (an aberration of a usual physical process), rather than the dream being a representation of madness.[1] The geography of treatment changed as well. Communities now kept the mad confined within their boundaries, and asylums proliferated, among them the notorious Hôpital Général, which at one point contained one percent of the population of Paris.

Accompanying the French political revolutions of the eighteenth century were psychiatric revolutions that challenged the confinement model. In the name of moral treatment the famous alienists (an interesting early term for psychiatrists) Pinel and Tuke struck off the chains of the mentally ill and recommended educational and social rehabilitation. What was truly revolutionary was the humanity they introduced through the concept of rehabilitating rather than confining the mentally ill. This treatment also involved a departure from a physical explanation for mental illness and substituted a failure in the psyche. The individual was now expected to take some responsibility for his or her condition, and this meant that he or she was made to feel guilty about its occurrence. Moreover, the conditions of the patient's early growth and development were related, for the first time, to his or her illness, thus implicating a role for relatives in madness.

A scant seventy-five years after the concepts of moral treatment were introduced in the United States, the forces of nature rather than nurture reasserted themselves in the struggle to explain mental illness. Intense interest was shown in family patterns of mental illness, and the popular literature was filled with contrasts between "good" and "bad" families, the former typically producing generations of religious leaders and educators and the latter, generations of feuding and lazy mental subnormals. This movement became affiliated with that barren marriage of biology and sociology known as social Darwinism, which held essentially that the principles of natural selection applied to social class. Accordingly, only cream and not scum could rise to the top of the social ladder. During the early part of this century, this movement powerfully involved itself in the establishment of restrictive immigration laws, many of which still exist.

This was essentially an effort at eugenics, keeping bad genes out of the country. There is a particular irony in this development since it has indeed been shown that the incidence and prevalence of serious mental illness is higher in first-generation immigrants, but this increased incidence does not accompany immigrant families into second and third generations, especially when their socioeconomic status rises.[2] In other words, these data would indicate that the stress of social dislocation and economic deprivation rather than the gene pool in immigrant populations is associated with the higher incidence of mental illness.

Freud and the Family

The developmental theories of mental illness that still have great currency today are predominantly Freudian in origin. Moreover, much of our current thinking about the family in general is based on Freudian and neo-Freudian inferences from observations of families of mental patients. Freud's well-known theories about developmental conflicts in families giving rise to neuroses have thus become widely accepted descriptions of normal development in the family. In like manner, Bateson and Jackson's astute observations about "double-bind communications" have been noted in far more general circumstances than the families of schizophrenics.[3] The description of families that emerges from these pathological studies is a bit reminiscent of Nietzsche's distinction between good and bad and good and evil.[4] The definition of good that one may derive from the study of evil is quite different from the definition that emerges when one starts with the good as a primary position and then derives a sense of the bad.

Starting, then, from an observation of the mentally ill, Freud laid the theoretical groundwork for a developmental psychology that posits that the child's resolution of instinctual conflicts and its progress through a course of oral, anal, phallic, and genital preoccupations was tied to the development of later mental health or illness. In particular, parental deprivation or overgratification of the urges typical of a given developmental state might result in developmental arrest. Conflicts at the oral state were postulated to lead to more severe forms of hysteria and schizophrenia, those at the anal state to obsessive compulsive disorders, and so on. Freud's use of the Oedipus metaphor provided an explanatory framework for a wide variety of psychological dysfunctions. Young children were described as having intense sexual and aggressive longings toward their parents, and Freud believed that in the resolution of these longings lay the necessary maturational steps toward developing healthy independent relationships. In his treatment Freud focused on the individual patient rather than the family, feeling that it was the unconscious fantasy life of the patient rather than the realities of the family situation that constituted the illness. Nonetheless, the groundwork was laid for an examination of the realities as well as the fantasies of family life and for an explanation of mental illness based on patterns of family interaction.[5]

Certain aspects of Freud's theories, notably the concept of "penis envy" with the accompanying idea that women experience themselves as castrated males, have been subjected to a host of appropriate criticism.[6] Both feminists and nonfeminists have suggested that perhaps this one-sided notion masks a profound envy on the part of men of women's creativity, which has been termed "womb-envy," or more whimsically, "Venus envy."[7] The absurd Freudian idea that, for a woman, having a child is a temporary replacement for a penis raises complementary questions about men's frantic struggles to be "creative" and to "make a mark upon the world" as an effort to compensate for the absence of a greater role in the process of biological creativity.

The relationship between the abnormal development of the mind—conscious and unconscious—and early life experience has been deeply explored by a host of other psychoanalytic writers, female and male. Anna Freud, Sigmund's daughter, pupil, and analysand, linked the nature of defense mechanisms such as denial and repression to early childhood experience and the resolution of various developmental stages. Nonetheless, she was forced to conclude her classic work, *The Ego and the Mechanisms of Defense*, with a mysterious reference to the "constitution of the particular individual"[8] in order to explain why a given individual might choose certain patterns of defense to resolve unconscious conflicts rather than others (e.g., obsessive-compulsive versus hysterical).

Margaret Mahler attached great importance to the early period of mother-child attachment, which she termed "symbiosis."[9] She linked childhood autism to a child's failure to "separate and individuate" from the mother. That is, in a symbiotic attachment, the child has no sense of self as separate from mother. Children who fail to learn to perceive themselves as different from mother become, from her point of view, severely disturbed.

The wealth of other psychoanalytic literature relating developmental failure to psychopathology has been thoroughly reviewed by Shainess, who emphasizes the importance of the mother's environment to the child's development.[10] She believes that an atmosphere of respect and nurturance for the mother is essential if she is to provide a similar atmosphere for the child. Further, the mother's basic attitude of acceptance or rejection is quickly and continuously conveyed to the child and helps create the child's sense of self. As she notes, the stresses attendant to mothering often unearth experiences and attitudes felt with great emotional force by the mother as a child.[11]

Family Systems Theories

In recent decades family theorists, descendants of psychoanalytic thinkers, have argued that family communication patterns, especially the mother's style of interacting, are responsible for creating schizophrenia in children. Bateson and Jackson, pioneers in this area, produced an intriguing theory of double-bind communication. In this communication, the parent overtly forbids the child to do something that she or he covertly encourages him or her to do, and does not allow the child to openly discuss the paradox. As an example, a mother may critically question an adolescent daughter about supposedly forbidden sexual behavior in such minute detail that she in effect encourages the daughter to have sexual experiences. The catch is that whatever the daughter does will disappoint the mother on some level, and the daughter will always be in the wrong. In such fashion, mothers, according to the theory, drive their young crazy.

While this theory could apply equally to both parents, in fact mothers have been singled out for special recognition. There is a subtle implication that mothers control the pattern of family communication and that they have a unique ability to invoke and maintain a pattern of double-bind communication for their own purposes and at the expense of all other members of the family:

> On the basis of our examination of the clinical data, we have been impressed by a number of observations, including: the helplessness, fear, exasperation, and rage which a double-bind situation provokes in the patient, but which the mother may serenely and un-understandingly pass over. We have noted reactions in the father that both create double-bind situations, or extend and amplify those created by the mother, and we have seen the father passive and outraged, but helpless, become ensnared in a similar manner to the patient.
>
> According to our theory, the communication situation described is essential to the mother's security, and by inference to the family homeostasis. If this be so, then when psychotherapy of the patient helps him become less vulnerable to mother's attempts at control, anxiety will be produced in the mother. Similarly, if the therapist interprets to the mother the dynamics of the situation she is setting up with the patient, this should produce an anxiety response in her.[12]

Small wonder! I have quoted this work at some length to indicate how thoroughly mothers have been scapegoated in this school of thought. Bateson and Jackson dismiss the fact that the particular mother they were describing had herself been psychotic. They note only that the mother had kept her hospitalization a secret. The mother's experience of distress is minimized. Such one-sided empathy—for the patient and not the mother—must raise questions.

That such theorizing has consequences in fact as well as in theory became clear to me when I and my colleagues sought to have the parents of one young but chronic schizophrenic inpatient come to the hospital for a conference. They refused, and we speculated about their lack of concern for the boy. With immense persistence, we finally arranged a meeting, only to discover that they were indeed quite caring. Why had they initially refused to come to the hospital? It turned out that their son had been treated on a ward in the same hospital that had been studied by Bateson and Jackson and was heavily influenced by their theories. For nine months he had been taught that he would recover by venting his anger at his parents for making him schizophrenic. Their reluctance to come to the hospital was no longer mysterious.

Lidz and his Yale group went so far as to give us the term "schizophrenogenic mother."[13] Such mothers were described as using their children to fulfill their own life goals while confusing these children with a pretense of caring. The bleak picture painted of these women and mothers is conveyed by the following passage:

> There were two mothers, Mrs. Nebb and Mrs. Newcomb, who completely dominated the lives of their passive husbands and children. We consider these women typical "schizophrenogenic" mothers in needing and using their sons to complete their own frustrated lives. Their sons had to be geniuses, and any faults in them or anything that went wrong with their lives were consistently blamed on others—classmates, doctors, teachers, and society in general. They believed that only they understood their sons. We could never really understand these mothers, for their incessant talk was driven and mixed up, displaying unbelievable obtuseness to any ideas not their own. While we have hesitated to call these women schizophrenic, they are certainly not reality-oriented and are very close to being psychotic.[14]

One need not be a psychiatrist to detect the authors' hostility toward these mothers. Their obvious inability to understand these women is at least honestly stated, but their befuddlement is peculiar given their overall enterprise—that of making apparently psychotic symptoms understandable in the light of family dynamics.

In fairness, the Yale group does provide a broader explanatory framework than just the schizophrenogenic mother. They describe patterns of marital "schism" or "skew" responsible for mental illness in children and are even open to the possibility of a genetic factor in schizophrenia, although they discount its importance (p. 187). In a publication some eight years later, Lidz dropped the term "schizophrenogenic mother" and replaced it with "schizophrenogenic family."[15]

Laing, a well-known existential writer, further elaborated on ways in which the family atmosphere may result in an experience of what he called "ontological insecurity," a sense that at any moment the rug may be pulled out from under one.[16] For a person experiencing ontological insecurity, dealings with others are not simple interactions over content but always constitute a threat to the very existence of the patient. Laing sees the patient as a scapegoat for the insecurity and confusion of the family. The patient constantly receives the message, not that he or she is merely wrong or inadequate, but that he or she does not deserve to exist. Laing comments usefully on the Yale group's terminology:

> In recent years, the concept of a schizophrenogenic mother has been introduced. Fortunately an early witch-hunting quality about the concept has begun to fade. This concept can be worked out in various rather different ways, but it can be stated

>in the following terms: there may be some ways of being a
>mother that impede rather than facilitate or "reinforce" any
>genetically determined inborn tendency there may be in the
>child towards achieving the primary developmental stages of
>ontological security. Not only the mother but also the total
>family situation may impede rather than facilitate the child's
>capacity to participate in a real shared world, as
>self-with-other.[17]

Indeed this is a far more reasonable discussion of the problem of schizophrenogenesis, but it overlooks the possibility that the process may occur in two directions—disordered family patterns may result from, as well as cause, disturbance in the child. This intriguing alternative is summarized by the ironic comment that "mental illness is inherited—I inherited it from my children." One team of researchers has in fact demonstrated that, at the least, the presence of a schizophrenic child is profoundly disruptive to the functioning of the parents.[18] They formed artificial families composed of schizophrenics and normal children with the parents of such children and then gave these artificially constructed "families" tasks to perform. They found that the parents of schizophrenics and normal children did not differ in their capacity to perform the tasks when working with normal children, either their own or others. However, the presence of a schizophrenic child in this artificial family grouping hampered any parent's ability to perform the cognitive task. Thus the direction of this research would suggest that observations of pathological patterns of family interaction may be as much the result as the cause of schizophrenia in a child.

There are several obvious objections to such data. First, these studies are somewhat artificial when dealing with the complexity of childhood development and family interaction. Performance on a cognitive task is hardly a measure of parenting. Second, it is well known that schizophrenia usually starts at the end of the second and beginning of the third decade of life. It is much rarer for a young child to be declared schizophrenic. Nonetheless, most clinicians would agree that, in retrospect, children who become schizophrenic in early adult life have usually demonstrated some serious signs of abnormality prior to this time, which may include social withdrawal, difficulty in school, and troubled relationships with siblings and parents.[19]

While this research has not provided answers, it has certainly raised questions. An unresponsive or unhappy infant may indeed shape very different parental behavior than a child who is cheerful and receptive. A dyadic pattern of interaction develops that is the product of parent and child, not simply the response of one to the other. Thus the observations of genuine differences in the parental behavior of normal versus schizophrenic offspring made by Bateson and Jackson, Lidz, Laing, and others may result from the fact that the family is in many cases more victim than cause of mental illness.

Biological Factors in Schizophrenia

Two lines of evidence in recent years, both biological, challenge developmental theories of schizophrenia. Hence, a century later we are returning to biological explanations of madness. First, twin studies demonstrated that identical twins (twins with the same genetic material) were far more likely to both have schizophrenia than were fraternal twins (twins reared together in the womb, but with different genetic material).[20] However, these studies are vulnerable to the justifiable criticism that, indeed, identical twins are raised more similarly than fraternal twins, and also that doctors and researchers are far more prone to look for and perhaps dubiously find similar mental conditions in identical twins.

Then Rosenthal, Kety, and others studied adopted children in Denmark and more convincingly demonstrated the genetic factor in schizophrenia.[21] They found that the occurrence of schizophrenia in a biological parent resulted in a roughly sevenfold increase in the likelihood of a child developing schizophrenia, regardless of the presence or absence of schizophrenia in the adoptive family in which the child was raised. These data cannot but constitute an assault on the family development theory of schizophrenogenesis.

In addition, within the last two decades psychopharmacologists have discovered a new class of drugs that are in many cases dramatically effective in reducing the symptoms, if not improving the course, of schizophrenia. These drugs seem to act on certain neurotransmitter receptor sites in the brain. There is compelling evidence that the effectiveness of antipsychotic drugs in blockading receptors to the neurotransmitter dopamine is proportional to their clinical effectiveness in reducing psychotic symptoms such as delusions and hallucinations.[22] These impressive drugs do not seem to influence the long-term course of the illness, however, and are not uniformly effective with all schizophrenics.

Biological theories of schizophrenia have appeared and appropriately disappeared with dismaying regularity, the famous and ultimately irrelevant "pink spot" found in the urine of schizophrenics being but one example. The pink spot was thought to be evidence of a biochemical defect in the brains of schizophrenics, but it turned out to result from the peculiar diet of psychiatric inpatients. Nonetheless, evidence is accumulating that such disorders as schizophrenia, at least in its borderline and chronic forms, have an important biological component, and there is good evidence that such serious disorders of mood as manic-depressive psychosis are likewise inherited and primarily biological disturbances.[23]

The fact that a biological intervention can either worsen or ameliorate the disease, plus the data supporting a genetic factor, raise serious questions about whether schizophrenia—that most devastating of mental illnesses—is indeed the result of a defect in mothering, or fathering, or parenting. Why, then, is schizophrenia usually the showcase argument for the damage wreaked by defective mothering? Probably because it is such a devastating illness and because the schizophrenic child easily appears a living indictment of the failure of mothering. Such a living indictment can be used to prove that imperfect performance of traditional female roles has a noxious effect on children.

A new direction has been emerging in recent years and involves treating families of the seriously mentally ill as victims, as well as causes, of the illness. If schizophrenia is viewed more as a biological than a developmental disease, then the analogy to illnesses such as diabetes seems more apt; efforts are then directed at helping families cope with the impact of the serious disturbance in the child, and the underlying assumption is that the families need special expertise and support in dealing with the illness rather than seeing them as invested in perpetuating the system that gave rise to the illness in the first place.[24] Recently a movement has developed among parents of the adult mentally ill that has resulted in self-help groups that provide crisis support, lectures, and political activism for families of the adult mentally ill. These family support groups, with names such as Parents of Adult Schizophrenics, are willing to publicly acknowledge that there is some serious mental illness in the family, but are much more inclined to attribute the illness to biological causes, sometimes affiliating with rather speculative theories of the origin of mental illness, such as the "orthomolecular school." This particular theory is attractive to many because it attributes the cause of schizophrenia to dietary rather than psychological nutrition and therefore provokes far less guilt in its adherents, while offering hope for a possible cure.

In like manner, some traditional mental health services are developing increasing interest in providing consultation and support to families of schizophrenics, instead of assuming that there have been mistakes in mothering and ill will toward the patient. The assumption is that the families are struggling to help an impaired offspring adjust as best he or she can and that information about coping strategies, associated medical problems, the use of medication, financial and vocational support, and the availability of services in a crisis can improve life for both the patient and the patient's family.

The linking of bad mothering with the development of schizophrenia is a particularly flagrant example of how a perceived difference within a class may be used to exploit the entire class. The emphasis on the importance of good mothering in helping the vast majority of offspring form relationships that are meaningful and mutually gratifying is minimized by the stark accusation that bad mothering leads to madness. This in turn is reinforced by that old standby, maternal guilt. We often feel responsible for things over which we have no control, and to the extent that a mother believes she is responsible for the psychological health of her child, the development of a major disruption in the child's life, be it physical or psychological, always occasions the question: "What could I have done to avoid this?" Certainly there are lessons to be learned about mothering and fathering, and we need to learn them, but blaming mothers, and even mothers and fathers, for the most severe of psychiatric disturbances has a stultifying effect and may serve to inhibit rather than foster important new experimentation in sharing and changing nurturing and breadwinning roles.

I have tried to demonstrate that the evidence for the link between mothering, fathering, and mental illness is weakest when the outcome is psychiatrically the most disastrous. From a psychodynamic and family systems point of view, it makes far more sense to assume that the quality of relatedness between child and parent influences to a greater extent the normal array of relationships and developments as the child matures, and there is little biological evidence of any significance to challenge this notion. So if we are relatively free to dismiss the extreme idea that mothers and fathers drive their young mad, we are still left to wonder how indeed they shape the normal development of their children. This is a broad and complex area, made the more so by changing concepts of male and female sex roles, which have altered, if not replaced, older understandings of "masculinity" and "femininity."

The debate within and outside the women's movement regarding what, if anything, constitutes uniquely female attributes and roles is particularly delicate when it comes to the importance of mothering, fathering, or parenting. Because we have been willing to believe that mothers do something special for their children—something that cannot be replaced by anyone other than the mother—mothers have been given an inequitable share of the responsibility for child care and undue blame for the mental illness of their children. Nonetheless, it would be unwise to throw out the baby with the bath water—that is, to ignore the importance of the parent-child relationship in human psychological development. To the extent that we downplay the importance of early experience on later development, both normal and pathological, we likewise denigrate the power that we have to shape the course of the next generation, as well as our responsibility for doing so. The question is, "How can we avoid scapegoating parents, and especially mothers, and at the same time learn from past mistakes about the best way to raise children and foster psychological growth?"

Times of social change provide both risks and opportunities in examining social institutions. It is simplistic to think that the perfect performance of traditional and highly differentiated social roles, which were dependent in turn on a certain ecoomic structure and level of affluence, is necessary for the mental health of our children. At the same time, children need to be fed, sheltered, loved, and accepted. One organizing principle for the reassignment of parenting roles is that of role flexibility. It is more important that nurturance come from a genuinely caring person than that it come from the same person all the time. While this statement may provoke disagreement, Kagan's research on early child-care facilities indicates that the quality of the facility and the quality of the child's relatedness to its mother determine developmental progress, rather than the simple quantity of time spent with the mother.[25]

The real strength of the family lies in this notion of role flexibility, that all members of the family are motivated to do what is necessary to preserve the well-being of its members. To the extent that we are comfortable in expecting nurturance from a father or breadwinning from a mother, we are twice as likely to provide the child with one or the other form of sustenance, should the other parent become unable or unwilling to do it. Furthermore, what a child learns when he or she sees a parent able to exchange roles is a kind of security. The importance of this security is underscored by a school of psychiatric theory not yet discussed, the existential one. Existential psychiatrists such as Minkowski, Binswanger, and Yalom, building on the philosophies of Kierkegaard, Husserl, Heidegger, and Sartre, among others, emphasize the distinction between a person and his or her attributes—social roles, ego ideals, fantasies about oneself, and so on.[26] Existential psychotherapists are impatient with concepts, ideas about the self, which are viewed as reifications, an existential trap into which we all fall. We come to confuse what we are with a kind of thinghood. We make ourselves into objects, and the goal of existential psychotherapy is to alter one's perspective of the relationship between one's attributes and one's self, to avoid confusing what one is with a collection of social roles and personal goals. The person dons these roles like a garment and learns to feel more like a person when she or he is willing and able to take them off as well as put them on. This is not to say that roles are invariably damaging or confining. Rather, what is authentically human about a person is the ability to assume a role, not the role itself. We are more than any of the concrete roles, attitudes, or goals we set for ourselves. We begin to lose ourselves when we start to identify too thoroughly with any role. Merely running from roles is not the answer either, from an existential point of view; it is rather choosing to be what we are without becoming completely defined and constricted by our choices. The term existentialism comes from the idea that existence is coexistent with essence. We are not imperfect approximations of some ideal, but constantly create ourselves in an unending process of being and becoming.

This existential perspective has implications for good parenting. Loving and nurturing a child need not mean being trapped in a stereotyped role of mothering or fathering. Both men and women may choose to nurture and set limits. There is reason to hope that the new diffusion of parenting responsibility and gender roles will teach children an underlying truth that has been obscured in the past by rigid segregation of roles—that is, the human capacity to care, relate, and nurture another human being, which is fundamental to life, regardless of who does it. It takes the strong ties of parenthood usually to provide this care consistently over a period of years, but parents who are able to nurture children while not feeling trapped or resentful in this nurturing role are more rather than less likely to convey a sense of authentic caring to their children.

In psychotherapy, patterns of parenting figure prominently. Patient and therapist often spend considerable time developing a perspective on what growing up in the patient's family was like. Current problems in the patient's life are often related to learned patterns in the family, and the patient's emotional relationship to the therapist, the transference, is explored for further information about learned patterns of relating. There is often a two-step process: first the patient learns to recognize fixed parental roles, idiosyncracies, and limitations and then, later, to forgive them. First the patient comes to see what his or her parents were, from one perspective, and then later to appreciate that they were more than that, that they did what they did in order to solve their own problems. The struggle for the patient is to see the parent as a person and not just a parent, as it is for the parent to see the patient as more than a child.

As an example, an adolescent girl was hospitalized because of a severe school phobia. She was, like many school phobics, bright and capable, but she suffered extreme anxiety at the thought of leaving home. She was the youngest of three daughters. Her mother was a warm but anxious and frightened woman; her father was a large, muscular man of the "strong, silent" variety. It emerged that the patient's difficulties had begun two generations earlier, when her maternal grandmother began dying of cancer. This woman had been the "matriarch" of the family and its strength. All her grown children lived near her, and they all gathered with their families each Sunday at her home. A physician mistakenly advised these children not to tell their mother her diagnosis, assuming that she could not tolerate the news. As a result, they spent a demoralizing year sitting in vigil by the mother's bedside, unable to discuss with her what was happening and unable to express or share their grief. The patient's mother never recovered from her own mother's painful death, and felt desperately lonely. Her daughter's fear of school was in fact an unconscious fear of leaving her mother alone. The unwritten premise operating in the family was that women are too weak to accept the harsh realities of life, and so no one had been able to deal with the loss. Gradually the family learned that the grandmother probably knew about and did in fact face her own death and that the equation of women with weakness was arbitrary. Both daughter and mother became more independent. The daughter became, in fact, an excellent student. The equation of silence with strength was challenged, and the father was asked to face directly emotional issues that had been previously considered "woman talk." Such an involvement had in the past been considered weakness for him. In essence, as they gave up old roles everyone started doing what they were supposedly unable to do: face major losses, attend school, discuss feelings.

We have been praising with faint damns, warning what can go wrong if the task is not done properly rather than observing what can and does go right. This is in part related to the tendency of the disciplines of psychiatry and psychology to focus on the abnormal and derive theories of the normal from it. This bias has profoundly affected the view of mothering much more than the view of fathering, and thus the importance attached to mothering has been a two-edged sword: It attributes power to women and at the same time accuses them of misusing it.

In a world of increasingly undifferentiated sex roles, joint custody of children, and single parenting by men as well as women, new theories of mental health and mental illness will have to take fuller account of the male parent and lay to rest the association of madness with malignant mothering.

Notes

1. M. Foucault, *Madness and Civilization: A History of Insanity in the Age of Reason* (New York: Vintage, 1973).

2. L. Srole et al., *Mental Health in the Metropolis* (New York: McGraw-Hill, 1962).

3. F. Bateson et al., "Toward a Theory of Schizophrenia," in *Theory and Practice of Family Psychiatry*, ed. J. G. Howells (New York: Brunner/Mazel, 1971), pp. 745–64.

4. F. Nietzsche, *The Birth of Tragedy and the Genealogy of Morals*, trans. F. Golffing (New York: Doubleday, 1956).

5. S. Freud, *Three Essays on the Theory of Sexuality*, in *The Standard Edition of the Complete Psychological Works of Sigmund Freud*, vol. 7 (London: Hogarth, 1953); idem, *New Introductory Lectures on Psycho-Analysis*, ibid., vol. 22 (1964).

6. K. Horney, *Feminine Psychology* (New York: Norton, 1967); C. Thompson, "'Penis Envy' in Women," *Psychiatry* 6, no. 2 (May 1943): 123–25; N. Shainess, "Women's Liberation—and Liberated Women," in *The World Biennial of Psychiatry and Psychotherapy*, vol. 2, ed. S. Arieti (New York: Basic, 1973), pp. 86–111; and J. Mitchell, *Psychoanalysis and Feminism* (New York: Pantheon, 1974).

7. W. Lederer, *The Fear of Women* (New York: Grune and Stratton, 1968).

8. A. Freud, *The Ego and the Mechanisms of Defense*, trans. C. Baines (New York: International Universities Press, 1946), p. 165.

9. M. S. Mahler, "Autism and Symbiosis, Two Extreme Disturbances of Identity," *International Journal of Psycho-Analysis* 39, no. 1 (1958): 77–83.

10. N. Shainess, "Mother-Child Relationships: An Overview," *Science and Psychoanalysis* 14 (1969): 64–88.

11. N. Shainess, "The Structure of the Mothering Encounter," *Journal of Nervous and Mental Disease* 136, no. 2 (February 1963): 146–61.

12. Bateson et al., "Toward a Theory of Schizophrenia," p. 759.

13. T. Lidz, S. Fleck, and A. R. Cornelison, *Schizophrenia and the Family*, Monograph Series on Schizophrenia No. 7 (New York: International Universities Press, 1965).

14. Ibid., p. 176.

15. T. Lidz, *The Origin and Treatment of Schizophrenic Disorders* (New York: Basic, 1973).

16. R. D. Laing and A. Esterson, "Sanity, Madness, and the Family," in *Families of Schizophrenics*, vol. 1 (New York: Basic, 1964).

17. R. D. Laing, *The Divided Self: An Existential Study in Sanity and Madness* (Harmondsworth, England: Penguin, 1960), p. 189.

18. J. H. Liem, "Effects of Verbal Communications of Parents and Children: A Comparison of Normal and Schizophrenic Families," *Journal of Consulting and Clinical Psychology* 42, no. 3 (June 1974): 438–50; E. G. Mishler and N. E. Waxler, "Family Interaction and Schizophrenia: An Approach to the Experimental Study of Family Interaction and Schizophrenia," *Archives of General Psychiatry* 15, no. 1 (July 1966): 64–74; idem, "Family Interaction Processes and Schizophrenia: A Review of Current Theories," *International Journal of Psychiatry* 2, no. 4 (September 1966): 375–413, reprinted from the *Merrill-Palmer Quarterly of Behavior and Development* 2, no. 4 (October 1965); idem, "Experimental Studies of Families," *Advances in Experimental Social Psychology* 5 (1970): 249–304; and N. E. Waxler, "Parent and Child Effects on Cognitive Performance: An Experimental Approach to the Etiological and Responsive Theories of Schizophrenia," *Family Process* 13, no. 1 (March 1974): 1–22.

19. R. A. Woodruff, D.W. Goodwin, and S. B. Guze, *Psychiatric Diagnosis* (New York: Oxford University Press, 1974).

20. A. J. Rosanoff et al., "The Etiology of So-called Schizophrenic Psychoses, with Specific Reference to Their Occurrence in Twins," *American Journal*

of Psychiatry 91 (1934): 247–86; I. I. Gottesman and J. Shields, "Contributions of Twin Studies to Perspectives in Schizophrenia," in *Progress in Experimental Personality Research*, vol. 3, ed. B. A. Maher (New York: Academic Press, 1966), pp 1–84; and M. Fischer, B. Harvald, and M. Hauge, "A Danish Twin Study of Schizophrenia," *British Journal of Psychiatry* 115, no. 526 (September 1969): 981–90.

21. S. S. Kety et al., "Mental Illness in the Biological and Adoptive Families of Adopted Schizophrenics," *American Journal of Psychiatry* 128, no. 3 (September 1971): 82–86; and D. Rosenthal and S. Kety, eds., *The Transmission of Schizophrenia* (Oxford: Pergamon, 1968).

22. S. H. Snyder, "The Dopamine Hypothesis of Schizophrenia: Focus on the Dopamine Receptor," *American Journal of Psychiatry* 133, no. 2 (February 1976): 197–202.

23. E. Slater and V. Cowie, *The Genetics of Mental Disorders* (London: Oxford University Press, 1971).

24. D. G. Langsley and D. M. Kaplan, *The Treatment of Families in Crisis* (New York: Grune and Stratton, 1968).

25. J. Kagan, R. B. Kearsley, and P. R. Zelazo, "The Effects of Infant Day Care on Psychological Development" (paper presented at a symposium on "The Effect of Early Experience on Child Development," American Association for the Advancement of Science, Boston, Mass., 19 February 1976).

26. E. Minkowski, *Lived Time: Phenomenological and Psychopathological Studies*, trans. N. Metzel (Evanston, Ill: Northwestern University Press, 1970); L. Binswanger, *Being-in-the-World* (New York: Basic, 1963); and T. D. Yalom, *Existential Psychotherapy* (New York: Basic, 1980).

7

SUSAN WESTERBERG PRAGER

Shifting Perspectives
on Marital Property Law

Historically, family law in the United States has been shaped by conceptions of appropriate male and female roles. More recently, concern over the disparate economic and social circumstances of men and women has been evidenced by the movement for equality between the sexes. This essay explores a few of the problems presented by the extension of equality principles to family law, particularly in the property relationships created by marriage.

At the end of the 1960s, much of American family law was still premised on the notion that within marriage men and women performed different roles that in turn called into play distinct rights and responsibilities. The wife remained at home, taking care of children, while her husband worked in the outside world. The husband had the legal right to manage community property because, after all, he had "earned" it; the contributions of the homemaker were not of equal weight. When a marriage ended by divorce, the mother, assumed to be more suitable, in part because she had previously cared for the children, was preferred as the custodial parent. A wife was entitled to financial support because she had fulfilled the common expectations of remaining at home. If, by chance, the husband had not worked outside the home, he was seen as unworthy of support.

During the 1970s fundamental changes displaced much of this law. Divorced parents began to be granted equal access to the custody of their children, the customary maternal preference for young children having been erased from the law.[1] The U.S. Supreme Court held that men, as well as women, must be eligible for alimony.[2] Community property states made the spouses coequal managers of community property, striking

I would like to thank Elizabeth Cheadle, Ginger Covitt, Patsy Schiff, Joan Vogel and Barrie Thorne for their comments on this essay and the Center for Research on Women at Stanford for creating the lecture series out of which it grew.

down the concept of male management that had previously pervaded the law.[3]

In addition to these and many other direct applications of equality principles by courts and legislatures, more subtle influences were present. No-fault divorce and constitutionally guaranteed rights to birth control are two examples of the relationship of the equality theme in family law reform. The move toward no-fault divorce [4] would have been unthinkable without the underlying premise that a woman ought to be able to fend for herself in the world, and in fact might prefer to do so rather than continue in a fundamentally unsatisfactory marriage. Conversely, what husband could discard a wife of many years if society believed that she was unable to function independently in the world? The series of Supreme Court decisions that ensured the right to birth control,[5] including the controversial abortion cases,[6] worked a fundamental change in the individual woman's ability to control the economic and social impact of childbearing. In turn, this control enabled women to plan for roles outside the home in ways not perceived possible in earlier years. This recent period contains many more instances of the impact of equal rights concerns on the law;[7] in fact, the equality theme in the law in the 1970s is undeniable.

While this period of feminist concern led to basic acceptance of the equality principle, examination of the law surrounding divorce reveals considerable confusion about the meaning of equality. It is unclear whether the focus should be on equality of opportunity or of result. The choice has enormous implications for the course the law ought to take. Moreover, the discussion of marital property law and divorce law that follows reveals that the confusion stems from far more than the difficulties in defining and implementing a policy of equality; it suggests that the focus on equality may obscure the need to accommodate other important social values.

Before analyzing the current marital property debate, this essay briefly describes the historical development of U.S. marital property law that led to two distinct systems, one based on sharing, the other on individualism. Next, it explores the recent debate from two vantage points: (1) the central role of equality concerns and (2) the extent to which the equality focus has distorted the debate. I argue that sharing theories are likely to be appropriate even if we achieve a world free of sex discrimination. I then comment on the rising use of private contracts between married people and consider the impact of no-fault divorce reforms, with particular attention to the problem of achieving equality. The conflicts discussed in each of these sections reflect considerable confusion about the nature of our objectives in a period of fundamental reconsideration of the law affecting marriage.

A Brief History of American Marital Property Law

Initially in the United States married women had no property rights, with marriage bringing about a unity of interests all lodged in the husband. Mid-nineteenth-century movements for reform, reflected in the married women's property acts * and the adoption of community property in parts of the American West, sought to grant married women the right to own and manage some property, at a minimum the property brought with them to the marriage or given to them thereafter. These reforms were fought bitterly; their opponents saw them as "radically wrong," "fundamentally altering the marriage relationship," and causing the "disintegration of marriage." At the California Constitutional Convention of 1849, strains of sentiments expressed in more recent years can be detected in the words of delegates who supported the traditional common law of marital property:

> This proposition, I believe, is calculated to produce dissension and strife in families. The only despotism on earth that I would advocate, is the despotism of the husband. There must be a head and there must be a master in every household; and I believe this plan by which you propose to make the wife independent of the husband, is contrary to the laws and provisions of nature —contrary to all the wisdom which we have derived from experience. This doctrine of woman's rights is the doctrine of those mental hermaphrodites, Abby Folsom, Fanny Wright, and the rest of that tribe.[8]

Though slightly more temperate, another delegate was similarly disturbed.

> [T]he principle of setting the wife up as an equal in everything whatever, to the husband—raising her from the condition of head clerk to partner . . . is contrary to nature, and contrary to the real interests of the married state.[9]

To these men, marriage was held together by little more than male dominance complemented by complete subjection of the wife. The institution of marriage was based on power and dependency; to tamper with these foundations, let alone accord the spouses equal status in property matters, would, it was feared, destroy the institution. Once the law introduced a separation of interests, conflict between the spouses was thought to be inevitable. Tensions within the marriage would set off property disputes, and property would be used to fight other battles. It was con-

---

* In 1839 Mississippi enacted the first married woman's property law. Maine and Michigan acted in 1844; New York did so in 1849. While every state except Virginia had reformed its law by 1875, judicial resistance to change made further legislation necessary.

sidered essential to avoid conflict by placing power in the husband alone. Definite views of maleness and male dignity, as well as the place of women in the culture, were at stake.

In contrast, one delegate who favored reform perceived mutual benefit growing out of individual interests:

> I believe that much opposition to the protection of the separate property of the wife arises from a degree of false pride on the part of the man. . . . I consider that the wife's interest is the husband's interest; and whatever can afford protection and security to her, must necessarily be to his advantage as well as hers.[10]

Another delegate damned the common law as "origin[ating] in a barbarous age, when the wife was considered in the light of a menial and had no rights."[11] The position of the wife had changed and the law should reflect her increased status:

> At the time the common law was introduced, woman occupied a position far inferior to that which she now occupies. As the world has advanced in civilization, her social position has been the subject of increased consideration, and by general consent of all intelligent men, she is now regarded as entitled to many of the rights in her peculiar sphere which were formerly considered as belonging only to man. This part of the common law is one of those portions belonging to the dark ages, which has not yet been expunged by the advance of civilization.[12]

These comments reflect reform ideas that were soon to sweep much of the nation as the married women's property acts gained momentum. Yet, in reviewing this history from the vantage point of the 1980s, we cannot help but reflect on how little the fundamental concerns that touch the nature of the marital relationship have changed.

The nineteenth-century reform movement produced two different legal theories of marital property law: the sharing-oriented community property of the Spanish civil law;[13] and the individualistically framed separate propertyal theories of marital property law: the sharing-oriented community property of the Spanish civil law;[13] and the individualistically framed separate property system created by the married women's property acts, which reformed the common law. Community property stresses the unity created by marriage, placing considerable emphasis on sharing of property. Earnings traceable to labor during the marriage are regarded as community property. The marriage is seen as a partnership in which both spouses equally share, reflecting the theory that both contribute to earnings, regardless of which spouse has directly earned the property. At the same time, community property systems recognize some separate property interests during the marriage. Separate property is seen as property not related to labor during marriage but acquired before marriage or received by gift or inheritance during marriage.

In contrast to community property, separate property systems, which dominated in the United States after the married women's property acts of the nineteenth century, conferred no special property rights from the fact of marriage. Rather, the married individuals functioned as property owners much as if they had never married. In this reformed common-law conception, the spouses are defined as separate individuals, each of whom can acquire and manage property.[14]

The separate property system can best be understood as a reaction to the English common law, which the nineteenth-century reformers attacked. In English common law, marriage brought about a single unified property interest with most of the incidents of ownership and all control residing in the husband. Upon marriage, a woman's property for most purposes became her husband's. He was even entitled to all her earnings. At common law the wife could not make contracts or engage in litigation. Blackstone's often quoted but exaggerated description of the common law as merging the spouses' interests into one person, the husband,[15] certainly contained a ring of truth.

The essential element of the reformed common law embodied in the married women's property acts was revolutionary when viewed in the context of the then prevailing common-law concept of marriage and the prerogatives and duties it imposed. The reform enactments regarded the married woman as the separate and individual owner of all property that would have been hers but for the marriage. The property a woman brought with her to the marriage, from whatever source, plus any gift or inheritance that came to her thereafter and any property earned by her during marriage, was her separate property. In their more audacious form, the acts granted married women *control* as well as ownership.

The reformed common law and the community property approaches represent distinctive views on the desirability of unifying the property interests of the wife and the husband. According to the individualistic premise of the reformed common law, common ownership is possible only by explicit choice. Not only is separation of property unfavored, but the spouses are regarded much like two unmarried individuals. By contrast, a community property law makes the assumption that common ownership is highly desirable and is to be preferred and encouraged over separate ownership. Thus, these systems manifest different judgments about the nature of the marital relationship and the assumptions and expectations of the spouses.

The Current Marital Property Debate

The first, and at present the strongest, feminist perspective that surged in the 1960s and '70s pointed out that the separate property system prevailing in most of the United States provided an illusory equality. In a society in which married women have traditionally assumed primary responsibility for the home and in which men have a primary position in the paid economy, a separate property system results in a world where husbands earn property and wives are unlikely to do so. Among other effects, such a legal system can reinforce the dependent status of women.*

The marital property law should, in this first reform view, reflect the division of labor often found in marriage by mandating a sharing of much of the property owned by the spouses. While the minority of community property jurisdictions have been grounded in this perspective for many years, relatively recent reforms in the vast majority of the noncommunity property states bring them closer to community property through the concept of "equitable division" of property upon divorce.[16] For example, in 1971 the Colorado legislature provided for division of "marital property" on divorce using community propertylike distinctions: Colorado subjects earnings traceable to labor during the marriage to equitable distribution but does not divide premarriage property, inheritances, or gifts. New Jersey's 1971 reform is more expansive in its application of sharing principles, encompassing in the equitable division all property acquired during the marriage, regardless of its source. States that have enacted equitable distributions have recognized the homemaker as having property rights at the end of the marriage. This recent reform perspective appears to root the need for sharing of property in the differentiation of roles based on the sex of the marital partners. The concern has been that women have been disadvantaged by the individually oriented system of the reformed common law because of patterns of child rearing, domestic labor, and access to incomes in the paid economy.

Interestingly, the current focus on equality has produced a second theme, one that leads to an emphasis on individual rather than shared property rights. This second feminist perspective assumes that the problem of inequality posed by the traditional economic structure of marriage is a short-run concern. In this conception, true economic and social equality of the sexes will ultimately emerge. At that point, sharing principles will become unnecessary and, in fact, will be destructive of individual rights to no important purpose. Once sex-based discrimination is a thing of the past, each spouse will in reality have property and the power that comes with it. Each can then own and manage his or her property as he or she deems best. Thus it is possible to argue, as Mary Ann Glendon has persuasively done,[17] that the future may well produce an individually

* Wives who have not developed or maintained positions in the paid economy are justifiably reluctant to opt out of the marriage, and divorce is even more difficult for the wife to sustain if the marital property system treats all accumulations of the period of the marriage as owned by the husband because he "earned" them.

oriented set of property laws rather than a marital partnership framework stressing common ownership.

Although those favoring separate and those advocating sharing principles ultimately diverge, both stem from a concern for equality. The recent literature is dominated by the notion that equality is the critical, perhaps exclusive, factor in shaping the property rights of married people. It suggests that to the extent that there is economic inequality, a sharing oriented system is required. When inequality is not present, a system based on individual rights is appropriate.

In my view the current preoccupation with equal rights may dangerously skew our vision of marital property policy questions and create a deceptive mode of analysis. While it is certainly true that sharing principles have been advanced in recent years because of the economic inequalities created by traditional marriage, it is questionable whether the need for sharing principles will vanish if those inequalities disappear. As long as marriage and other similar close personal relationships continue to reflect sharing behavior, there is, I believe, a place for sharing principles in marital property law. Marital sharing principles are not dependent on a social structure in which one or the other spouse relinquishes the earner role. Rather, the need for the sharing philosophy stems from the dynamics of marriage and similar relationships.

In marriage, most of us seek an alliance with another individual who will believe in us; who will be loyal to us; who will help us function in a demanding, often hostile world; and who will help make life satisfying. In exchange we will try to do the same. These needs and the expectations they create shape the frame of mind with which decisions are made during marriage. The expectation of stability and continuity and the desire for a shared life suggest that married people are unlikely to make decisions on an individually oriented basis; rather, the needs of each person tend to be taken into account. Thus, married people will often make different decisions from those they would make if there were no marriage or marriagelike relationship functioning.

The pervasive influence of sharing behavior and expectations may be best illustrated by examples of common behavior patterns. Two-earner marriages are the principal focus of discussion, since they constitute the most favorable context for the individualistic view. Each example assumes a world in which equality has been achieved in employment opportunity and in the social acceptance of chosen, rather than sex-determined, roles.* While these admittedly intuitive perceptions of common behavior patterns are no substitute for empirical study, they nonetheless suggest

* This is not to suggest that people living in such a world would be likely to conform to one particular behavior pattern with respect to the relationship of work to family life or that the dominant pattern could be predicted with any accuracy.

the presence and strength of sharing assumptions in two-earner marriages.

Career choices that confront the spouses at varied times during marriage constitute one area in which attitudes about the relationship influence the choices made. Employment decisions determine many aspects of the couple's personal life and have significant impact on the acquisition and management of property. Where will they live? Are moves likely? How much income can be anticipated? To what extent will the particular work of one spouse create stress for that spouse and perhaps for both? How will work affect their ability to be together? By and large, it is not practicable for each spouse in the two-earner marriage to make employment decisions on a completely individualized basis, for each decision affects both spouses in direct ways.*

Some couples may attempt to make employment choices that maximize opportunities for both of them, given the fact that they want to live together. In a marriage of two professionals, each may decide to forego his or her first choice of employment because its location does not afford sufficiently desirable options to the other. For example, a wife may accept a management position in Los Angeles that is an improvement over her New York job but decline a better position in a small city because her husband, an interior designer, would find significantly less challenging business there. The husband, who has an established design clientele in New York, may agree to move to Los Angeles, where opportunities will be acceptable, but, because he will have to rebuild reputation and contacts, less attractive than in New York.†

In some marriages one spouse's career will be subordinated temporarily,[18] perhaps because of the need for education or the presence of children. Educations may be obtained in serial fashion in order to maximize economic potential, with each spouse supporting the other while he or she is in school. The decision to have children may have significant career and

* It is, of course, insensitive and misleading to characterize the employment posture of lower-income couples as involving real choices. The observations made in this discussion of employment decisions reflect a middle-class perspective. But this is not to ignore the impact of marital property principles for those with low incomes. Although there is a tendency to exclude low-income couples from the marital property policy debate on the rationale that there is unlikely to be any property that could be divided at the end of the relationship, significant categories of property are indeed available. I have in mind here enforced savings such as social security and pension interests.

† At first glance separation of property might seem appropriate in these circumstances, for the example would suggest the decisions have resulted in similar impact on each spouse. But while each has foregone the choice he or she would have made but for the relationship, the impact on each might not be equal. There may be disparate effects on earning potential or professional status. More important, what impact should the frame of mind of the spouses in making these mutual accommodations have on the marital property concepts applied to them? In other words, does such an accommodation reflect expectations of separate or shared property rights?

property ramifications. Some couples believe that at least one of them should spend considerable time with children, particularly when they are young, or they may find no practical alternatives for child care. This can entail terminating employment or reducing the work load for some period. Even assuming that neither spouse temporarily foregoes employment to care for children, at least one partner must stand ready in emergencies and be flexible enough to reclaim children when child care arrangements end.*

Other couples may conclude that it is desirable to structure their choices to give permanent priority to the advancement of one of them rather than equalize opportunities. Typical reasons for this choice might include one earner being less marketable than the other, one spouse having a stronger need for recognition outside the family, one partner showing greater achievement potential than the other, or one spouse pursuing a career (e.g., military or foreign service) that makes it difficult for decisions about the other's career to be given equal consideration. Sacrifices involved in subordinating one spouse's career, temporarily or permanently, are promoted by the notion that the relationship will be permanent, an expectation that can be shattered when the relationship ends unexpectedly.[19]

Still other couples may see the two-earner marriage as an opportunity to reduce the importance of work. Having two shared incomes may make it economically possible for both to work less or hold less demanding jobs. This may seem desirable for numerous personal reasons including considerations of health or the attraction of more leisure time. The expectation of a stable relationship in which both partners earn money helps make possible the option of reduced employment.†

Like employment choices, decisions concerning family finances reflect fundamental assumptions about property and the marital relationship. Two broad categories of behavior seem common; one involves separation of property and the other, the pooling of assets.

Some spouses segregate earnings by maintaining separate accounts. This choice furthers or helps satisfy the individual's need for exclusive control over at least some aspects of life. Often spouses may select such an arrangement because they find it difficult to agree on certain economic

---

* Both are not free to travel on business; both are not necessarily available for overtime or flexible hours. Although some may truly try to share responsibilities for children, many will conclude that it is more functional for one of them to do so.

† Suppose, for example, that the spouses decide it would be desirable to retire at the same time, meaning that one of them will have to retire early and forego full benefits. Yet their combined financial resources make this alternative workable, and they see social benefits such as adjusting to retirement together and having more time to spend with one another. Now suppose that after a year of perhaps too much togetherness, they separate. Should each spouse retain his or her separate property, including the disproportionate retirement benefits, or should sharing principles be employed to equalize the impact of the retirement decisions?

matters or because it is convenient to have separate accounts. When the married individuals each contribute equally to common expenses, including proportionate shares of consumables and asset-building expenses such as house payments, it is unlikely that sharing expectations are present, unless they are developed in the employment or other contexts.

When the spouses are less exacting—one purchasing food and the other making mortgage payments—sharing attitudes are more likely to exist. Here, it seems, individual control may well have effectuated some of the spouses' needs for freedom of choice for such things as clothing and entertainment.* But individual control may not reflect an expectation of separate property rights. If the spouses were forced to think about whether one of them or both owned the house, what would they be likely to conclude? [20]

Far more common than segregating earnings is the pattern of pooling property with control in one or both spouses. When married individuals treat the property they each earn as one common fund, their actions clearly reflect a sharing assumption. It is important to recognize that this attitude may well be present even when title to all assets is not jointly held. [21]

If these examples accurately reflect typical choices made by two-earner couples, they suggest that sharing attitudes are pervasive even in marriages in which individualistic expectations might be expected to be strongest and that these attitudes are founded upon certain fundamental assumptions about the relationship.

Rather than detail the arguments for sharing concepts in marriage, it may be useful to begin to assess the problems each of the two marital property systems might present in the future. Here the central issue may well be the relationship of the principle of individualism to marriage. Conversations with my students have helped clarify some of the sources of the highly individualistic separate property view, in particular, a deeply felt psychological need on the part of some to view property as exclusively their own.

Perhaps the fear of divorce or a sense of its inevitability underpins the ideology of the separate property supporters. For many people today, the possibility that marriage will end in divorce looms large and is bound to shape perceptions of what a fair marital property law should contain. The separate property concept would resolve the particularly troublesome question of dependency in the marital relationship by refusing to reflect any dependency. Traditionally, the imposition of sharing principles has

---

* Often individual control is attractive because it satisfies the need for some privacy with respect to expenditures. But for many, individual management seems desirable simply because it eliminates the confusion that can result when both spouses transact business out of the same account.

been used to provide support for the dependent spouse when the relation-ship ends. In contrast, a separate property structure sends a signal that dependency will not be rewarded. In this way, the marital property law becomes a tool of social engineering designed to foster economic and psychic independence.* A separate property system encourages each per-son to function as an earner by refusing to compensate a spouse who remains in the home for a significant period.

The absence of sharing principles can thus be used to discourage the establishment of dependency relationships. But if many couples in fact make decisions with the special exigencies of the marital relationship in mind, a system of property law that assumes that decisions ought to be made on an individual basis may produce two different ill effects.

First, one spouse may ultimately be treated unfairly if the couple does not alter its behavior to conform to the individualistic orientation of the separate property model. This, it seems to me, is an important question for those feminists who believe that our social structure should admit and support a diversity of life styles including the one-earner or role-divided marriage. Certainly, the family relationship continues to be valued by many people, including many who are concerned about the status of women in the culture. Furthermore, in structuring the marital property law, we should not assume that if sex-determined status disappears in the future, both spouses will function equally as earners or both will in fact earn. It is possible that the elimination of sex-based discrimination will not produce such a world, at least not for some significant proportion of the population. For example, chronic unemployment may continue, causing a significant number of one-earner relationships. In addition, many spouses, male and female, may well care for children on a full-time basis. If mar-riage ends while one spouse is engaged in this role, particularly if that spouse is substantially less employable because of prolonged absences from the work force or interrupted schooling, protection becomes impor-tant. In other words, the achievement of equality does not necessarily spell the end of the division of functions within a family; it simply ends the routine assignment of function based on sex.

In addition to the potential injustice to one spouse, the push to re-structure behavior along individualistic lines can have other repercussions. If behavior is indeed responsive to a separatist legal structure that suggests putting oneself first, other social values are likely to suffer. By dictating that a married person behave as if unmarried with respect to certain choices or suffer the consequences of subsequent property disadvantage, the individually oriented model works to reward self-interested choices that can be detrimental to the continuation of the marriage. At the same

* This, of course, assumes that the spouses are aware of the law and structure their behavior accordingly.

time it punishes conduct of accommodation and compromise so important to furthering and preserving the relationship. From a social engineering standpoint, an individualistic property system may begin to produce behavior that is at cross-purposes with other values, such as stability and cooperation in marital relationships.

For purposes of analysis, the foregoing discussion has tested sharing principles in the context of a world that does not yet exist. Moreover, there is serious doubt that the functionally sex-neutral world will ever materialize; economic and cultural factors may continue to impede change.* Even the full achievement of true equality of opportunity may not produce equality in fact. This suggests that for the foreseeable future, the sharing-oriented reformers are likely to continue to gain ground. At the same time, the law must accommodate an increasing diversity of personal perspectives, some of which reflect sharing attitudes and some of which prefer individualism.

The Growing Interest in Private Contracts

In part because the question of desirable marital property policy involves important and conflicting values, the alternative solution of private contracts has been receiving much attention. Lenore Weitzman in her important 1974 article, *Legal Regulation of Marriage: Tradition and Change*, proposed marriage contracts as a method to alter the legal restrictions traditionally placed on married people.[22] The formal written contract may be used to address a number of individual needs and expectations. While the law has traditionally negated the availability of contracts to govern the incidents of marital relationship, recently there are indications that contracts freely and fairly established will be upheld at least in some important respects.† Furthermore, even provisions that may not be enforceable in the event of dispute may accomplish their goals simply by being articulated at the outset. Popular interest in the use of contracts to set forth expectations about the marital relationship, as well as contracts in lieu of marriage, is evidenced by the fact that lawyers are now frequently called upon to draft them. In contrast, as recently as ten years ago, their use was reserved for the wealthy or the person with children by a previous marriage who entered a second marriage late in life.

In this brief essay let me simply raise some of my doubts about the

---

* The earnings gap between men and women has continued to widen, and women still bear a heavier burden of child care than men, both as married and single parents. In addition, seniority and other labor policies may, depending on economic conditions, lead to the disproportionate loss of jobs for women on a "last in, first out" basis.

† The legal trend, led by Florida and California, points to enforcement of all property-related provisions, except those affecting child support.

wisdom of encouraging private contracts. The factors that make it difficult to sustain marital relationships also limit the usefulness of an agreement shaped by attitudes present at one particular point in time. The constant, often imperceptible, shifting of attitudes means that the premises of a relationship may change in unanticipated ways; new responses must be found, earlier positions are reversed. It would be a most unusual agreement that could adequately cope with the fluctuating nature of the relationship and the individual goals of its partners.

Agreements can serve important purposes, such as increasing self-awareness and an appreciation of the marital partner's perceptions on a wide range of questions, but they are by no means an all-encompassing remedy or a complete substitute for a generally applicable system of marital property law. In fact, encouraging agreements may lead to unfair results because it is unlikely that people will consciously reassess the premises of their relationship and amend their contracts to reflect changed circumstances or assumptions.[23] In addition, laws that required or even assumed the existence of contracts would impose a greater hardship on the poor and the less educated members of society. Furthermore, a mandatory agreements scheme seems largely unenforceable, particularly in the light of the trend toward unformalized relationships.

In short, while formal agreements will probably play a greater role in marital property law, they will not eliminate the need for generally applicable principles. Nor does the rising use of private agreements suggest that one or another conception of property ownership is gaining favor. The increasing diversity of life styles indicates that a significant number of couples will choose private agreements over the prevailing marital property system, whether it be based on individual or shared ownership.[24]

The Impact of the No-Fault Divorce Reform

The shift to a marital breakdown or no-fault divorce system reflects an important shift in emphasis. Appropriately, the reasons for divorce are now private matters. Once the married individuals determine that the marriage has failed, the state will sanction a divorce without inquiring into the reasons for it.

However, none of us who heralded California's 1970 no-fault divorce reform foresaw its ramifications, particularly for many homemakers.[25] While few would want to return to the fault-based divorce law, the challenge in recent years has been to grapple with the unfairness that has often resulted from the principle of divorce at the option of one partner irrespective of the reasons for the breakdown of the marriage. Under the earlier law, a divorce could be obtained only by the "innocent" spouse who had been wronged by specified acts of the other, such as adultery or cruelty. Basic acceptance of the concept of equal rights was an implicit precondition for this shift away from the old law. Unless we assumed that the wife discarded by her husband could function on her own, how could the new law be justified? Yet the rising interest in the 1970s in programs for displaced homemakers suggests the gap between the theory of equality and the reality for many women.[26]

In addition to the equality theme, the individualistic principle was also strongly present in divorce reform. These reforms tended to assume that wives and husbands were entitled to pursue their individual happiness, regardless of the impact on others in the family who wanted the family to continue. The early 1970s witnessed an unfortunate period of the application of new rules on people who had predicated many years of marriage on the old ones. Women married twenty to thirty years were told they must work at any job they could get if they were physically able to do so. In *Marriage of Dennis*, a 1973 California case, the fifty-year-old wife who had not worked outside the home during her quarter-century marriage was awarded spousal support of $200 a month for the first year and $100 a month for the next three years.[27] Prior to the marriage, the wife had been a riveter, and at one point during the marriage she had done some work as a seamstress, earning about seven dollars a week, until she had had to discontinue that work because of eye problems. The trial court would have terminated all her support after four years; the appellate court left open the possibility that the wife might need support thereafter. Both courts completely rejected the wife's contention that she should not have to work under the circumstances.

Fortunately, the unfairness of such responses rapidly became apparent, and a counter action took hold. In *Marriage of Brantner*, the trial court awarded $200 per month spousal support for two years, with gradual reductions to the point that after the seventh and eighth years of $50 a month, the wife would receive no support.[28]

Justice Gardner expressed the views of the outraged appellate court:

> In the case at bench we are faced with a woman who, during the last 25 years, has borne 2 children and confined her activities to those of a mother and housewife. These activities, vital though they may be, do not qualify her to embark on a lucrative career in the highly competitive job market. Had she not been married those 20-odd years, she might now be well qualified as a typist, truck driver or tinsmith. Opportunities for developing skills in those fields were denied her when she, and presumably her husband, decided that she would follow that most important but somewhat nonglamorous and definitely nonsalaried occupation of housewife and mother. Assuming she does not become blind,

her experience as a homemaker qualifies her for either of two
positions, charwoman or babysitter. A candidate for a well
paying job, she isn't. . . .[29]

The court explicitly recognized the abuses made possible by the no-fault
divorce reform:

> The new Family Law Act has been heralded as a bill of rights for
> harried former husbands who have been suffering under
> prolonged and unreasonable alimony awards. However, the act
> may not be used as a handy vehicle for the summary disposal of
> old and used wives. A woman is not a breeding cow to be
> nurtured during her years of fecundity, then conveniently and
> economically converted to cheap steaks when past her prime. If a
> woman is able to do so, she certainly should support herself. If,
> however, she has spent her productive years as a housewife and
> mother and has missed the opportunity to compete in the job
> market and improve her job skills, quite often she becomes,
> when divorced, simply a "displaced homemaker."[30]

The court made clear that it did not want to foster dependence unnecessarily, but at the same time it recognized that the earning spouse might bear
continuing responsibility based on the spouses' earlier choices.

> A marriage license is not a ticket to a perpetual pension and, as
> women approach equality in the job market, the burden on the
> husband will be lessened in those cases in which, by agreement
> of both parties, the wife has remained employed or at least has
> had the opportunity to maintain and refresh her job skills during
> marriage. However, in those cases in which it is the decision of
> the parties that the woman becomes the homemaker, the
> marriage is of substantial duration and at separation the wife is to
> all intents and purposes unemployable, the husband simply has
> to face up to the fact that his support responsibilities are going to
> be of extended duration—perhaps for life. This has nothing to
> do with feminism, sexism, male chauvinism or any other trendy
> social ideology. It is ordinary common sense, basic decency and
> simple justice.[31]

As *Brantner* indicates, spousal support has become more easily available
after long marriages when the economic circumstances of the former
spouses present need, typically on the part of the wife, and demonstrate
the husband's ability to pay.

One question that needs greater exploration is whether it is appropriate to discard the concept of responsibility in divorce law. Certainly we
would not want fault in its previous incarnation, which focused on isolated
selected behavior such as adultery and acts thought to be cruel. Yet

perhaps the fact that often one person wants to continue the marriage ought to be relevant to considerations of property division and spousal support. The difficulty in addressing this question is whether some greater fairness based upon expectations can be established without reintroducing the evils of the earlier fault-based law. One way to reconcile these goals is to retain the concept of divorce at the option of one partner but emphasize that there may well be continuing responsibility based not simply on the agreement to marry but on actual reliance during the ongoing marriage. Some of the criteria of both alimony and equitable distribution of marital property may already reflect this perspective.

Feminist perspectives, particularly the call for equality, contributed greatly to the changes that occurred in family law in the 1970s. At the same time, our inability to precisely define equality has created considerable, and fundamental, confusion in creating and applying the law. Throughout the discussion of marital property law, I have attempted to point out the need to focus on behavior and values developed during the ongoing marital relationship. If I am correct that sharing attitudes are likely to prevail within marriage even *if* sex discrimination disappears, then it would be wrong for the law to emphasize individualistically oriented property rights. Individualism can still be recognized by preserving such choices as the right to divorce, but reliance interests formed during the functioning marriage ought to be protected in the marital property laws.

I would hope that the healthy ferment about the meaning of equality and individualism will not obscure the simple and important point that the major contribution of this recent period is our ability to focus on the subject for the first time since the 1920s, with every confidence that our inquiry is an important one. This, in itself, is a contribution of enormous significance.

Notes

1. Freed and Foster report that as of 1 August 1979, thirty states have rejected, by statute or court decision, the "tender years" doctrine that presumes the mother should receive custody of young children. Eleven states follow a version of this doctrine that allows the custody presumption to be subordinated to the best interests of the child. Only four states clearly give preference to a "fit" mother. Ten states have enacted laws specifically "desexing" child custody. At least twenty-two other states have enacted statutes equalizing parental rights to child custody. Freed and Foster, *Divorce in the Fifty States*, 5 Fam. L. Rptr. 4027, 4035–36 (1979). These developments and the attendant uncertainty in custody results may well explain the recent interest in the alternative of joint custody.

2. *See* Orr v. Orr, 440 U.S. 268 (1979), which held that the Alabama statutory scheme of imposing alimony obligations on husbands but not wives violated the Equal Protection Clause of the Fourteenth Amendment.

3. Each of the eight community property states has adopted some form of equal management law. The dominant approach led by Washington in 1972 is to permit either spouse acting alone to manage community property, regardless of which spouse directly earned the property. *See, e.g.,* Cal. Civ. Code § 5125 (West 1980).

4. In 1970 California led the nation in developing a marital breakdown standard for divorce, eliminating the fault-based grounds such as cruelty and adultery. As of 1 August 1979, 35 states had enacted irretrievable breakdown grounds. Of these, 18 have superimposed this standard on traditional fault and period of separation grounds. *See* Freed and Foster, *supra* note 1 at 4029.

5. In Griswold v. Connecticut, 381 U.S. 479 (1965), the U.S. Supreme Court held that a constitutional right of privacy exists to protect a married couple's right to birth-control advice and devices. Eisenstadt v. Baird, 405 U.S. 438 (1972), extended this privacy right to any individual, married or single.

6. The landmark decision in Roe v. Wade, 410 U.S. 113 (1973), established the individual woman's right to abortion in the first trimester of pregnancy for any reason. Several years later, the Court struck down spousal and parental consent requirements for abortion. Planned Parenthood of Missouri v. Danforth, 428 U.S. 52 (1976). Of course the Supreme Court does not operate in a vacuum. These legal changes occurred because of changing attitudes about the issue of abortion.

7. A number of the Supreme Court cases struck down laws that discriminated against fathers and, through them, their children. For example, in Weinberger v. Wiesenfeld, 420 U.S. 636 (1975), a father successfully challenged the Social Security Act provisions that granted certain benefits to female, but not male, surviving spouses with minor children; in Stanley v. Illinois, 405 U.S. 645 (1972), an unwed father successfully challenged the state's presumption that an unwed father was an unfit parent in circumstances where, had the mother been the survivor, she would have been presumed to be fit.

8. J. Browne, *Report of the Debates in the Convention in California* 260 (1850) (remarks of Mr. Botts).

9. *Id.* at 261 (remarks of Mr. Lippitt).

10. *Id.* at 259 (remarks of Mr. Tefft).

11. *Id.* at 264 (remarks of Mr. Jones).

12. *Id.* at 263 (remarks of Mr. Dimmick).

13. The community property system reached the United States through the Spanish civil law that was continued in Texas, Louisiana, California, New Mexico, and Arizona. Washington, Nevada, and Idaho followed, completing the minority of states that follow community property principles. For a discussion of the development of the California law, see Prager, *The Persistence of Separate Property Concepts in California Community Property System:* 1849–1975, 24 UCLA L. REV. 1 (1976).

14. For a detailed analysis of the common law of marital property, see Johnston, *Sex and Property: The Common Law Tradition, The Law School Curriculum, and Developments Toward Equality,* 47 NYU L. REV. 1033 (1972).

15. "By marriage, the husband and wife are one person in law: (*1*) that is the very being or legal existence of the woman is suspended during the marriage or at least is incorporated and consolidated into that of the husband. . . ." W. BLACKSTONE, COMMENTARIES *442. By contrast, it was Blackstone's view that "in the civil law the husband and the wife are considered as two distinct persons." *Id.* at *444.

16. Many years ago a few of the separate property jurisdictions altered their laws to provide some division on divorce. As early as 1889, Kansas provided for a "just and reasonable division of property acquired by the parties jointly during their marriage." Oklahoma's 1893 modification of the reformed common law was apparently heavily influenced by the Kansas law as well as the community property theories. In 1970, the Uniform Marriage and Divorce Act was proposed as a model for the states to follow. As revised in 1973, § 307 alternative A of the act provides for equitable apportionment of the property of either or both spouses. The act has no legal effect and force until individual states choose to enact all or part of its provisions. However, the promulgation of the act has furthered the marital property reform movement. By the summer of 1980, less than a handful of states continue the pattern of separate property without any provision for some sharing on divorce. New York has adopted an equitable distribution system effective 19 July 1980. 1980 N.Y. Adv. Legis. Serv. 429, 434–36 (to be codified as N.Y. Dom. Rel. Law § 236).

17. Glendon, *Is There a Future for Separate Property?* 8 FAM. L. Q. 315 (1974).

18. In one small sample of two-career families Holmstrom found a tendency in the spouses to alternate the priorities given to each individual's career. First one and then the other spouse's advancement would receive preference. L. HOLMSTROM, *The Two-Career Family,* 33–35 (1972).

19. The unfairness that can result when a marriage ends after one spouse has made professional sacrifices to help advance the other is well known to lawyers who counsel clients in the divorce context. How often a client will articulate the disappointment and hurt that can accompany lost expectations by saying: "But I thought *we* were working toward a goal together, and that we would later enjoy the

benefits." Admittedly, current social standards exacerbate these feelings. The instance of the wife who worked to put her husband through medical school and who then did not return to school illustrates that the reliance involved is likely to have severe consequences. A similar frustration of expectations would occur when the marital relationship ends by death, unless sharing theories are continued. Is it appropriate to conclude that when it becomes more socially desirable for women to vigorously pursue employment, no consideration should be given to the sharing expectations implicit in circumstances where one spouse's career assumes priority for some period of time? As Jessie Bernard has pointed out, even relatively brief work interruptions have an impact on achievement. J. BERNARD, *Women And The Public Interest*, 179–86 (1971).

20. In one relatively recent case, after years of pooling earnings, the wife began to support the family with her earnings and the husband used his earnings to make investments. Upon divorce, the court, applying New York's separate property system, awarded all investments to the husband over the wife's objections. Wirth v. Wirth, 38 App. Div. 2d 611, 326 N.Y.S. 2d 308 (1971). Wirth rather graphically illustrates how a separate property system frustrates the expectations of the spouses formed during the ongoing relationship.

21. The tendency of the spouses to pool all their property is likely to be stronger as total family income decreases. Rheinstein observed: "As long as a marriage functions, spouses of modest means rarely earmark their assets as 'his' and 'hers.'" Rheinstein, *The Transformation of Marriage and the Law*, 68 NWU L. REV. 463, 475 (1973). The family that must spend all money coming to it in order to acquire the necessities of life is unlikely to think of certain property as the husband's because earned by him and other property as the wife's because obtained by her. The only assets accumulated by these families are likely to result from forced savings, things that the spouses cannot directly control or manage, such as employment-connected and governmental benefits. These easy-to-overlook forms of property are of growing importance in our society.

22. Weitzman, *Legal Regulation of Marriage: Tradition and Change*, 62 CALIF. L. REV. 1169 (1974).

23. A 1976 California case illustrates how such contracts can fail to reflect changed circumstances. In order to protect the pregnant woman from possible loss of her teaching job, the parties entered into what they expected to be only a "temporary" marriage. On this assumption, they executed a premarriage contract providing that their earnings and all other property acquired during marriage would be held as separate property. The "temporary" marriage lasted almost nine years. Despite the changed expectations that could reasonably be implied from these facts, the California Supreme Court upheld the validity of the premarriage contract, and the wife was awarded no property upon the dissolution of the marriage. *In re* Marriage of Dawley, 17 Cal. 3d 342, 551 P.2d 323, 131 CAL. RPTR. 3 (1976).

24. Lenore Weitzman has found that in a sample of California couples who entered into marriage contracts, the large majority provided for ownership of property along community property principles, suggesting that the motivation for the contract was not related to any need to modify the marital property law in force. Weitzman, *Contracts for Intimate Relationships*, 1 ALT. Lifestyles 303 (1978).

25. See, for example, Comment, *The End of Innocence: Elimination of Fault in California Divorce Law*, 17 UCLA L. REV. 1303 (1970).

26. For example, in 1975 the California legislature provided for legislative findings and declarations relating to displaced homemakers; in 1977, the legislature provided for job services, counseling, health care, and placement for displaced homemakers. See CAL. GOVT. CODE §§ 7300 *et seq.*

27. *In re* Marriage of Dennis, 35 Cal. App. 3d 279, 110 CAL. RPTR. 619 (1973).

28. *In re* Marriage of Brantner, 67 Cal. App. 3d 416, 136 CAL. RPTR. 635 (1977).

29. *Id.* at 420.

30. *Id.* at 419.

31. *Id.* at 420.

8

WILLIAM J. GOODE

Why Men Resist

Although few if any men in the United States remain entirely untouched by the women's movement, to most men what is happening seems to be "out there" and has little direct effect on their own roles. To them, the movement is a dialogue mainly among women, conferences of women about women, a mixture of just or exaggerated complaints and shrill and foolish demands to which men need not even respond, except now and then. When men see that a woman resents a common male act of condescension, such as making fun of women in sports or management, most males are still as surprised as corporation heads are when told to stop polluting a river.

For the time being, men are correct in this perception if one focuses on the short run only. It is not often that social behavior deeply rooted in tradition alters rapidly. Over the longer run, they are not likely to be correct, and indeed I believe they are vaguely uneasy when they consider their present situation. As against numerous popular commentators, I do not think we are now witnessing a return to the old ways, a politically reactionary trend, and I do not think the contemporary attack on male privilege will ultimately fail.

The worldwide demand for equality is voiced not only by women; many groups have pressed for it, with more persistence, strength, and success over the past generation than in any prior epoch of world history. It has also been pressed by more kinds of people than ever before: ethnic and racial groups, castes, subnational groups such as the Scots or Basques, classes, colonies, and political regimes. An ideal so profoundly moving will ultimately prevail, in some measure, where the structural bases for traditional dominance are weakened. The ancient bases for male dominance are no longer as secure as they once were, and male resistance to these pressures will weaken.

Males will stubbornly resist, but reluctantly adjust, because women will continue to want more equality than they now enjoy and will be unhappy if they do not get it; because men on average will prefer that their

131

women be happy; because a majority of either sex will not find an adequate substitute for the other sex; and because neither will be able to build an alternative social system alone. When dominant classes or groups cannot rig the system as much in their favor as they once did, they will work within it just the same; to revise an old adage, if that is the only roulette wheel in town, they will play it even if it is honest and fair.

To many women, the very title of my essay is an exercise in banality, for there is no puzzle. To analyze the peculiar thoughtways of men seems unnecessary, since ultimately their resistance is that of dominant groups throughout history: They enjoy an exploitive position that yields them an unearned profit in money, power, and prestige. Why should they give it up?

The answer contains of course some part of the truth, but we shall move more effectively toward equality only if we grasp much more of the truth that bitter view reveals. If it were completely true, then the greater power of men would have made all societies male-vanity cultures, in which women are kept behind blank walls and forced to work at productive tasks only with their sisters, while men laze away their hours in parasitic pleasure. In fact, one can observe that the position of women varies a good deal by class, by society, and over time, and no one has succeeded in proving that those variations are the simple result of men's exploitation.

Indeed there are inherent socioeconomic contradictions in any attempt by males to create a fully exploitative set of material advantages for all males. Moreover, there are inherent *emotional* contradictions in any effort to achieve full domination in that intimate sphere.

As to the first contradiction, women—and men in the same situation—who are powerless, slavish, and ignorant are most easily exploitable, and thus there are always some male pressures to place them in that position. Unfortunately, such women do not yield much surplus product. In fact, they do not produce much at all. Women who are freer and are more in command of productive skills, as in hunting and gathering societies and increasingly in modern industrial ones, produce far more, but they are also more resistant to exploitation or domination. Without understanding that powerful relationship, men have moved throughout history toward one or the other of these great choices, with their built-in disadvantages and advantages.

As to emotional ties, men would like to be lords of their castle and to be loved absolutely—if successful, this is the cheapest exploitative system—but in real life this is less likely to happen unless one loves in return. In that case what happens is what happens in real life: Men care about the joys and sorrows of their women. Mutual caring reduces the degree to which men are willing to exploit their wives, mothers, and sisters. More interesting, their caring also takes the form of wanting to prevent *other* men from exploiting these women when they are in the outside world. That is, men as individuals know that *they* are to be trusted, and so should have great power, but other men cannot be trusted, and so the laws should restrain such fellows.

These large sets of contrary tensions have some effect on even those contemporary men who do not believe that the present relations between men and women are unjust. Both sets, moreover, support the present trend toward greater equality. In short, men do resist, but these and other tensions prevent them from resisting as fully as they might otherwise, while not so much as a cynical interpretation of their private attitudes would expect. On the other hand, they do resist somewhat more strenuously than we should predict from their public assertion in favor of, for example, equal pay, or slogans like "liberty and justice for all."

This exposition is necessarily limited. Even to present the latest data on the supposed psychological traits of males would require more space than is available here. I shall try to avoid the temptation of simply describing men's reactions to the women's movement, although I do plan to inform you of men's attitudes toward some aspects of equality. I shall try to avoid defending men, except to the extent that explaining them may be a defense. And, as is already obvious, I shall not assert that we are on the brink of a profound, sudden change in sex-role allocations, in the direction of equality, for we must never underestimate the cunning or the staying power of those in charge. Finally, because all of you are also observers of men, it is unlikely that I can bring forward many findings that are entirely unknown to you. At best, I can suggest some fruitful, perhaps new, ways of looking at male roles. Within these limitations, I shall focus on the following themes:

1. As against the rather narrow definition of men's roles to be found in the current literature on the topic, I want to remind you of a much wider range of traditionally approved roles in this and other cultures.
2. As against the conspiracy theory of the oppression of women, I shall suggest a modest "sociology of the dominant group" to interpret men's behavior and thinking about male roles and thus some modest hypotheses about why they resist.
3. I shall point to two central areas of role behavior, occupations and domestic tasks, where change seems glacial at present and men's resistance strong.
4. As against those who feel that if utopia does not arrive with the next full moon, we should all despair, I shall point to some processes now occurring that are different from any in recorded history and that will continue to press toward more fundamental changes in men's social positions and roles in this as well as other countries of the world.

The Range of Sex Roles

Let me begin by reminding you of the standard sociological view about the allocation of sex roles. Although it is agreed that we can, with only small error, divide the population into males and females, the biological differences between the two that might affect the distribution of sex roles— which sex is supposed to do which social tasks, which should have which rights—are much too small to determine the large differences in sex-role allocation within any given society or to explain the curious doctrines that serve to uphold it. Second, even if some differences would give an advantage to men (or women) in some tasks or achievements, the overlap in talent is so great that a large minority of men (or women) could do any task as well as could members of the other sex. Third, the biological differences are too fixed in anatomy and physiology to account for the wide diversity of sex-role allocation we observe when we compare different societies over time and cultures.

Consequently, most of sex-role allocation must be explained by how we rear children, by the sexual division of labor, by the cultural definitions of what is appropriate to the sexes, and by the social pressures we put on the two sexes. Since human beings created these role assignments, they can also change them. On the other hand, these roles afford large advantages to men (e.g., opportunity, range of choices, mobility, payoffs for what is accomplished, cultivation of skills, authority, and prestige) in this and every other society we know. Consequently, men are likely to resist large alterations in roles. They will do so even though they understand that in exchange for their privileges, they have to pay high costs in morbidity, mortality, and failure.[1] As a consequence of this fact about men's position, it can be supposed that they will resist unless their ability to rig the system in their favor is somehow reduced. It is my belief that this capacity is in fact being undermined somewhat, though not at a rapid rate.

A first glance at descriptions of the male role, especially as described in the literature about mass media, social stereotypes, family roles, and personality attributes, suggests that the male role is definite, narrow, and agreed upon. Males, we are told, are pressed into a specific mold. For example, ". . . the male role prescribes that men be active, aggressive, competitive, . . . while the female role prescribes that women should be nurturant, warm, altruistic . . . and the like."[2] The male role requires the suppression of emotion, or "the male role, as personally and socially defined, requires men to appear tough, objective, striving, achieving, unsentimental. . . . If he weeps, if he shows weakness, he will likely be viewed as unmanly. . . ." Or: "Men are programmed to be strong and 'aggressive.'"[3]

We are so accustomed to reading such descriptions that we almost believe them, unless we stop to ask, first, how many men do we actually know who carry out these social presciptions (i.e., how many are emotionally anesthetized, aggressive, physically tough and daring, unwilling or unable to give nurturance to a child)? Second, and this is the test of a social role, do they lose their membership cards in the male fraternity if they fail in these respects? If socialization and social pressures are so all-powerful, where are all the John Wayne types in our society? Or, to ask a more searching question, how seriously should we take such sex-role prescriptions if so few men live up to them?

The key fact is not that many men do not live up to such prescriptions; rather, it is that many other qualities and performances are also viewed as acceptable or admirable, and this is true even among boys, who are often thought to be strong supporters of sex stereotypes. The *macho* boy is admired, but so is the one who edits the school newspaper, who draws cartoons, or who is simply a warm friend. There are at least a handful of ways of being an admired professor. Indeed a common feminist complaint against the present system is that women are much more narrowly confined in the ways they are permitted to be professors, or members of any occupation.

But we can go further. A much more profound observation is that oppressed groups are *typically* given narrow ranges of social roles, while dominant groups afford their members a far wider set of behavior patterns, each qualitatively different but each still accepted or esteemed in varying degrees. One of the privileges granted, or simply assumed, by ruling groups, is that they can indulge in a variety of eccentricities while still demanding and getting a fair measure of authority or prestige. Consider in this connection, to cite only one spectacular example, the crotchets and quirks cultivated by the English upper classes over the centuries.

Moreover, if we enlarge our vision to encompass other times and places, the range becomes even greater. We are not surprised to observe Latin American men embrace one another, Arab or Indian boys walk together hand in hand, or seminary students being gentle. The male role prescriptions that commonly appear in the literature do not describe correctly the male ideal in Jewish culture, which embodied a love of music, learning, and literature; an avoidance of physical violence; an acceptance of tears and sentiment, nurturance, and a sensitivity to others' feelings. In the South that I knew half a century ago, young rural boys were expected to nurture their younger siblings, and male-male relations were ideally expected to be tender, supporting, and expressed occasionally by embraces. Among my own kin, some fathers then kissed their school-age sons; among Greek-Americans in New York City, that practice continues many decades later. Or, to consider England once more, let us remember the admired men of Elizabethan England. True enough, one ideal was the violent, daring Francis Drake and the brawling poet Ben Jonson. But men also expressed themselves in kissing and embracing, writing love poems to one another, donning decorative (not to say gaudy and efflorescent) clothing, and studying flowers as well as the fiery heavens.

We assert, then, that men manage to be in charge of things in all societies but that their very control permits them to create a wide range of ideal male roles, with the consequence that large numbers of men, not just a few, can locate rewarding positions in the social structure. Thereby, too, they considerably narrow the options left for feminine sex roles. Feminists especially resent the narrowness of the feminine role in informal interaction, where they feel they are dealt with only as women, however this may be softened by personal warmth or affection.

We can recognize that general relationship in a widespread male view, echoed over the centuries, that males are people, individuals, while women are lumped together as an aggregate. Or, in more modern language: Women have roles, a delimited number of parts to play, but men cannot be described so simply.

Nor is that peculiar male view contradicted by the complaint, again found in all major civilizations, that women are mysterious, unpredictable, moved by forces outside men's understanding, and not controllable. Even that master of psychodynamics Sigmund Freud expressed his bewilderment by asking, "What do women want?" Men have found their women difficult to understand for a simple reason: They have continued to try to think of them as a set of roles (above all else, mothers and wives), but in fact women do not fit these roles, not only not now, but not in the past either. Some women were great fighting machines, not compliant; some were competitive and aggressive, not nurturant; many were incompetent or reluctant mothers. They have been queens and astronomers, moralists and nurturers, leaders of religious orders as well as corporations, and so on. At any point, men could observe that women were ignoring or breaking out of their social molds, and men experienced that discrepancy as puzzling. However, it is only recently that many have faced the blunt fact that there is no feminine riddle at all: Women are as complex as men are, and always will escape the confinements of any narrow set of roles.

The Sociology of Superordinates

That set of relationships is only part of the complex male view, and I want to continue with my sketch of the main elements in what may be called the "sociology of superordinates." That is, I believe there are some general principles or regularities to be found in the view held by superordinates—here, the sex-class called males—about relations with subordinates, in this instance women. These regularities do not justify, but they do explain in some degree, the modern resistance of men to their new social situation.[4] Here are some of them:

1. The observations made by either men or women about members of the other sex are limited and somewhat biased by what they are most interested in and by their lack of opportunity to observe behind the scenes of each others' lives.[5] However, far less of what men do is determined by women; what men do affects women much more. As a consequence, men are often simply less motivated to observe carefully many aspects of women's behavior and activity because women's behavior does not usually affect what men propose to do. By contrast, almost everything men do will affect what women *have* to do, and thus women are motivated to observe men's behavior as keenly as they can.

2. Since any given cohort of men know they did not create the system that gives them their advantages, they reject any charges that they conspired to dominate women.

3. Since men, like other dominants or superordinates, take for granted the system that gives them their status, they are not aware of how much the social structure, from attitude patterns to laws, pervasively yields small, cumulative, and eventually large advantages in most competitions. As a consequence, they assume that their greater accomplishments are actually the result of inborn superiority.

4. As a corollary to this male view, when men weigh their situation, they are more aware of the burdens and responsibilities they bear than of their unearned advantages.

5. Superiors, and thus men, do not easily notice the talents or accomplishments of subordinates, and men have not in the past seen much wisdom in giving women more opportunities for growth, for women are not capable of much anyway, especially in the areas of men's special skills. Thus, in the past, few women have embarrassed men by becoming superior in those areas. When they did, their superiority was seen, and is often still seen, as an odd exception. As a consequence, men see their superior position as a just one.

6. Men view even small losses of deference, advantages, or opportunities as large threats. Their own gains, or their maintenance of old advantages, are not noticed as much.[6]

Although the male view is similar to that of superordinates generally, as the foregoing principles suggest, one cannot simply equate the two. The structural position of males is different from that of superordinate groups, classes, ethnic populations, or castes. Males are, first, not a group, but a social segment or a statistical aggregate within the society. They share much of a common destiny, but they share few if any *group* or *collective* goals (within small groups they may be buddies, but not with all males). Second, males share with certain women whatever gain or loss they experience as members of high or low castes, ethnic groups, or classes. For example, women in a ruling stratum share with their men a high social rank, deference from the lower orders, and so on; men in a lowly Indian caste share that rank with their women, too. In modern societies, men and women in the same family are on a more or less equal basis with respect to "inheritance, educational opportunity (at least under-graduate), personal consumption of goods, most rights before the law, and the love and responsibility of their children." [7] They are not fully equal, to be sure, but much more equal than are members of very different castes or social classes.

Moreover, from the male view, women also enjoy certain exemptions: "freedom from military conscription, whole or partial exemption from certain kinds of heavy work, preferential courtesies of various kinds." Indeed, men believe, on the whole, that their own lot is the more difficult one. [8]

Most important as a structural fact that prevents the male view from being simply that of a superordinate is that these superordinates, like their women, do not live in set-apart communities, neighborhoods, or families. Of course, other such categories are not seqestered either, such as al-coholics, ex-mental patients, or the physically handicapped; but these are, as Goffman points out, "scattered somewhat haphazardly through the social structure." That is not so for men; like their women, they are allocated to households in a nonrandom way, for "law and custom allow only one to a household, but strongly encourage the presence of that one." [9]

A consequence of this important structural arrangement is that men and women are separated from their own sex by having a stake in the organization that gives each a set of different roles, or a different emphasis to similar roles; women especially come to have a vested interest in the social unit that at the same time imposes inequalities on them. This coali-tion between the two individuals makes it difficult for members of the same sex to join with large numbers of persons of their own sex for purposes of defense or exploitation. This applies equally to men and women.

One neat consequence may be seen in the hundreds of family law provisions created over the centuries that seem to run at cross-purposes. Some gave more freedom to women in order to protect them from preda-tory or exploitative males (i.e., in the male view, *other* men), and some took freedom away from women and put it in the hands of supposedly good and kindly men (i.e., heads of families, *themselves*). Or, in more recent times, the growing efforts of some fathers to press their daughters toward career competence so that they will not be helpless when abandoned by their future husbands, against those same fathers' efforts to keep their daughters docile and dutiful toward their protecting fathers.

You will note that male *views* are not contradictory in such instances, even though their *actions* may be. In coalition with their women, they oppose the exploitative efforts of outside men; within the family unit, however, they see little need for such protections against themselves, for they are sure of their own goodheartedness and wisdom.

That men see themselves as bound in a coalition with their families and thus with their daughters and wives is the cause of much common male resistance to the women's movement, while some have instead become angered at the unfair treatment their wives and daughters have experienced. The failure of many women to understand that complex male view has led to much misunderstanding.

Responses of Superordinates to Rebellion [10]

First, men are surprised at the outbreak. They simply had not known the depth of resentment that many women harbored, though of course many women had not known it either. Second, men are also hurt, for they feel betrayed. They discover, or begin to suspect, that the previously contented or pleasant facade their women presented to them was false, that they have been manipulated to believe in that presentation of self. Because males view themselves as giving protection against anyone exploiting or hurting their women, they respond with anger to the hostility they encounter, to the discovery that they were deceived, and to the charge that they have selfishly used the dominant position they feel they have rightfully earned.

A deeper, more complex source of male anger requires a few additional comments, for it relates to a central male role, that of jobholder and breadwinner. Most men, but especially most men outside the privileged stratum of professionals and managers, see their job as not yielding much intrinsic satisfaction, not being fun in itself, but they pride themselves on the hard work and personal sacrifice they make as breadwinners. In the male view, men make a gift of all this to their wives and children. [11]

Now they are told that it was not a gift, and they have not earned any special deference for it. In fact, their wives earned what they received, and indeed nothing is owing. If work was a sacrifice, they are told, so were all the services, comforts, and self-deprivations women provided. Whatever the justice of either claim, clearly if you think you are giving or sacrificing much to make gifts to someone over a period of time, and then you learn he or she feels the gifts were completely deserved, for the countergifts are asserted to have been as great and no gratitude or special debt was incurred, you are likely to be hurt or angry.[12]

I am reasonably certain about the processes I have just described. Let me go a step further and speculate that the male resentment is the greater because many fathers had already come to suspect that their children, especially in adolescence, were indifferent to those sacrifices, as well as to the values that justified them.[13] Thus, when women too begin to assert that men's gifts are not worth as much as men thought, the worth of the male is further denied.

Some Areas of Change and Nonchange

Although I have not heard specific complaints about it, I believe that the most important change in men's position, as they experience it, is a loss of centrality, a decline in the extent to which they are the center of attention. In our time, other superordinates have also suffered this loss: colonial rulers, monarchs and nobles, and U.S. whites both northern and southern, to name a few.

Boys and grown men have always taken for granted that what they were doing was more important than what the other sex was doing, that where they were, was where the action was. Their women accepted that definition. Men occupied the center of the stage, and women's attention was focused on them. Although that position is at times perilous, open to failure, it is also desirable.

Men are still there of course, and will be there throughout our lifetime. Nevertheless, some changes are perceptible. The center of attention shifts to women more now than in the past. I believe that this shift troubles men far more, and creates more of their resistance, than the women's demand for equal opportunity and pay in employment.

The change is especially observable in informal relations, and men who are involved with women in the liberation movement experience it most often. Women find each other more interesting than in the past, and focus more on what each other is doing, for they are in fact doing more interesting things. Even when they are not, their work occupies more of their attention, whether they are professionals or factory workers. Being without a man for a while does not seem to be so bereft a state as it once was. I also believe that this change affects men more now than at the time of the suffragist movement half a century ago, not only because more women now participate in it but also because men were then more solidary and could rely on more all-male organizations and clubs; now, they are more dependent on women for solace and intimacy.

As a side issue, let me note that the loss of centrality has its counterpart among feminist women too, and its subtlety should be noted. Such women now reject a certain type of traditional centrality they used to experience, because its costs are too great. Most women know the experience of being the center of attention: When they enter a male group, conversation changes in tone and subject. They are likely to be the focus of comments, many of them pleasurable: affectionate teasing, compliments, warmth. However, these comments put women into a special mold, the stereotyped female. Their serious comments are not welcomed or applauded, or their ideas are treated as merely amusing. Their sexuality is emphasized. Now, feminist women find that kind of centrality less pleasant—in fact, condescending—and they avoid it when they can. In turn, many men feel awkward in this new situation, for their repertory of social graces is now called boorish.

Although I have noted men's feelings of hurt and anger, I want to emphasize that I believe no backlash of any consequence has been occurring, and no trend toward more reactionary male attitudes exists. Briefly, there is a continuing attitude change on the part of both men and women, in favor of more equality. The frequent expressions of male objection, sometimes labeled "backlash" in the popular press, can be attributed to two main sources: (1) The discovery, by some men who formerly did pay lip service to the principle of equality, that they do not approve of its concrete application; and (2) active resistance by men and women who simply never approved of equality anyway and who have now begun to oppose it openly because it can no longer be seen as a trivial threat. Most of this is incorrectly labeled "backlash," which ought instead to refer only to the case in which people begin to feel negative toward a policy they once thought desirable, because now it has led to undesirable results. Those who oppose women's rights like to label any support they get as backlash because thereby they can claim that "women have gone too far."

It may surprise you to learn that it is not possible to summarize here all the various changes in public opinion about sex roles, as attitudes have shifted over the past generation, simply because pollsters did not bother to record the data. They often did not try to find out about social trends and thus only rarely asked the same questions in successive decades. One unfortunate result is that one of the most fiercely debated events of this period, the women's liberation movement, almost does not appear in the polls.[14]

The single finding that seems solid is that no data show any backward or regressive trend in men's attitudes about women's progress toward equality. The most often repeated question is not a profound one: whether a respondent would vote for a qualified woman for President. Favorable answers rose from about one-fourth of the men in 1937 to two-thirds in 1971, and to four-fifths among men and women combined in 1975. Another repeated question is whether a married women should work if she has a husband able to support her, and here the answers of men and women combined rose from 18 percent in 1936 to 62 percent in 1975. In contrast to these large changes, a large majority favored equal pay, in principle at least, as early as 1942, and later data report no decrease.

In 1953, 21 percent of men said it made no difference whether they worked for a man or woman, and that figure rose slightly to 32 percent in 1975.[15] Polls in 1978 show that a large majority of the nation, both men and women, was in favor of the enforcement of laws forbidding job discrimination against women or discrimination in education; and most agreed that more women should be elected to public office.[16]

A plurality of only about 40 percent held such favorable opinions in 1970. On such issues, men and women do not differ by much, although, until recently, men's attitudes were somewhat more favorable. Divisions of opinion are sharper along other lines: The young are in favor more than the old, the more educated more favorable than the less educated, city dwellers more than rural people, blacks more than whites. Whatever the differences, clearly no substantial amount of male backlash has appeared. Through men's eyes, at least the *principle* of equality seems more acceptable than in the past. Their resistance is not set against that abstract idea. Modest progress, to be sure, but progress nonetheless.

I cannot forego making reference to a subvariety of the backlash, which has been reported in hundreds of articles, that is, that more men are impotent because of women's increased sexual assertiveness. This impotence, we are told, appears when women discover the delights of their own sexuality, make it clear to their men that they will play coy no more, and indeed look at their men as sexual objects, at least sometimes.

The widespread appearance of male impotence as an answer to, or an escape from, increased female willingness would certainly be news,[17] but it violates the sexual view of most men, and, much worse, it runs counter to the only large-scale data we have on the topic.[18] The male view may be deduced, if you will permit the literary reference, from traditional pornography, which was written by men and expressed male fantasies. Briefly, in such stories, but entirely contrary to real life, everything went smoothly: At every phase of the interaction, where women in real male experience are usually indifferent if not hostile, the hero encounters enthusiasm, and in response he himself performs miracles of sexual athleticism and ecstasy.

Nothing so embroidered is found in social science data, but it seems reasonably certain that in the five-year period ending in 1970, the married men of the United States increased the frequency of their lovemaking with their wives. Doubtless, there were pockets of increased impotence, but with equal security we can assert that most husbands did not have that experience.

The reason is clear, I think: The message of permission had finally been received by women, and they put it into action. In millions of how-to-do-it books and articles, they were not only told to enjoy themselves but were urged to do so by seducing their men. Since the most important sex organ is the human mind, these changes in the heads of both men and women caused changes in the body. Without question, the simplest and most effective antidote to male impotence, or even lassitude and nonperformance, is female encouragement and welcome. Even if a few cases of the backlash of impotence have occurred, that has not, I think, been a widespread trend among males in our time, as a psychological response to women's move toward some equality in sexuality itself. To this particular change among women, men have offered little resistance.

Domestic Duties and Jobs

So far, the opinion data give some small cause for optimism. Nevertheless, all announcements of the imminent arrival of utopias are premature. Men's approval of more equality for women has risen, but the record in two major areas of men's roles—the spheres of home and occupation— gives but little reason for optimism. Here we can be brief, for though the voluminous data are very complex, the main conclusions can easily be summarized.[19] The striking fact is that very little has changed, if we consider the society as a whole and focus on changes in behavior.

Let us consider the domestic role of men. They have contributed only slightly more time to their duties in the home than in the past—although "the past" is very short for time budgets of men's child-care and homemaking activities. By contrast, the best record now indicates that homemakers without jobs spend somewhat less time at their domestic tasks then they did ten years ago. Working wives allocate much less time (26–35 hours a week) to the home than do stay-at-home wives (35–55 hours), but *husbands* of working wives do almost as little as husbands of stay-at-home wives (about 10–13 hours weekly). We hear much these days about Russian husbands who expect their wives to hold jobs and also take care of housework and child care, but so do American husbands. Moreover, that is as true of the supposedly egalitarian Swedish or Finnish husbands as it is of the German and French ones.[20]

Of course, there are some differences. If a child two years or younger is in the house, the father does more. Better-educated husbands do a bit more, and so do younger husbands. But the massive fact is that men's domestic contribution does not change much whether or not they work, and whether or not their wives work.[21] Still more striking is the fact that the past decade has shown little change in the percentage of women who want their husbands to take a larger share of domestic work, though once again it is the vanguard of the young, the educated, and the black who exhibit the largest increase. Studies have reported that only about 20 to 25 percent of wives express the wish for more domestic participation by their husbands, and that did not change greatly until the late 1970s.[22]

With reference to the second large area of men's roles, job holding, we observe two further general principles of the relations between superordinates and those at lesser ranks. One is that men do not, in general, feel threatened by competition from women if they believe the competition is fair and women do not have an inside track. Men still feel that they are superior and will do better if given the chance. Without actually trying the radical notion of genuinely fair competition, they have little reason to fear as yet: Compared with women, they were better off in wages and occupational position in the 1970s than in the 1950s.

The second principle is that those who hold advantaged positions in the social structure (men, in this case) can perceive or observe that they are being flooded by people they consider their inferiors—by women, blacks, or the lower classes—while the massive statistical fact is that only a few people are rising by much. There are several causes of this seeming paradox.

First, the new arrivals are so visible, so different from those who have held the jobs up to this time. The second cause is our perception of relative numbers. Since there are far fewer positions at higher job levels, only a few new arrivals constitute a fair-sized minority of the total at that level. Third, the mass media emphasize the hiring of women in jobs that seem not to be traditional for them, for that is considered news. Men's structural position, then, causes them to perceive radical change here, and they resist it.

Nevertheless, the general conclusion does not change much. The amount of sex segregation in jobs is not much different from the past.[23] More important, there is no decrease in the gap between the earnings of men and women; at every job level, it is not very different from the past, and in the period from 1955 to 1971 the gap actually became somewhat larger. That is, a higher percentage of women entered the labor force, and at better wages than in the past, but men rose somewhat faster than they.

Although the mass figures are correct, we need not discount all our daily observation. We see women entering formerly masculine jobs from garbage collecting to corporate management. That helps undermine sex stereotypes and thereby becomes a force against inequality. For example, women bus drivers were hardly to be found in 1940, but they now make up 37 percent of that occupation; women bartenders now form 32 percent of that occupation, but a generation ago made up only 2.5 percent.[24] Although occupational segregation continued strong in the 1970s, it did decline in most professions (e.g., engineering, dentistry, science, law, medicine) between 1960 and 1970. That is, the percentage of women in these professions did rise.[25] Women now constitute over one-fourth of the law school classes in the higher-ranking law schools of the country. In occupations where almost everyone was once male, it is not possible to recruit, train, and hire enough women to achieve equality in a few years, but the trend seems clear.

A secondary effect of these increasing numbers should be noted. Percentages are important, but so are absolute numbers. If women lawyers increase from about seven thousand to forty thousand, they become a much larger social force, even though they may be only about 10 percent of the total occupation. When women medical students, while remaining a small percentage of their classes, increase in number so that they can form committees, petition administrators, or give solidarity to one another against the traditional masculine badgering and disesteem, they greatly increase their impact on discriminatory attitudes and behavior. That is, as their rise in numbers permits the formation of real groups, their power mounts faster than the numbers or even (except at the start) the percentages. Thus, changes occur even when the percentage of the occupation made up of women is not large.

Bases of Present Changes

Most large-scale, objective measures of men's roles show little change over the past decade, but men do feel now and then that their position is in question, their security is somewhat fragile. I believe they are right, for they sense a set of forces that lie deeper and are more powerful than the day-to-day negotiation and renegotiation of advantage among husbands and wives, fathers and children, or bosses and those who work for them. Men are troubled by this new situation.

The conditions we live in are different from those of any prior civilization, and they give less support to men's claims of superiority than perhaps any other historical era. When these conditions weaken that support, men can rely only on previous tradition, or their attempts to socialize their children, to shore up their faltering advantages. Such rhetoric is not likely to be successful against the new objective conditions and the claims of aggrieved women. Thus, men are correct when they feel they are losing some of their privileges, even if many continue to laugh at the women's liberation movement.

The new conditions can be listed concretely, but I shall also give you a theoretical formulation of the process. Concretely, because of the increased use of various mechanical gadgets and devices, fewer tasks require much strength. As to those that still require strength, most men cannot do them either. Women can now do more household tasks that men once felt only they could do, and still more tasks are done by repair specialists called in to do them. With the development of modern warfare, there are few if any important combat activities that only men can do. Women are much better educated than before.

With each passing year, psychological and sociological research reduces the areas in which men are reported to excel over women and discloses far more overlap in talents, so that even when males still seem to have an advantage, it is but a slight one. It is also becoming more widely understood that the top posts in government and business are not best filled by the stereotypical aggressive male but by people, male or female, who are sensitive to others' needs, adept at obtaining cooperation, and skilled in social relations. Finally, in one sphere after another, the number of women who try to achieve rises, and so does the number who succeed.

Although the pressure of new laws has its direct effect on these conditions, the laws themselves arise from an awareness of the foregoing forces. Phrased in more theoretical terms, the underlying shift is toward the decreasing marginal utility of males, and this I suspect is the main source of men's resistance to women's liberation. That is, fewer people believe that what the male does is indispensable, nonsubstitutable, or adds such a special value to any endeavor that it justifies his extra "price" or reward. In past wars, for example, males enjoyed a very high value not only because it was felt that they could do the job better than women but also because they might well make the difference between being conquered and remaining free. In many societies, their marginal utility came from their contribution of animal protein through hunting. As revolutionary heroes, explorers, hunters, warriors, and daring capitalist entrepreneurs, men felt, and doubtless their women did too, that their contribution was beyond anything women could do. This earned men extra privileges of rank, authority, and creature services.

It is not then as individuals, as persons, that males will be deemed less worthy in the future or their contributions less needed. Rather, they will be seen as having no claim to *extra* rewards solely because they are members of the male sex-class. This is part of a still broader trend of our generation, which will also increasingly deny that being white, or an upper-caste or upper-class person, produces a marginally superior result and thus justifies extra privileges.

The relations of individuals are subject to continuous renegotiation as people try to gain or keep advantages or cast off burdens. They fail or succeed in part because one or the other person has special resources or lacks that are unique to those individuals. Over the long run, however, the outcome of these negotiations depends on the deeper social forces we have been describing, which ultimately determine which qualities or performances are more or less valued.

Now, men perceive that they may be losing some of their advantages and that more aspects of their social roles are subject to public challenge and renegotiation than in the past. They resist these changes, and we can suppose they will continue to do so. In all such changes, there are gains and losses. Commonly, when people at lower social ranks gain freedom, those at higher ranks lose some power or centrality. When those at the lower ranks also lose some protection, some support, those at the higher ranks lose some of the burden of responsibility. It is also true that the care or help given by any dominant group in the past was never as much as members believed, and their loss in political power or economic rule was never as great as they feared.

On the other hand, I know of no instance when a group or social stratum gained its freedom or moved toward more respect and then had its members decide that they did not want it. Therefore, although men will not joyfully give up their rank, in spite of its burdens, neither will women decide that they would like to get back the older feminine privileges, accompanied with the lack of respect and material rewards that went with those courtesies.

I believe that men perceive their roles as being under threat in a world that is different from any in the past. No society has yet come even close to equality between the sexes, but the modern social forces described here did not exist before either. At the most cautious, we must concede that the conditions favoring a trend toward more equality are more favorable than at any prior time in history. If we have little reason to conclude that equality is at hand, let us at least rejoice that we are marching in the right direction.

Notes

1. Herbert Goldberg, *The Hazards of Being Male* (New York: Nash, 1976); and Patricia C. Sexton, *The Feminized Male: Classrooms, White Collars, and the Decline of Manliness* (New York: Random House, 1969).On the recognition of disadvantages, see J. S. Chafetz, *Masculine/Feminine or Human?* (Itasca, Ill.: Peacock, 1974), pp. 56 ff.

2. Joseph H. Pleck, "The Psychology of Sex Roles: Traditional and New Views," in *Women and Men: Changing Roles, Relationship and Perceptions*, ed. Libby A. Cater and Anne F. Scott (New York: Aspen Institute for Humanistic Studies, 1976), p. 182. Pleck has carried out the most extensive research on male roles, and I am indebted to him for special help in this inquiry.

3. For these two quotations, see Sidney M. Jourard, "Some Lethal Aspects of the Male Role," p. 22, and Irving London, "Frigidity, Sensitivity and Sexual Roles," p. 42, in *Men and Masculinity*, ed. Joseph H. Pleck and Jack Sawyer (Englewood Cliffs, N.J.: Prentice-Hall, 1974). See also the summary of such traits in I. K. Braverman et al., "Sex-Role Stereotypes: A Current Appraisal," in *Women and Achievement*, ed. Martha T. S. Mednick, S. S.. Tangri, and Lois W. Hoffman (New York: Wiley, 1975), pp. 32–47.

4. Robert Bierstedt's "The Sociology of the Majority," in his *Power and Progress* (New York: McGraw-Hill, 1974), pp. 199–220, does not state these principles, but I was led to them by thinking about his analysis.

5. Robert K. Merton, in "The Perspectives of Insiders and Outsiders," in his *The Sociology of Science* (Chicago: University of Chicago Press, 1973), pp. 99–136, has analyzed this view in some detail.

6. This general pattern is noted at various points in my monograph *The Celebration of Heroes: Prestige as a Social Control System* (Berkeley: University of California Press, 1979).

7. Erving Goffman, "The Arrangement Between the Sexes," *Theory and Society* 4 (1977): 307.

8. Hazel Erskine, "The Polls: Women's Roles," *Public Opinion Quarterly* 35 (Summer 1971).

9. Goffman, "Arrangement Between the Sexes," p. 308.

10. A simple analysis of these responses is presented in William J. Goode, *Principles of Sociology* (New York: McGraw-Hill, 1977), pp. 359 ff.

11. See Joseph H. Pleck, "The Power of Men," in *Women and Men: The Consequences of Power*, ed. Dana V. Hiller and R. Sheets (Cincinnati: Office of Women's Studies, University of Cincinnati, 1977), p. 20. See also Colin Bell and Howard Newby, "Husbands and Wives: The Dynamic of the Deferential Dialectic," in *Dependence and Exploitation in Work and Marriage*, ed. Diana L. Barker and Sheila Allen (London: Longman, 1976), pp. 162–63; as well as Richard Sennett and Jonathan Cobb, *The Hidden Injuries of Class* (New York: Vintage, 1973), p. 125. On the satisfactions of work, see Daniel Yankelovich, "The Meaning of Work," in

The Worker and the Job, ed. Jerome Rosow (Englewood Cliffs, N.J.: Prentice-Hall, 1974), pp. 19–49.

12. Whatever other sacrifices women want from men, until recently a large majority did *not* believe men should do more housework. On this matter, see Joseph H. Pleck, "Men's New Roles in the Family: Housework and Child Care," to appear in *Family and Sex Roles,* ed. Constantina Safilios-Rothschild, forthcoming. In the mid-1970s, only about one-fourth to one-fifth of wives agreed to such a proposal.

13. Sennett and Cobb, *The Hidden Injuries of Class,* p. 125.

14. To date, the most complete published summary is that by Erskine, "The Polls: Women's Roles," pp. 275–91.

15. Stephanie Greene, "Attitudes Toward Working Women Have 'A Long Way to Go,' " *Gallup Opinion Poll,* March 1976, p. 33.

16. *Harris Survey,* 16 February 1978; see also *Harris Survey,* 11 December 1975.

17. It is, however, in harmony with one view expressed by many women (as well as men), that men in the past were a bit necrophiliac (i.e., they preferred to hop on unresponsive women, take their quick crude pleasure, and hop off). It does not accord much with what we know of people generally (they gain more pleasure when their partner does) or even of bawds and lechers (they brag about the delirium they arouse in the women they seduce).

18. See Charles F. Westoff, "Coital Frequency and Contraception," *Family Planning Perspectives* 6 (Summer 1974): 136–41.

19. The most extensive time budget data on a cross-national basis are found in A. Szalai, ed., *The Use of Time* (The Hague: Mouton, 1972). The most useful summary of the data on the above points is in Joseph H. Pleck, "The Work-Family Role System," *Social Problems* 24 (1977): 417–27. See also his "Developmental Stages in Men's Lives: How Do They Differ From Women's?" (National Guidance Association, Hartland, Michigan, 1977), mimeo.

20. Elina Haavio-Mannila, "Convergences Between East and West: Tradition and Modernity in Sex Roles in Sweden, Finland, and the Soviet Union," in Midnick et al., *Women and Achievement,* pp. 71–84. Further data will appear in J. Robinson, *How Americans Use Time,* forthcoming.

21. Pleck, "Men's New Roles in the Family." For details on men's contribution to child care, see Philip J. Stone, "Child Care in Twelve Countries," in Szalai, *The Use of Time.*

22. These data are to be found in Pleck, "Men's New Roles in the Family." However, 1977 data show that in Detroit this figure has risen to over 60 percent: Arland Thornton and Deborah S. Freedman, "Changes in the Sex Role Attitudes of Women 1962–1977," *American Sociological Review* 44 (October 1979): 833.

23. The expansion of women's jobs has occurred primarily in "female" jobs or through new occupations defined as female or (less frequently) by women taking over formerly male jobs. See Council of Economic Advisers, *Economic Report of the President,* 1973, p. 155; and Barbara R. Bergman and Irma Adelman, "The 1973 Report of the President's Council of Economic Advisors: The Economic Role of Women," *American Economic Review,* September 1973, pp. 510–11. In 1960, about

24 percent of the labor force was made up of women in occupations where women are predominant; in 1970, the figure was 27 percent according to Myra H. Strober, "Women and Men in the World of Work: Present and Future," in Cater et al., *Women and Men: Changing Roles, Relationships, and Perceptions*, pp. 128–33.

24. Jean Lipman-Blumen, "Implications for Family Structure of Changing Sex Roles," *Social Casework* 57 (February 1976): pp. 67–79.

25. Victor R. Fuchs, "A Note on Sex Segregation in Professional Occupations," *Explorations in Economic Research* 2, no. 1 (Winter 1975): 105–11.

9

CLAIR (VICKERY) BROWN

Home Production
for Use in a Market Economy

self pity's
→ standing up

"How would I describe myself? It'll sound terrible–just a housewife. (LAUGHS.) It's true. What is a housewife? You don't have to have any special talents. I don't have any.

"Oh–I even painted the house last year. How much does a painter get paid for painting a house? (LAUGHS.) What? I'm a skilled craftsman myself? I never thought about that. Artist? No. (LAUGHS.) I suppose if you do bake a good cake, you can be called an artist. But I never heard anybody say that. I bake bread too. Oh gosh, I've been a housewife for a long time. (LAUGHS.)

"I never thought about what we'd be worth. I've read these things in the paper: If you were a tailor or a cook, you'd get so much an hour. I think that's a lot of baloney.

"What am I doing? Cooking and cleaning. (LAUGHS.) It's necessary, but it's not really great."

Theresa Carter,
from Stud Terkel's WORKING

Housework is taken for granted in our postindustrial economy, although the work done within the privacy of the home comprises the number-one full-time occupation and virtually all adults engage in it to some degree. Why have we largely ignored an essential work activity that is a major determinant of our well-being? Precisely because it is so essential and because, until recently, it has changed little.

Housework, or the work performed within the home economy, consists of child rearing and the provision of food, clothing, and shelter. This

Barrie Thorne, David Matza, Lois Greenwood, Lenore Weitzman, Todd Easton, Myra Strober, Harold Wilensky, and Joanne Kliejunas provided helpful comments and discussions on a previous draft.

151

work satisfies basic human needs, and the functioning of the home economy must be taken for granted in order to ensure reproduction and to free part of the adult population for work activities outside the home. Even the threat of a disruption of basic housework services affects the smooth functioning of the society and the market economy. No wonder, then, that the recent rapid changes we have been witnessing in our family structure have precipitated the declaration of social crisis along with political resistance to change. The future of the family, which serves as a catchword for the future of women's role within the society, has gained high priority on the agenda of national social problems.

This essay analyzes the structural characteristics of home production and then uses the analysis to discuss how the home economy is related to the growing market economy. A source of conflict between these two economies stems from the fact that the production processes in the home economy are time-intensive and fulfill basic human needs, yet the work done in the home has declined in relative (although not absolute) importance as a determinant of the family's material standard of living because the goods and services purchased in the marketplace have become more important in defining the family's consumption position.

This analysis delineates the interactions between the home and market economies by two stages. During the first stage, many of the production processes of the home economy were taken over by the market economy. During the second stage, which has been underway for at least half a century, the market economy provided new goods and services never produced by the home economy. If the family wanted to consume these goods and services, they had to enter the marketplace both as workers (to earn money) and as consumers (to purchase the goods).

After discussing these historical trends, this essay documents how the shift toward fewer people per household has increased the resources needed per person to meet the basic needs of shelter, transportation, and housework. In addition, more fluid marital patterns have undermined the role of the family in providing income security for wives and have increased wives' need for an independent, dependable source of income other than their husband's income.

The essay then discusses the problems inherent in switching one's work effort between the home and market economies because of the different work and value structures of the two economies. These differences post barriers to rapidly and smoothly changing the current division of labor by sex between the two economies.

Housework: The Provision of Essential Services

As feminist social historians have noted, the stability of the family has long been a social concern, and keeping women's primary work role within the home has been the major focus of this concern.[1] The threatened disruption of the family, and along with it a breakdown in the functioning of the home economy, is distinguished in the current crisis by the rise in the importance of paid work for wives and mothers outside the home. In order to discuss the economic importance of ongoing change in the family, we need to understand the basic characteristics of housework and how the home economy has been affected by economic growth.

The home economy produces a "good home life," primarily through providing the four basic housework services (child rearing and the provision of food, clothing, and shelter) along with satisfying personal relationships. Even the adult without children must take care of her (his) food, clothing, and shelter needs. Because some housework is a necessity, it must be readily obtainable under normal circumstances; otherwise, it could not have become a necessity.

"Necessity" is a nebulous concept because it is defined precisely only through death, and the point of death comes at different levels of deprivation for different individuals. This approach to absolute necessity became economically obsolete before it was ever adequately defined. Since an economically mature country can afford the broader test of relative deprivation, the concept of necessity expanded beyond those items necessary for the support of life to include items that are necessary to be integrated into the society. This broader concept of necessity is even more muddled, however, as the determination of "socially necessary" becomes a political football.

Housework has components that fit into both concepts of necessity—some housework is needed to support and reproduce life at a subsistence level, and other housework is needed to reproduce child and adult behavior that is socially acceptable. Housework activities above these two levels can be viewed as producing value above necessity (e.g., leisure for the housewife or nonnecessity work that enhances the family's life). An outsider's division of these categories of housework most likely would differ from the housewife's categorization of her own work, but the categorization provides a division of housework into the two groups of necessity and above-necessity activities.

When the wife has primary responsibility for the home, she can engage in paid labor only after making sure the necessity housework activities are done. Then she can compare the value to the family of the above-necessity housework with the value of the goods and services she can buy with her paycheck. Part of the analysis by economists of women's work decisions has been misdirected because the necessity component of housework has either been ignored (or judged to be significantly small) or has been assumed to be available for purchase in the marketplace.

The family's valuation of the fruits of the wife's work does not occur in a vacuum. For example, the family's comparison of the mother's supervision of children after school with a large entertainment budget depends to a large extent on what other families in the neighborhood are doing. And although the primary determinant of the amount of necessity housework is the family composition, especially the number and ages of the children, this too is affected by social custom.

The housewife performs a broad range of daily services at times that are dictated by human needs—for example, satisfying the need for food must be done at specified times and responding to a baby's needs must occur as the need arises. Other activities may be performed at times chosen by the homemaker—for example, housecleaning and shopping. Most importantly, a full-time homemaker is on call twenty-four hours a day, and she provides her family with flexibility in using her services, especially in providing personalized care and attention.

These timing problems characterize both necessity and above-necessity chores and constrain the homemaker's ability to decide how to allocate her time among different work activities. In addition, market work must be done in blocks of time at specified hours. But these scheduling rigidities are only part of the limitations faced by the wife in her "choice" of work activities. Most importantly, she faces the situation that most services provided within the home cannot be substituted with goods and services bought in the marketplace. This point has not been obvious to economists and needs elaboration.

What's Wrong with Economic Analyses of the Home Economy

In most economic models, the household is viewed as producing consumption by combining time with market goods and services (e.g., meals are produced with the time spent shopping for and preparing store-bought items). The family is viewed as facing a large array of possibilities of how to use its time and money to produce a given set of consumption bundles. More specifically, the wife is viewed as having a great deal of flexibility in deciding how to combine her time with market goods in producing her "output," such as meal preparation, a clean house, and neat clothing. However, very little substitution between the homemaker's time and market goods has actually been observed in the homemaking process. There is evidence that both employed and full-time homemakers use the same techniques in running their homes, with the employed wife using few market goods and services to substitute for her own input of time.[2] The main substitution tends to be between the wife's market work and her leisure time. Lack of substitution of time and market goods in housework means that the way a family lives—its material standard of living versus its personalized care—is dramatically affected by whether the wife works full-time at home or whether she also works for pay outside the home.

The lack of substitution between housework and purchased goods and services reflects the more basic lack of comparability between services provided by the homemaker and the goods and services purchased in the marketplace. The home economy specializes in producing mothering and the nurturing of family members along with personalized care in providing food, clothing, and shelter. The marketplace produces sophisticated medical care, advanced education, the means for transportation and communication, urban housing, and the ability to pool risk through insurance, as well as mass-produced food, clothing, cars, and other consumer durables. The family's evaluation of these dissimilar home-produced and market-produced goods and services will be a major determinant of whether the wife works exclusively at home or also has a job. The family's evaluation will vary with its circumstances and experiences over time.

The wife's work decision about having a paid job should be viewed as a decision by her and her husband (although not necessarily without conflict) about the family's needs or desire for her mothering and nurturing services weighed against its needs or desire for the market goods and services that can be purchased with her paycheck. Although the cost to the family of the wife's housework is her foregone earnings in the labor market, her market wage will not accurately reflect the marginal cost of her time because of the constraints she faces in scheduling her activities at home and at a job. In addition, the full-time homemaker's provision of round-the-clock care of family members' needs makes it impossible to equate the value of her time with her replacement cost (i.e., the wage rate such services would command in the marketplace). The personalized and on-call nature of her work prevents us from evaluating the services of the housewife as a combination of so many hours of chauffeur, cook, babysitter, and laundress per day. In the real world, the household could not contract to buy these services in the small amounts of time and at the random hours that the housewife actually performs these duties. Even in those instances where the contracting of some services occurs, the service is more impersonalized and must be directed by someone (usually the housewife). The purchased services usually do not reflect the kind of service the housewife provides because she intimately knows the family members she is serving and takes responsiblilty for organizing and providing the care as it is needed.

The "new home economics," the name adopted by the neoclassical school for their work on the family,[3] has done little to increase our understanding of the home economy because its positivist methodological approach only provides a logical, rationalistic framework for a *post hoc* measurement of family behavioral response to economic variables. Because a family is assumed to make the best of its given economic situation, its observed behavior is optimal by assumption, and the differences between households that appear to be economically identical are theoretically "explained" by unidentified preference structures. Problems of conflict among family members are admitted but ignored.

Even more seriously, the question of what options are available to the family is not addressed, since one of the tenets of neoclassical theory is that the marketplace responds to people's needs and desires rather than that people's needs and desires are formed by the marketplace. Choice, in an economic sense, is assumed to exist on the basis that if people are willing to pay the market value (i.e., the opportunity costs or exchange value of the resources used) for a good or service, then the market will provide the good or service. However, when there are large fixed costs and information problems, such as in housing, few people may be willing to take the risk associated with individually experimenting with different kinds of housing that would allow for more flexibility in family arrangements, even though collectively the demand for experimental housing might justify the cost. Since the functioning of the home economy is intimately tied to the family arrangement and the housing situation, people's choice of how to provide the necessities produced by the home economy depends on the options available to them in how they set up their households. If the housing stock does not include certain arrangements, such as communal kitchens and dining rooms, we cannot automatically assert that people have voluntarily rejected this housing arrangement in favor of private kitchens.

The importance of this point will become clearer after we look at how the relative importance of the home economy for family consumption standards has declined with economic growth and how the absolute importance of the home economy in the national economy has increased with changes in family arrangements.

The Impact of Rising Standards of Living on the Contribution of Housework

The relationship between the home and market economies has gone through two distinct stages. Early industrialization began the process of transferring some production processes (e.g., clothmaking, sewing, canning foods) from the home to the marketplace. Although the home economy could still produce these goods, the processes were arduous and the market economy was usually more efficient. Soon, the more important second stage was evident—the marketplace began producing goods and services that had never been produced by the home economy, and the home economy was unable to produce them (e.g., electricity and electrical appliances, the automobile, the telephone, television, advanced education, sophisticated medical care). In the second stage, the question of whether the home economy was less efficient in producing these new goods and services was irrelevant; if the family were to enjoy these fruits of industrialization, they would have to be procured in the marketplace. The traditional ways of taking care of these needs in the home, such as in nursing the sick, became socially unacceptable (and, in most serious cases, probably were less successful). Just as the advent of the automobile made the use of the horse-drawn carriage illegal and then impractical, and the advent of television changed the radio from a source of entertainment to a source of background music, so most of the fruits of economic growth did *not* increase the options available to the home economy to either produce the good or service or purchase it in the market. Growth brought with it increased *diversity* in consumption goods, but *not* increased flexibility for the home economy in procuring these goods and services. Instead, economic growth brought with it increased consumer reliance on the marketplace. In order to consume these new goods and services, the family had to enter the marketplace as wage earners and consumers. The neoclassical model that views the family as deciding whether to produce goods and services directly or to purchase them in the marketplace is basically a model of the first stage. It cannot accurately be applied to the second (and current) stage.

The process of urbanization was an important part of the economic growth that changed consumption patterns to include market goods and services that made living in dense areas more feasible and desirable. The movement of the population from the farm or from abroad to the city or the suburb displayed distinct but complex patterns. In 1910, one-third of all households still lived on a farm; by 1970, fewer than 1 in 20 households lived on a farm. Urban population rose from 46 percent in 1910 to 73 percent in 1970. After World War II, the suburban population doubled from 14 percent in 1950 to 27 percent in 1977.[4] Urban distribution networks facilitated the mass marketing of the modern consumer goods made possible by technological innovation and capital formation.

Advances in medical technology and the growing social acceptance of birth control and abortion increased women's control over the number and, more importantly, the timing of their children. As a result, the number of years devoted to child rearing declined. Currently the median age of the mother at the birth of her last child is under thirty years.[5] In a majority of families, the mother has completed her childbearing and has her youngest child in public school by the time she has turned thirty-five. Faced with a life expectancy of over seventy years, women can no longer view the time-intensive role of mothering as a lifetime career.

The dramatic improvement in the material standard of living since World War II can be demonstrated with a few observations from the Consumer Expenditure Surveys of 1950 and 1972 (for the average middle-income family of four):

1. The percent of after-tax income spent on recorded expenditures declined from 111 percent to 92 percent.
2. The percent of after-tax income spent on food declined from 33 percent to 19 percent.
3. The percent of after-tax income spent on clothing declined from 12 percent to 6 percent.
4. The proportion of after-tax income spent on transportation increased from 13 percent to 18 percent, primarily reflecting the increased ownership of cars.
5. Insurance and retirement increased from 5 percent to 7 percent.
6. Shelter expenditures increased from 11 percent to 13 percent (as home ownership increased from 57 percent to 72 percent for this group), and house furnishing expenditures declined from 7 percent to 4 percent.[6]

The primary housework activities of meal preparation and clothing care have been using a declining share of the family's budget; hence a housewife's efforts to decrease expenditures in these areas by direct work activities (e.g., baking from scratch) or more careful shopping made less difference in their relative impact on the family's budget in 1972 than they did in 1950. This decrease in the relative economic importance of housework probably also affects the significance a wife attaches to her work in the home. Purchases of food and clothing, 45 percent of the average middle-income family's disposable income in 1950, accounted for only 25 percent of their income in 1972. Twenty percent of the family's budget that had previously been spent on food and clothing now became freed for other kinds of expenditures, primarily transportation, insurance and retirement, and homeownership.

As a growing proportion of the family's budget is being spent on market goods and services that are not directly related to housework activities, the family's ability to consume these items depends primarily on its purchasing power (i.e., its money income) and not on its time available for housework activities. The output of the home economy has declined in relative importance as a determinant of the family's total consumption standard; however, housework still remains important as a necessity.

Budget studies show that families have used economic growth both to increase the command over material goods and to lessen financial strain by reducing expenditures as a proportion of disposable income. However, most families have not used increasing affluence to increase their time available for leisure or other nonpaid activities. To the contrary, the hours devoted to market work per family have increased, as have the number of activities that go through the marketplace. Some social scientists have viewed this unfolding of events as a paradox; the Greek philosophers had predicted that an affluent society would use time above that needed to produce necessities to enjoy the good life, defined in terms of noneconomic satisfactions.[7] This has not occurred, as the following figures show.

Real per capita income in 1972 was 60 percent higher than in 1950, and this increase reflected both higher real wages and more workers per family. If we look at the families in the top 60 percent of the income distribution, we see that only 20 to 30 percent of the wives in husband-wife families were in the labor force in 1950; by 1972, 60 percent of the families in these middle- and upper-middle-income groups had more than one earner in the labor market, and 10 to 30 percent had more than two earners. In addition, nonearned income, primarily transfer payments and income from assets, became increasingly important over the period. In 1972, the typical middle-income family had at least two earners and income in addition to their earnings.[8] At the same time, changes were occurring in living arrangements, and these changes have important implications for how we use our economic resources, especially the time required for housework.

The Resources Needed by Different Families

The living arrangement of families simultaneously determines their needs, which reflect the age and number of family members, and their resources, which reflect the economic power of the adults (i.e., their control over wages and hours of work). Setting up a household entails large fixed costs that include procuring shelter, household furnishings, and a means of transportation. These fixed costs result in economies of scale with increased family size, since it involves the sharing of capital among household members. As a result, a decline in the nation's average household size means an increase in the resources needed to provide the basic housing and equipment needed by the population.

The period from 1940 to 1975 witnessed a decline in average household size from 3.7 to 2.9 persons.[9] This decline reflects primarily an increase in the number of unrelated individuals living alone, reinforced by a decrease in families living together as well as a decrease in the number of children per family since the mid-1960s. Over this period, the population of the country grew 62 percent, the number of nuclear families increased 76 percent, and primary individuals (i.e., individuals who do not live with relatives) increased an astonishing 352 percent.

The phenomenal growth in primary individuals resulted from an increased tendency for both younger and older adults to maintain their own households. In 1950, only 43 percent of unrelated individuals lived alone; by 1975, 73 percent did. The one-adult household jumped from 7 percent of all households in 1940 to 21 percent in 1976.

Although families sharing housing were never a large group during this period, group-family housing became almost nonexistent. Less than 5 percent of all families shared homes in 1976 (down from around 16 percent in 1940). Family groups that in the past tended to double up and young and retired adults who tended to live with their families are now buying more privacy. Whatever the reasons for the rapid growth of one-person households, the economic outcome is clear: Our society is using an increasing amount of resources per capita to provide housing, household furnishings, and transportation. To what extent this reflects our state of affluence or to what extent this reflects the inflexibility of our existing institutions remains an open question.

The fixed money costs of setting up a household are only part of the relatively large fixed costs associated with smaller households; in addition there are time economies of scale. Table 1 gives the economies of scale observed at the poverty threshold. For example, a one-adult household required $43 of income per week in 1973 and 31 hours of household work time to stay above poverty. By contrast, the one adult with one child household required $58 per week, an increase of $15 (35%); it also required 57 hours of housework time, an increase of 26 hours (84%). With the

Table 1. Economies of Scale at the Poverty Threshold

Household	One-Adult Income Index	One-Adult Time Index
	Weekly Figures	
One adult with:		
0 children	1.00	1.00
1 child	1.35	1.84
2–3 children	1.81	1.97
4–5 children	2.47	2.03
6 or more children	3.16	2.23
Two adults with:		
0 children	1.35	1.39
1 child	1.63	2.00
2–3 children	2.19	2.13
4–5 children	2.98	2.19
6 or more children	3.26	2.39

Source: The "one-adult indices" were calculated by dividing the time or money requirements for each household type by the corresponding requirement for the one-adult household. The calculations for the income figures are based on the Social Security Administration's poverty thresholds, and the calculations for the time figures are based on the time requirements derived in Clair Vickery, "The Time Poor: A New Look at Poverty," *Journal of Human Resources* 12, no. 1 (Winter 1977).

addition of one to two more children, the money needed increased $20 (81%), while the time needed increased 4 hours (97%). Major economies of scale in terms of income are experienced with the addition of the first (and additional) children, and major economies of scale in terms of time are experienced with the addition of the second (and additional) children. In the two-adult household, money economies of scale also begin with the second person; time economies of scale also begin with the second child. In both kinds of households, the first child substantially raises the required housework time, and additional children only slightly increase the (already substantial) time required.[10]

As family groupings have become more fragmented, the home economy has become less efficient because the smaller household does not capture the benefits of the scale economies. The impact has been most obvious in the growing housing shortage where the rapid proliferation of new households has pushed vacancy rates downward and housing prices upward. In addition, the unforeseen increases in the price of energy over the past six years have caused energy costs to become a large part of shelter costs. This price development makes the smaller household even less efficient because energy usage is part of the scale economies of shelter.

The growth in real income has allowed the individualization of consumption activities as the economic need to band together as family members has declined and the ability to buy privacy has increased. The result has been an increase in our work activities and resources that go toward fulfilling necessities, as well as an increased reliance on the marketplace. Economic analyses of the family have ignored this source of inefficient behavior and instead have focused on the economic returns from specialization in housework. These trends toward fragmentation of family groupings and equalization of work roles by sex are inefficient in terms of producing the resources used to satisfy basic needs, although they may not be inefficient in terms of the more general efficiency criteria of satisfying needs or desires above the level of necessity. Unfortunately, economists have not addressed the more general question of whether there is a more efficient way of satisfying the observed quest for greater flexibility in household arrangements and for women's economic independence. Both goals have a major impact on the functioning of the home economy.

The Changing Role of the Home Economy

The demand by the women's movement for economic independence and the equalization of sex roles has brought into clear relief the contrasts and contradictions between the home economy and the market economy, for these differences between the two economies have helped perpetuate the inequality between the sexes. Because women have been prepared to run the home economies when they assume their roles as wives and mothers, their sense of identity and personal power are grounded in this economy. The market economy and home economy have their own value structures, their own work structure, and reward different behaviors. For this reason, movement between the two economies is difficult and usually involves personal conflict.[11] The two economies can be contrasted by five major characteristics:

1. *Supervision*. The housewife is her own supervisor during the day as she performs her chores within the home. Although she responds to the demands and needs of other family members, she is in charge of deciding how to provide the personalized care. At a paid job, most workers have a formal supervisor who decides what work needs to be done in what manner and ensures that the work is actually performed.

2. *Pay*. The housewife gives her services within the home economy; in return, the family shares the husband's earnings (or in the absence of the children's father, she qualifies for a government welfare check or a government-enforced maintenence check from the father). Although the work performed within the home economy varies little by the income of the husband, the earnings that the wife and children share vary tremendously. There is no systematic relationship between the output of her work efforts and the family income. No provision is made for sickness, and the housewife is on call twenty-four hours a day. In a paid job the worker has a formal or informal contract that stipulates a rate of pay for a job performed. Rules govern behavior on the job, sick leave, vacation days, and hours of work.

3. *Mobility*. The housewife's job in the home economy depends on the agreement with her husband to share his income and her labor as a family unit. If she becomes dissatisfied with her job, her choices are to improve the job (or otherwise to change her attitude toward her job) or to quit. Quitting is not a clear-cut option, however, since some home economy must still exist in order to provide food, clothing, and shelter for the children and the separated parents. Because of the essential nature of the housewife's job, "changing jobs" for her boils down to continuing working (i.e., caring for the children) without a guarantee of pay; "changing jobs" means a complete change in life style with a greatly reduced income. The market economy provides for less dramatic changes if a worker is dissatisfied with a job and is unable to effect changes at the current workplace. Although options are restricted by the market jobs available, and changing jobs is a stressful process, the worker still faces more than the two options of continuing on the current job or working for little or no pay.

4. *Measure of Value*. The housewife works in a personalized economy that caters to children's and husband's needs, and the measure of value is

not quantified. In fact, economists have tried unsuccessfully to quantify the value of the home economy through its reflection in the market economy, primarily because the outputs of the home and market economies are not the same. The home economy focuses on individual and family well-being, and its personalized care and nurturing cannot be given a price tag by comparing the services of the home economy with what a family is willing to pay for occasional substitutes (e.g., child care, meals out, maid service), since the occasional substitute is not comparable to a permanent replacement. Asked about the comparison, many housewives would agree with Theresa Carter quoted at the start of this essay: "I think that's a lot of baloney." So far the marketplace has not provided a permanent replacement for the services provided in the home economy. In contrast, the employed woman knows precisely the value of her work since the marketplace uses the exchange value (i.e., the rate of pay) as its measure of value for the work performed.

5. *Personal behavior.* The home economy is based on the concept of mutual aid and service to others, and this cooperative behavior is necessary for the home economy to function. It can be viewed primarily as a noncompetitive economy, while the market economy is a competitive economy that rewards the individual. A woman who has worked primarily in the home economy is at a disadvantage in the market economy, which has a different reward structure and different value system. If the woman carries with her cooperative and service values of the home economy, she is likely to end up working for a low monetary reward when she seeks the approval of others and a sense of worth from service to others, both reflections of the reward system of the home economy. Since money and individual advancement are not part of the reward structure of the home economy, a woman who takes the value structure of the home economy with her into the market economy will be at a disadvantage in demanding equitable compensation for her work according to the values of the market economy.

These conflicts between the value and reward structures of the home and market economies have caused deep divisions among feminist social scientists in discussing the future of the home economy. Women, who have had responsibility for running the home economy, realize the importance of the home economy for rearing children. At the same time, they realize the role the home economy has played in keeping women in a subordinate role through economic dependence on the husband. Since the home economy takes care of necessities, we cannot hold its functioning in abeyance until we agree on how to restructure it. At one extreme we hear cries for saving the values of the home economy at the expense of equality for women; at the other extreme, we hear cries for destroying the home economy and turning its functions over to the marketplace or state in order to achieve equality for women. Faced with these two dismal prospects, many women (and men) have had to search for some alternative. As is usually the case, compromise positions seem to promise too much to everyone and please no one, since they tend to gloss over the underlying conflict between the home and market economies.

As the household has shrunk in size and as market activities have become more important, the dichotomy between the large, impersonal, efficient market economy and the small, personalized, inefficient home economy grows. Do viable alternatives to these extremes exist? If they exist, are there any signs of the mechanisms that will produce the necessary insitutional changes? Although more and more people are experimenting with nontraditional family arrangements, these experiments do not yet point to the widespread acceptance of new family forms. Possible ways for families or individuals to pool capital equipment, share housing, and engage in a quasi-barter system of exchanging skills within a neighborhood setting remain unexplored. Examples of such potentially pooled activities include car repair, plumbing and household repairs, small carpentry and remodeling jobs, gardening, electrical work, as well as the traditional jobs of child care and meal preparation. Although the social institutions through which these exchanges might occur do not yet exist, the economic forces promoting such changes are increasing. One example of a possible pooling arrangement is to allow neighborhoods to use the public school system to set up systems of car repair and small carpentry jobs. Another possibility is for the government to experiment with setting up new-style apartments for older people that would allow each person to have a separate living space and at the same time share kitchens or bathrooms. This set-up would allow the sharing of food preparation, which is their major housework activity.

The Future of Home Economy

As the social customs enforcing lifetime marriages have weakened, marriage with its explicit sharing of money income and housework no longer provides income security for the wife. These shifts in family institutions have increased the need for most adults to have some direct control over their money income, and this control is usually achieved through paid labor.

Wives' work responsibilities in the home have been influenced by these social changes and by economic growth in two important ways. First, their homework-based bargaining power diminished as homemaking activities declined in value relative to the family's total consumption activities. As the jobs available to women expanded and as their control over conception grew, the wife was drawn to paid labor in order to in-

crease her economic contribution to the family, her input in family decision making, and her own self-esteem, as well as to increase her financial
security in the event of divorce. Second, since the majority of families
came to have a wife employed at least part of the time, each family became
increasingly dependent on the wife's earnings to maintain its relative income position and participate in consuming the fruits of economic growth.

At the same time that each adult's need for economic independence
has grown, the family and the individual have both become more dependent on the marketplace, this dependence on wage labor mitigated somewhat by government programs of unemployment compensation, welfare
benefits, and social security. This long-run trend toward the marketplace
producing more and better goods and services that have become part of the
commonly accepted living standard for most families raises the question of
how much economic growth has reduced financial strain. The entrance of
the wife into paid labor also does not necessarily reduce the family's
financial stress, especially when one spouse is unemployed. Although the
risk of the family having no money income declines when both spouses are
in the labor market, the family's incidence of unemployment increases as
each worker faces the risk of unemployment. Unless the wife's working
increases the family's savings and decreases its financial commitments, her
employment will not decrease the financial strain that accompanies unemployment. Once the wife becomes regularly employed, she can no
longer act as a buffer stock of labor, entering the labor market as a temporary waitress or office clerk when her husband is unemployed or involved
in a work stoppage. The family's financial pressures will continue to be
determined not only by their income level but also by their material
aspirations, which may be fueled by economic growth and the wife's
entrance into paid labor.

As the number of paid work hours per family has grown, the time
available for nonmarket work, for interpersonal relationships, and for family life in general has declined. How can we get off this treadmill? The
decisions of each family and society as a whole are interrelated, so that no
family feels it can cut back its market work until other families also cut
back their market work. Otherwise, the family's economic position relative to its peer group will fall. The labor movement and the government
could both promote social discussion of policies that would allow families
greater flexibility in organizing the husband's and wife's work and simultaneously encourage a better balance of paid and nonpaid activities. Programs such as legislation to do away with mandatory overtime or to decrease the standard workweek through amendment of the Fair Labor
Standards Act would be steps in the right direction of reducing the paid
work hours for both men and women.

In looking at the role that families play in our economy, I conclude that as the home economy's functions decline in relative terms, the family's ability to procure higher earnings by increasing the paid work time of its members will reach a dead end. As we experience the personal costs of our economic gains, then perhaps we will be willing to rethink the relative importance of economic gains versus our noneconomic needs for love, self-development, and satisfying relationships that come with good home and community life. Central to these issues are the evolving work roles of men and women in the home and market economies. If our society goes toward more equal work roles between men and women, we will necessarily go toward increasing the work done by men within the home and the time spent by men in family life. One role of the economist in this analysis is to reevaluate the gains from specialization of work roles at a time when the activities performed in the home have become less important in determining the living standards of the family. At the same time, we need to search for alternative ways of providing the services normally produced by the home economy, such as meal preparation and child care, that are no longer provided efficiently by small households and yet need to be produced within a cooperative setting that reflects the values of the home economy.

As Theresa Cook said, "Cooking and cleaning. It's necessary, but it's not really great."

Notes

1. See Barbara Ehrenreich and Deirdre English, *For Her Own Good* (New York: Doubleday Anchor 1978); and Sheila M. Rothman, *Woman's Proper Place* (New York: Basic, 1978).

2. Clair Vickery, "Women's Economic Contribution to the Family," in *The Subtle Revolution: Women at Work*, ed. Ralph Smith (Washington, D.C.: Urban Institute, 1979); Myra H. Strober and Charles B. Weinberg, "Stragegies Used by Working and Nonworking Wives to Reduce Time Pressures," *Journal of Consumer Research*, March 1980, pp. 338–48.

3. See, for example, Gary S. Becker, "A Theory of the Allocation of Time," *Economic Journal*, September 1965, pp. 493–517; idem, "The Economics of Marriage," *Journal of Political Economy*, July/August 1973, pp. 813–46; Supplement on New Economic Approaches to Fertility, *Journal of Political Economy*, March/April 1973, pt. 2; and Jacob Mincer, "Labor Force Participation of Married Women," in

Aspects of Labor Economics, ed. H. Gregg Lewis (Princeton: Princeton University Press, 1962), pp. 63–105.

4. U.S. Bureau of the Census, *Historical Statistics of the United States, Colonial Times to 1970*, 1976, Series A-73, A-82, A-350, A-352. The definition of "urban area" varies by year.

5. Hugh Carter and Paul C. Glick, *Marriage and Divorce: A Social and Economic Study* (Cambridge, Mass.: Harvard University Press, 1976), p. 145; updated by Glick in a paper presented at the annual meeting of the Population Association of America in Montreal, 30 April 1976.

6. This analysis of expenditure patterns draws from my earlier work, "Women's Economic Contribution." These same patterns of *changes* in expenditures are observed across all income groups in addition to the middle-income family reported here.

7. Staffan B. Linder, *The Harried Leisure Class* (New York: Columbia University Press, 1970); see also Harold Wilensky, "The Uneven Distribution of Leisure: The Impact of Economic Growth on 'Free Time,'" *Social Problems* 9 (Summer 1961).

8. U.S. Bureau of the Census, *Statistical Abstract of the United States: 1976*, Table Nos. 636, 630, 2; U.S. Bureau of the Census, *Current Population Reports*, Series P-60, Nos. 80 and 90.

9. This discussion of changes in living arrangements draws from Clair Vickery, "The Changing Household: Implications for Devising an Income Support Program," *Public Policy*, Winter 1978, pp. 121–51.

10. Similar economies of scale are observed at other income levels. Equivalency tables for the hypothetical Department of Labor budgets (lower, moderate, and higher cost budget) for urban families can be found in U.S. Bureau of Labor Statistics, *Revised Equivalence Scale for Estimating Equivalent Incomes or Budget Costs by Family Type*, Bulletin No. 1570-2, November 1968. Time-budget studies across income groups are reported in Kathryn E. Walker and Margaret E. Woods, *Time Use: A Measure of Household Production of Family Goods and Services* (Washington, D.C.: American Home Economics Association, 1976).

11. A study of these issues as they relate to the displaced homemaker has been done by Lois Greenwood, *Toward a Theory of Women and Powerlessness: A Study of the Displaced Homemaker*, forthcoming Ph.D. dissertation, University of California, Berkeley.

10

RAYNA RAPP

Family and Class in Contemporary America: Notes Toward an Understanding of Ideology

T his essay is grounded in two contexts, one political and one academic. The political context is that of the women's movement, in which a debate seems always to be raging concerning the future of the family. Many of us have been to an archetypical meeting in which someone stands up and asserts that the nuclear family ought to be abolished because it is degrading and constraining to women. Usually, someone else (often representing a Third World position) follows on her heels, pointing out that the attack on the family represents a white middle-class position and that other women need their families for support and survival. Evidently both speakers are, in some senses, right. And just as evidently they aren't talking about the same families. We need to explore those different notions of family if we are to heal an important split in our movement. To do so, we must take seriously the things women say about their experiences in their families, especially as they vary by class.

The University of Michigan's Women Studies Program called this paper into being, gave it a first airing, and contributed a stimulating set of discussions. Subsequent presentation of these ideas at the New School for Social Research, the URPE Spring conference on Public Policy, and the Anthropology Department of the University of Northern Colorado provided invaluable feedback. I especially want to thank Jill Cherneff, Ingelore Fritsch, Susan Harding, Mike Hooper, Janet Siskind, Deborah Jay Stearns, Batya Weinbaum, and Marilyn Young for their comments. The women of Marxist-Feminist Group II posed the questions that led me to write this paper; they supplied, as always, the supportive context within which the meaning of my work has been discussed. Above all, Gayle Rubin deserves my thanks for her general intellectual aid, and the specific editorial work she did in turning my primary process into a set of written ideas. originally published in a special issue of the *University of Michigan Papers in Woman's Studies*. Subsequently published in *Science and Society* 42 (1978): 278–300, and reprinted by permission of the author and *Science and Society*.

The second context out of which this essay grows is the academic study of the contemporary American family. Over the last few years, in reading eclectically in sociology, demography, urban planning, and policy literature, I've been trying to sort out what is known (or not known) about women's experiences in their families. Here, too, a debate is raging over the future of the family. On the one hand, there is a tremendous alarmism that presages the end of the family—recent books have included titles such as *The Fractured Family;* journals on family coordination and counseling, and courses at every level from high school through graduate studies speak of the family in crisis. On the other hand, *Here to Stay* (to name but one title) and a spate of studies reanalyzing the divorce rates reassure us that the American family is simply changing, but not disappearing. This debate seems to mystify the subject it claims to clarify.[1] This is not surprising, since the family is a topic that is ideologically charged. In order to get some understanding of the importance of ideology in analyses of the family, there are two fields to which we ought to turn for perspective. One is the recent work that has been done on the history of the family.[2] A great many innovative studies reveal similar issues in historical perspective; for as long as modern records have been kept concerning families, it seems that people have been speculating on the future of the institution. The last decade of social history should caution us to moderate our alarmism. At the least, we have learned that all societies contain a multiplicity of family forms whose structural arrangements respond to complex conditions.

The second field that adds perspective to the issue is anthropology, which studies the family and kinship systems both at home and abroad. Anthropology reminds us that we are *all* participant observers when we study the American family. It has been pointed out that our understandings often get in the way and more often express the ideology and norms of our culture than an analysis. This word of warning leads me to examine not only what differing groups of people *say* about their families but what they actually *do* in their families. It also leads me to examine the ways in which I think the concept of family itself is ideological in social science.

The archetypical political debaters arguing over the meaning of the family aren't talking about the same families. Neither are the social scientists. We need to make a distinction between families and households, and to examine their relation to one another. The entities in which people actually live are not families, but households (as any census taker, demographer, or fieldworking anthropologist will tell you). Households are the empirically measurable units within which people pool resources and perform certain tasks. Goody analyzes them as units of production, reproduction, and consumption.[3] They are residential units within which personnel and resources get distributed and connected. Households may vary in their membership composition and in their relation to resource allocation, especially in a system such as our own. That is, they vary systematically in their ability to hook into, accumulate, and transmit wealth, wages, or welfare. This seems a simple unit to define.

Families, on the other hand, are a bit more slippery. In English we tend to gloss "family" to mean household. But analytically, the concept means something else. For all classes of Americans, the word has at least two levels of meaning.[4] One is normative: Husbands, wives, and children are a set of relatives who should live together (that is, the nuclear family). The other meaning includes a more extended network of kin relations that people may activate selectively. That is, the American family includes the narrower and broader webs of kin ties that are "the nuclear family" and all relations by blood and marriage. The concept of family is presumed in America to carry a heavy load of affect. We say "blood is thicker than water," "till death do us part," "you can choose your friends, but not your relatives," and so on. What I will argue in this essay is that the concept of family also carries a heavy load of ideology.

The reason for this is that the family is the normative, correct way in which people get recruited into households. It is through families that people enter into productive, reproductive, and consumption relations. The two genders enter them differently. Families organize households, and it is within families that people experience the absence or presence, the sharing or withholding, of basic poolable resources. "Family" (as a normative concept in our culture) reflects those material relations; it also distorts them. As such, the concept of family is a socially necessary illusion which simultaneously expresses and masks recruitment to relations of production, reproduction, and consumption—relations that condition different kinds of household resource bases in different class sectors. Our notions of family absorb the conflicts, contradictions, and tensions actually generated by those material, class-structured relations that households hold to resources in advanced capitalism. "Family," as we understand (and misunderstand) the term, is conditioned by the exigencies of household formation, and serves as a shock absorber to keep households functioning. People are recruited and kept in households by families in all classes, yet the families they have (or don't have) are not the same.

Having asserted that households and families vary by class, we now need to consider that third concept, class. If ever a concept carried a heavy weight of ideology, it is the concept of class in American social science. We have a huge and muddled literature that attempts to reconcile objective and subjective criteria, to sort people into lowers, uppers, and middles, to argue about the relation of consciousness to material reality.[5] I will say only the following: "Social class" is a short-hand for a process, not a thing. That process is the one by which different social relations to the means of production are inherited and reproduced under capitalism. As the concept is developed by Marx, the process of capital accumulation generates and constantly deepens relations between two categories of people: those who are both available and forced to work for wages because they own no means of production, and those who control those means of production. The concept of class expresses a historical process of expanding capital. In the process, categories of people get swept up at different times and places and deposited into different relations to the means of production and to one another. People then get labeled blue collar or white collar; they may experience their social existence as mediated by ethnicity or the overwhelming legacy of slavery and racism. Yet all these categories must be viewed in the light of the historic process of capitalist accumulation in the United States. To a large extent, what are actually being accumulated are changing categories of proletarians. Class formation and composition is always in flux; what gets accumulated in it are relationships. Under advanced capitalism, there are shifting frontiers which separate poverty, stable wage-earning, affluent salaries, and inherited wealth. The frontiers may be crossed by individuals, and in either direction. That is, both upward and downward mobility are real processes. The point is, "class" isn't a static place that individuals inhabit. It is a process determined by the relationships set up in capital accumulation.

Returning to the initial distinction between family and household, I want to explore how these two vary among differing class sectors in contemporary America and to draw a composite picture of the households formed around material relations by class, and the families which organize those households. I will argue that those families mean different things by class, and by genders as well, because classes and genders stand in differing material relations to one another. I'll further argue that their meanings are highly ideological.

I'd like to begin with a review and interpretation of the studies done on the working-class family. Studies span the postwar decades from the late 1940s to the present. They are regionally diverse, and report on both cities and suburbs. The data provided by researchers such as Berger, Gans, Komarovsky, Howell, Rubin, and others reveal a composite portrait.[6] The most salient characteristic of household organization in the working class is dependency on hourly wages. Stable working-class households participate in relations of production, reproduction, and consumption by sending out their labor power in exchange for wages. "Sending out" is important: there is a radical split between household and work place, yet the resources upon which the household depends come from participation in production outside of itself. How much labor power a working-class household needs to send out is determined by many things:

the cost of reproducing (or maintaining) the household, the work careers and earning trajectories of individual members, and the domestic cycle (that is, the relations between the genders and the generations, which specify when and if wives and adolescent children are available to work outside the home). Braverman [7] estimates that the average working-class household now sends out 1.7 full-time equivalent workers. That figure tells us that a high percentage of married women and teen-aged children are contributing their wages to the household. In many ways, the work patterns for nineteenth-century European capitalism described by Tilly and Scott [8] still leave their mark on the contemporary American working class household; it is not only male heads of households upon whom survival depends.

What the working class sends out in exchange for basic resources is labor power. Labor power is the only commodity without which there can be no capitalism. It is also the only commodity for which the working class controls its own means of production. [9] Control over the production of labor power undoubtedly affected women's experiences historically, as it does today. [10] In the early stages of industrialization, it appears that working-class households literally produced a lot of babies (future labor-power) as their strategy for dealing with a market economy. [11] Now workers produce fewer children, but the work of servicing them (social reproduction) is still a major process that goes on in the household. Households are the basic units in which labor power is reproduced and maintained. This takes place in a location radically removed from the work place. Such relations therefore appear as autonomous from capital, but of course they are not; without wages, households are hard to form and keep functioning; without the production of a disciplined labor force, factories cannot produce and profit.

The work that gets done in households (primarily by women) is not simply about babies. Housework itself has recently been rediscovered as work, and its contribution to arenas beyond the household is clear. [12] At the least, housework cuts the reproduction costs of wage workers. Imagine if all those meals had to be bought at restaurants, those clothes cleaned at laundry rates, those beds made by hotel employees! Housework is also what women do in exchange for access to resources that are bought by their husband's wages. As such, it is a coin of exchange between men and women. As housework is wageless, it keeps its workers dependent on others for access to commodities bought with wages. It makes them extremely vulnerable to the work conditions of their men. When women work (as increasingly they do), their primary definition as houseworker contributes to the problems they encounter in entering the paid labor force. They are available for part-time (or full-time) work in the lowest paid sectors of the labor market, in jobs which leave them less economically secure than men. Participation in the "sexregated" labor market then reinforces dependency upon the earnings of other household members and the continued importance of women's domestic labor.[13]

Of course, these rather abstract notions of "household participation" in the labor market or in housework are experienced concretely by family members. Working-class families are normatively nuclear. They are formed via marriage, which links men and women "for love" and not "for money." [14] This relation is of course both real and a socially necessary illusion. As such, it is central to the ideology of the family. The cultural distinction between love and money corresponds to the distinction between private family life in the home and work life outside the home. The two are experienced as opposite; in fact they are interpenetrating. The seeming autonomy to exchange love at home expresses something ideological about the relation between home and work: one must work for the sake of the family, and having a family is the "payoff" for leading a good life. Founding a family is what people do for personal gratification, for love, and for autonomy. The working-class family literature is full of life histories in which young women saw "love" as a way to get out of their own, often difficult families. Rubin's interviews, for example, are full of teen-aged girls who said, "When I grow up, I'll marry for love, and it will be better than my parents' marriage." You may marry for love, but what you mainly get is babies. Forty to 60 percent of teen-aged pregnancies are conceived premaritally, and approximately 50 percent of working-class women marry in their teen years.[15] It's a common experience to go from being someone's child to having someone's child in under a year. This is not exactly a situation that leads to autonomy.

For men, the situation is complementary. As one of the young working-class men in Rubin's study puts it:

> I had to work from the time I was thirteen and turn over most of my pay to my mother to help pay the bills. By the time I was nineteen, I had been working for all those years and I didn't have anything—not a thing. I used to think a lot about how when I got married, I would finally get to keep my money for myself. I guess that sounds a little crazy when I think about it now because I have to support the wife and kids. I don't know *what* I was thinking about, but I never thought about that then.[16]

What you get from the romance of love and marriage is in fact not simply a family but a household, and that's quite another matter. Romance is implicated in gender identity and ideology. We are all aware of the cultural distinction made between the sexual identity of a good and a bad girl; a good girl is one who accumulates her sexual resources for later investment. Autonomy means escaping your childhood family to become an adult with your own nuclear family. For young men, the identity process includes the cultural role of wild boy—one who "sows some wild oats," hangs out on street corners, perhaps gets in trouble with the police, and drinks.[17] Ideally, the good girl domesticates the wild boy; she gives him love, and he settles down and goes out to work. Autonomy means becoming an adult with your own nuclear family as an escape. But of course, autonomy is illusive. The family is classically seen as an escape from production, but in fact it is what sends people into relations of production, for they need to work to support their families. The meaning of production is simultaneously denied and experienced through family relations; working-class wives say of a good husband that he works steadily, provides for the kids, and never harms anyone in the family. The complementary statement is uttered by working-class husbands, who define a good wife as one who keeps the kids under control when he comes home from a hard day's work, and who runs the household well.[18] To exchange love is also to underwrite both the necessity and the ability to keep on working. This is the heritage that working-class families pass on, in lieu of property, to their children.

The family expresses ideology in another sense as well—the distinction between norms and realities. The norms concerning families are that people should be loving and sharing within them and that they should be protective. The reality is too often otherwise, as the recent rising consciousness of domestic violence indicates. Even without domestic violence, there are more commonplace stresses to which families are often subjected. Rubin found in her study that 40 percent of the adults she interviewed had an alcoholic parent.[19] Fifty percent had experienced parental desertion or divorce in their childhood. National statistics confirm these figures.[20] About half the adults in her study had seriously destabilizing experiences within their families. The tension generated by relations to resource base can often tear households apart. Under these conditions, to label the working-class personality "authoritarian" seems a cruel hoax. When the household is working, it expresses work discipline.

Ideology is expressed in gender role in families in another sense as well. Throughout the urban kinship literature, across classes and ethnic groups, the work of reproducing families is in part undertaken by larger kinship groups (the family in the broader sense of relatives). Family networks in this larger sense are women-centered and tend to be serviced by women. There exists a large literature on women-centered kinship networks in which it is usually assumed that women minister to kinship because they minister to families in general. Sylvia Yanagisako suggests that there is also a symbolic level to the kinship work which women do; ideologically, women are assigned to "inside, home, private" domains, while men are seen to represent the outside world.[21] Nuclear families are under cultural constraints to appear as autonomous and private. Yet they are never as private in reality as such values might indicate. The ideal autonomy of an independent nuclear family is constantly being contradicted by the realities of social need, in which resources must be pooled, borrowed, shared. It is women who bridge the gap between what a household's resources really are and what a family's position is supposed to be. Women exchange babysitting, share meals, lend small amounts of money. When a married child is out of work, his (or her) nuclear family turns to the mother, and often moves in for a while. The working-class family literature is filled with examples of such pooling.[22] To the extent that women "represent" the family, they facilitate the pooling needed at various points in the domestic cycle. Men maintain, at least symbolically, the autonomy of their families. Pooling is a norm in family behavior, but it's a hard norm to live with, to either meet or ignore. To comply with the demands of the extended family completely is to lose control over material and emotional resources; to refuse is very dangerous, as people know they will need one another. The tightrope act that ensues is well characterized in the classic mother-in-law story, which usually concerns a young wife and her husband's mother. The two women must figure out a way to share the small services, the material benefits, and the emotional satisfactions one man brings to them both in their separate roles of mother and wife. The autonomy of the younger woman is often compromised by the elder's needs; the authority of the mother is sometimes undermined by the demands of the wife. Women must constantly test, strain, and repair the fibers of their kinship networks.

Such women-centered networks are implicated in a process that has not yet been discussed. We have spoken of production and reproduction as they affect the working-class household and family. We ought briefly to mention consumption as well. As a household function, consumption includes turning an amount of wages into commodities so that labor power may be reproduced. This is often women's work. And work it really is. Weinbaum and Bridges tell us that the centralization and rationalization of services and industry under advanced capitalism may be most efficient from the point of view of capital, but it leaves a lot of unrewarding, technical work to be done by women in supermarkets, in paying bills, in dealing with huge bureaucracies.[23] Women experience the pay packet in terms of the use values it will buy. Yet their consumption work is done in the world of exchange value. They mediate the tension between use and exchange, as exemplified in the classic tales concerning domestic quarrels over money in which the man blames the woman for not making his pay check stretch far enough. In stable working-class neighborhoods, the consumption work is in part done by women united by family ties who exchange services, recipes, sales information, and general life style skills.

Kinship networks are part of "community control" for women. As Seifer notes, working-class women become involved in political issues that threaten the stability of their neighborhoods.[24] Perhaps one reason is that their neighborhoods are the locus of extended families within which both work needs and emotional needs are so often met.

When everyone submits to the conditions described here "for the sake of the family," we see the pattern that Howell labels settled living.[25] Its opposite, in his words, is hard living, a family life style that includes a lot of domestic instability, alcohol, and rootlessness. I want to stress that I am here departing from a "culture of poverty" approach. The value of a label like hard living is that it stresses a continuum made up of many attributes. It is composed of many processes with which the working class has a lot of experience. Given the national statistics on alcoholism, desertion, divorce, premarital pregnancy, and the like, everyone's family has included such experiences, either in its own domestic cycle or in the wider family network.[26] Everyone had a wild brother, or was a bad girl, or had an uncle who drank too much or cousins who got divorced. In each of such cases, everyone experienced the pooling of resources (or the lack of pooling) as families attempted to cope with difficult, destabilizing situations. In a sense, the hard livers keep the settled livers more settled: The consequences of leaving the normative path are well-known and are not appealing. This, too, is part of the working-class heritage. In studies by Seifer, Howell, and Rubin, young women express their hopes of leaving a difficult family situation by finding the right man to marry. They therefore marry young, with little formal education, possibly about to become parents, and the cycle begins again.

Of course, hard living is most consistently associated with poverty in the urban family literature. For essentially political reasons, black poverty has more frequently been the subject of social science analysis than has white poverty, but the pattern is found across races. Black Americans have survived under extremely difficult conditions; many of their household and family patterns have evolved to deal with their specific history, while others are shared with Americans of similar class and regional backgrounds. The problems of household formation under poverty conditions are not unique to any group of people; some of the specific, resilient solutions to those problems may be. Because we know far more about black families in poverty than we do about whites, I'll draw a composite picture of households and families using studies that are primarily black.[27] Even when talking about very poor people, analysts such as Liebow, Hannerz, Valentine, and Stack note that there are multiple household types, based on domestic cycles and the relative ability to draw on resources. Hannerz, for example, divides his black sample into four categories.[28] Mainstreamers live in stable households composed of husband, wife, and children. The adults are employed, and either own their own homes or aspire to do so. Their households don't look very different from the rest of the working class. Swingers (Hannerz' second type) are younger, single persons who may be on their way into mainstream life, or they may be tending toward street-families (type three), whose households are headed by women. This type is most important for our study. The fourth category is composed of street men who are peer-oriented, and predominantly hard-core unemployed or underemployed. They are similar to the men of *Tally's Corner*.[29] While Hannerz and Liebow both give us a wealth of information about what men are doing, they don't analyze their domestic arrangements in detail. Carol Stack,[30] who did her field work from the perspective of female-centered households, most clearly analyzes household formation of the very poor. She presents us with domestic networks: extremely flexible and fluctuating groups of people committed to resource pooling, to sharing, to mutual aid, who move in and out from under one another's roofs.

Given the state of the job market, welfare legislation, and segregated slum housing, households are unstable. These are people essentially living below socially necessary reproduction costs. They therefore reproduce themselves by spreading out the aid and the risks involved in daily life. For the disproportionally high numbers who are prevented from obtaining steady employment, being part of what Marx called the floating surplus population is a perilous endeavor. What this means in human terms is not only that the poor pay more (as Caplowitz tells us) [31] but that the poor share more as well. Stack's monograph contains richly textured descriptions of the way that food, furniture, clothing, appliances, kids, and money make the rounds between individuals and households. She subtitles one chapter, "What Goes Round Comes Round" and describes the velocity with which pooling takes place. People try to give what they can and take what they need. Meeting consumption requirements is hard work under these conditions, and domestic networks get the task done. The pleasures and pressures of such survival networks are predominantly organized around the notion of family.

Meyer Fortes tells us that "domestic groups are the workshops of social reproduction." [32] Whatever else they do, the families that organize domestic networks are responsible for children. As Ladner and Stack [33] remind us, poverty, low levels of formal education, and early age for first pregnancy are highly correlated; a lot of young girls have children while they are not fully adults. Under these circumstances, at least among black families, there is a tremendous sharing of the children themselves. On the whole, these are not kids who grow up in "isolated nuclear families." Stack, for example, found that 20 percent of the ADC (Aid to Dependent Children) children in her study were being raised in a household other than that which contained the biological mother. In the vast majority of cases, the household was related through the biological mother's family. Organizing kinship networks so that children are cared for is a primary function of families. Men, too, often contribute to child rearing. Like women, they share out bits and pieces of whatever they have. While some men make no contribution, others may be simultaneously contributing to sisters, to a mother and aunt, as well as to wives or lovers. They may sleep in one household, but bring groceries, money, and affection to several others.[34] Both Stack and Ladner analyze the importance of a father's recognition of his children, by which act he links the baby to his own kinship network. It is family in the broader sense of the term that organizes social reproduction.

Family may be a conscious construction of its participants. Liebow, Stack, Ladner and others describe fictive kinship, by which friends are turned into family. Since family is supposed to be more reliable than friendship, "going for brothers," "for sisters," "for cousins," increases the commitment of a relationship, and makes people ideally more responsible for one another. Fictive kinship is a serious relationship. Stack (who is white) describes her own experience with Ruby, a black woman with whom she "went for sisters." When Ruby's child was seriously ill, Stack became deeply involved in the crisis. When the baby was admitted to the hospital, she and Ruby rushed over for visiting hours. They were stopped by a nurse, who insisted that only the immediate family could enter. Ruby responded, "Caroline here is my sister, and nothing's stopping her from visiting this baby." And they entered, unchallenged. Ruby was correct; under the circumstances, white Caroline was her sister.[35]

Liebow notes that fictive kinship increases the intensity of relationships to the point where they occasionally explode: The demands of brothers and sisters for constant emotional and material aid may lead to situations that shatter the bonds. Fictive kinship is a prime example of family-as-ideology. In this process, reality is inverted. "Everybody" gets a continuous family, even though the strains and mobility associated with poverty may conspire to keep biological families apart. The idiom of kinship brings people together despite centrifugal circumstances.

It is important not to romanticize this pattern. It has enormous benefits, but its participants also pay high costs. One of the most obvious costs is leveling: Resources must be available for all and none may get ahead. Variations in the chance for survival are smoothed out in domestic networks via sharing. Stack tells the story of a central couple, Calvin and Magnolia, who unexpectedly inherit a sum of money. While the money might have enabled them to ensure their own security, it is gone within a few months. It disappears into the network to pay off bills, buy clothing for children, allow people to eat better.[36] Similar stories are told by Hannerz, Liebow, and Howell. No one gets ahead because individual upward mobility can be bought only at the price of cutting off the very people who have contributed to one's survival. Upward mobility becomes a terribly scarring experience under these circumstances. To get out, a person must stop sharing, which is unfamilial, unfriendly, and quite dangerous. It also requires exceptional circumstances. Gans [37] speaks of the pain that working-class children face if they attempt to use school as a means to achieve mobility, for they run into the danger of being cut off from their peer group. The chance for mobility may occur only once or twice in a lifetime—for example, at specific moments in a school career or in marriage. People rarely get the occasion, and when they do, to grasp it may simply be too costly. The pressures to stay in a supportive and constraining network, and to level out differences may be immense. They contribute to the instability of marriage and the normative nuclear family, for the old networks compete with the new unit for precious resources.

The family as an ideological construction is extremely important to poor people. Many studies show that the poor don't aspire to less "stable families," if that term is understood as nuclear families. They are simply much more realistic about their life chances. Ties to family, including fictive family, are the lifelines that simultaneously hold together and sustain individuals. My guess is that among the poor, families do not exhibit the radical split between "private, at home" and "public, at work" found in families of the stable working class. Neither work relations nor household relations are as continuous or as distinct. What *is* continuous is the sharing of reproduction costs throughout a network whose resources are known to all. There can be no privatization when survival may depend on rapid circulation of limited resources. In this process, women don't "represent" kinship to the outside world. They become the nodal points in family nets which span whatever control very poor people have over domestic and resource-getting arrangements. Families are what make the huge gap between norm and reality survivable.

It is particularly ironic that the ideology of family, so important to poor people, is used by ruling class ideologues to blame the poor for their own condition. In a society in which *all* Americans subscribe to some version of the normative nuclear family, it is cruelty to attack "the black family" as pathological. Mainstream culture, seeing the family as "what you work for" (and what works for you), uses "family language" to stigmatize those who are structurally prevented from accumulating stable resources. The very poor have used their families to cement and patch tenuous relations to survival; out of their belief in "family" they have invented networks capable of making next-to-nothing go a long way.[38] In response, they are told that their notion of family is inadequate. It isn't their notion of family that is deficient, but the relationship between household and productive resources.

If we now return to the political debate that opened this essay, I believe we can see that there are two different concepts of family at work. To achieve a normative family is something many categories of Americans are prevented from doing because of the ways that their households plug into tenuous resource bases. And when normative families are achieved, it is at substantial and differential costs to both men and women.

Having considered the meaning of family and household among class sectors with regular or unstable relations to wages, we should now consider those sectors for whom resource bases are more affluent. Analyzing the family and household life of the middle class is a tricky business. The term "middle class" is ambiguous; a majority of Americans identify themselves as part of it whenever they answer questionnaires, and the category obviously carries positive connotations. Historically, we take the notion from the Marxian definition of the petty bourgeoisie: that category of people who own small amounts of productive resources and have control over their working conditions in ways that proletarians do not. The term signifies a stage in proletarianization in which small-scale entrepreneurs, tradesfolk, artisans, and professionals essentially stand outside the wage-labor/capital relation. That stage is virtually over: There are ever fewer small-scale proprietors or artisans working on their own account in post–World War II America. We now use the term to refer to a different sector—employees in corporate management, government and organizational bureaucrats of various kinds, and professionals, many of whom work directly or indirectly for big business, the state, and semipublic institutions. On the whole, this "new middle class" is dependent on wages; as such, it bears the mark of proletarianization. Yet the group lives at a level that is quite different from the wage levels of workers.[39] Such a category is obviously hard to define; like all class sectors, it must be historically situated, for the middle class of early-twentieth-century America differs markedly from that of our own times. To understand what middle class means for the different groups, we need to know not only their present status but also the ethnic and regional variations in class structure within which their families entered America.

In a sense, the middle class is a highly ideological construction that pervades American culture; it is, among other things, the perspective from which mainstream social scientists approach the experiences of all the other sectors they attempt to analyze. To analyze the middle class's household formations and family patterns, we have to examine not only the data available on all the people who claim to be middle class but also explore the biases inherent in much of social science. This is a task beyond the scope of the present essay. Instead, I merely suggest a few tentative ideas as notes toward future research.

Households among the middle class are obviously based on a stable resource base that allows for some amount of luxury and discretionary spending. When exceptional economic resources are called for, nonfamilial institutions usually are available in the form of better medical coverage, expense accounts, pension plans, credit at banks, and so on. Such households may maintain their economic stability at the cost of geographical instability; male career choices may move households around like pieces on a chessboard. When far from family support networks, such households may get transitional aid from professional moving specialists, or institutions like the Welcome Wagon.[40] Middle-class households probably are able to rely on commodity forms rather than kinship processes to ease both economic and geographic transitions.

The families that organize such households are commonly thought to be characterized by egalitarian marriages.[41] Rubin comments that "egalitarian marriage" may be a biased gloss for a communication pattern in which the husband's career is in part reflected in the presentation of his wife.[42] To entertain intelligently, and instill the proper educational and social values in the children, women may need to know more about the male world. They represent the private credentials of family to the public world of their men at work. If this is the case, then "instrumental communication" might be a more appropriate term.

I am not prepared at this point to offer an analysis of middle-class kinship patterns, but I have a few hunches to present:

1. At this level, kinship probably shifts from the lateral toward the lineal. That is, resources (material and economic) are invested lineally, between parents, children, and grandchildren, and not dispersed into larger networks, as happens with working-class and poor families. Such a pattern would of course vary with geographical mobility, and possibly with ethnicity. There is usually a greater investment across generations, and a careful accumulation within them. This kind of pattern can be seen, for example, in the sums invested in children's educations, setting up professional practices, wedding gifts (in which major devolvement of property may occur), and so forth.

2. Perhaps friendship, rather than kinship, is the nexus within which the middle class invests its psychic and "familial" energies. Friendship allows for a great deal of affective support and exchange but usually does not include major resource pooling. It is a relation consistent with resource accumulation rather than dispersal. If the poor convert friendship into kinship to equalize pooling, it seems to me that the middle class does the converse: It reduces kinship exchanges, and replaces them with friendship, which protects them from pooling and leveling.[43]

There is one last sector of the American class system whose household and family patterns would be interesting to examine—the upper class, sometimes identified as the ruling class or the very rich. Once again, I limit myself to a few tentative observations. As one sociologist (either naive or sardonic) commented, "We know so little about the very wealthy because they don't answer our questionnaires." Indeed! They fund them rather than answer them. The few studies we do have (by authors such as Domhoff, Amory, Baltzell, Veblen) are highly suggestive. The upper class, they tell us, seems to hang together as a cultural phenomenon. They defend their own interests corporately, and have tremendous ideological importance.

We know very little about the household structure of the very rich. They are described as having multiple households that are recomposed seasonally [44] and filled with service workers rather than exclusively with kin and friends. While there is a general tendency toward "conspicuous consumption," we have no basic information on the relation of their resource bases to domestic arrangements.

When we turn to the family structure of the very rich, some interesting bits and pieces emerge (which may possibly be out of date). Families are described as extremely lineal and concerned with who they are rather than what they do. People have access to one another through their control of neighborhoods, schools, universities, clubs, churches, and ritual events. They are ancestor-oriented and conscious of the boundaries that separate the "best" families from all others. Families are obviously the units within which wealth is accumulated and transmitted. Yet the link between wealth and class is not so simple; some of the "best" families lose fortunes but remain in the upper class. Mobility is also possible. According to Baltzell,[45] under certain circumstances it is possible for nonmembers to enter the class via educational and work-related contacts. What emerges from the literature is a sketch of a group that is perhaps the only face-to-face subculture that America contains.

Women serve as gatekeepers of many of the institutions of the very rich.[46] They launch children, serve as board members at private schools, run clubs, and facilitate marriage pools through events like debuts and charity balls. Men also preside over exclusive clubs and schools, but different ones. The upper class appears to live in a world that is very sex-segregated. Domhoff mentions several other functions that very rich women fulfill. These include (1) setting social and cultural standards and (2) softening the rough edges of capitalism by doing charity and cultural work. While he trivializes the cultural standards that women set to things like dress and high art, I think he has alerted us to something more important. In the upper class, women "represent" the family to the outside world. But here, it is an outside world that is in many senses created by their own class (in the form of high cultural institutions, education, social welfare, and charity). Their public presence is an inversion of reality; they appear as wives and mothers, but it is not really their family roles but their class roles that dictate those appearances. To the extent that "everyone else" either has a wife/mother or is a wife/mother, upper-class women are available to be perceived as something both true and false. What they can do because of their families (and, ultimately, for their families) is utterly, radically different from what other women who "represent" their families can do. Yet what everyone sees is their womanness as family members rather than class members. They influence our cultural notions of what feminine and familial behavior should be. They simultaneously become symbols of domesticity and public service to which others may aspire. The very tiny percentage of very wealthy women who live in a sex-segregated world and have no need to work are thus perceived as benevolent and admirable by a much larger group of women whose relation to sex-role segregation and work is not nearly so benign. "Everybody" can yearn for a family in which sex-role segregation is valued; nobody else can have a family in which it is valued as highly as theirs. In upper-class families, at least as they present themselves to "the public," we see a systematic confusion of cultural values with the values of family fortunes. We have here an excellent illustration of how the ideas of the ruling class become part of the ruling ideas of society.

At each level of American society, households vary systematically as to resource base and their ability to tap wealth, wages, and welfare. Households are organized by families (which means relatives both distant and close, imaginary and real). Families both reflect and distort the material relations within which households are embedded. The working-class and middle-class households may *appear* isolated from the arenas in which production takes place. But, in fact, their families are formed to generate and deepen relations to those work processes that underwrite their illusion of autonomy. Women's experience with "the family" varies systematically by class because class expresses the material and social relations upon which their household bases rest. We need to explore their transformatory potential as well as the constraints that differential family patterns provide.

Women have structurally been put in the position of representing the contradictions between autonomy and dependence, between love and money, in the relations of families to capitalism. The ideological role that women have played needs to be demystified as we struggle toward a future in which consumption and reproduction will not be determined by capitalist production, in which households will not have access to such uneven resource bases, and in which women will neither symbolically nor in their real relations be forced to bridge the gap between affective norms and contradictory realities under the name of love. To liberate the notion of voluntary relations which the normative family is supposed to represent, we have to stop paying workers off in a coin called love.

Notes

1. The demographic concerns are clearly outlined in Mary Jo Bane, *Here to Stay: American Families in the Twentieth Century* (New York, 1976); historical issues of rapid change are briefly reviewed in Lois Decker O'Neill, "The Changing Family," *Wilson Quarterly*, Winter 1977; the political issues and public policy concerns are presented with polemical flair in Michael Novak, "The Family Out of Favor," *Harper's Magazine*, April 1976.

2. Overviews of the history of the family literature may be found in Elizabeth H. Pleck, "Two Worlds in One: Work and Family," *Journal of Social History*, December 1976: 178–95; Christopher Lasch, "The Family and History," *New York Review of Books* 22 (1975–76): 18, 19, 20; and Louise Tilly and Joan Scott, *Women, Work and Family* (New York, 1978). They all stress the complex relation between political-economic and ideological change that both condition and are conditioned by family patterns.

3. Jack Goody, "The Evolution of the Family," in *Household and Family in Past Time*, ed. Peter Laslett and Richard Wall (Cambridge, 1972).

4. Ibid. Also see David M. Schneider and Raymond T. Smith, *Class Differences and Sex Roles in American Kinship and Family Structure* (Englewood Cliffs, 1973).

5. There is a vast literature on this subject. Its mainstream interpretations in relation to family research are reviewed in Luther B. Otto, "Class and Status in Family Research," *Journal of Marriage and the Family* 37 (1975): 315–32. Marxist perspectives are presented in Charles H. Anderson, *The Political Economy of Social Class* (Englewood Cliffs, 1974); Anderson, *Toward a New Sociology* rev. ed.; (Homewood, Ill., 1974); Alfred Szymanski, "Trends in the American Class Structure," *Socialist Revolution*, no. 10 (July–August 1972); and Harry Braverman, *Labor and Monopoly Capital: The Degradation of Work in the Twentieth Century* (New York, 1974).

6. This composite is drawn from the works of Bennett Berger, *Working Class Suburb: A Study of Auto Workers in Suburbia* (Berkeley, 1968); Herbert J. Gans, *The Urban Villagers* (New York, 1962); Gans, *The Levittowners* (New York, 1967); Louise Kapp Howe, ed., *The White Majority: Between Poverty and Affluence* (New

York, 1970); Joseph Howell, *Hard Living on Clay Street* (New York, 1973); Mirra Komarovsky, *Blue Collar Marriage* (New York, 1962); Lillian Rubin, *Worlds of Pain* (New York, 1976); Joseph A. Ryan, ed., *White Ethnics: Life in Working Class America* (Englewood Cliffs, 1973); Nancy Seifer, "Absent From the Majority: Working Class Women in America," Middle America Pamphlet Series, National Project on Ethnic America, American Jewish Committee, 1973; Seifer, *Nobody Speaks for Me: Self-Portraits of American Working Class Women* (New York, 1976); Arthur B. Shostak, *Blue Collar Life* (New York, 1969); Richard Sennett and Jonathan Cobb, *The Hidden Injuries of Class* (New York, 1972); Patricia Cayo Sexton and Brendan Sexton, *Blue Collars and Hard Hats* (New York, 1971); and Studs Terkel, *Working* (New York, 1972).

7. Braverman, *Labor and Monopoly Capital*.

8. Louise Tilly and Joan Scott, "Women's Work in Nineteenth Century Europe," *Comparative Studies in Society and History* 17 (1975): 36–64.

9. See Ira Gernstein, "Domestic Work and Capitalism," *Radical America* 7 (1973): 101–30.

10. Linda Gordon, *Women's Body, Women's Right: A Social History of Birth Control in America* (New York, 1976).

11. Louise Tilly, "Reproduction, Production and the Family among Textile Workers in Roubaix, France" (paper presented at the Conference on Social History, February 1977).

12. The economic value of housework has been the subject of vigorous debate in Marxist literature in recent years. The debate was begun with the publication of Mariarosa Dalla Costa, "Women and the Subversion of the Community," *Radical America* 6 (1972): 67–102; and continued by Wally Secombe. "The Housewife and Her Labour Under Capitalism," *New Left Review* 83 (1974): 3–24; Jean Gardiner, "Women's Domestic Labour," *New Left Review* 89 (1975): 47–71; Lise Vogel, "The Earthly Family," *Radical America* 7 (1973): 9–50; Gerstein, "Domestic Work and Capitalism"; and others. See also Heidi I. Hartmann, "Capitalism and Women's Work in the Home, 1900–1930" (Ph.D. dissertation, Yale University, 1974); and Joann Vanek, "Time Spent in Housework," *Scientific American*, November 1974, 116–20, for American case historical materials, and Nona Glazer-Malbin, "Review Essay: Housework," *Signs* 1:905–22, for a review of the field.

13. For historical, sociological, and political-economic analyses of women's economic position in the labor market, see the special issue of *Signs*, Barbara B. Reagan and Martha Blaxall, eds., "Women and the Workplace," 1, no. 3, pt. 2 (1976). See also U.S. Bureau of the Census, *Statistical Abstract of the U.S.*, 1974, for statistical data on demography and workforce participation rates of women.

14. Schneider and Smith, *Class Differences and Sex Roles in American Kinship and Family Structure*, chap. 5.

15. Rubin, *Worlds of Pain*, chap. 4.

16. Ibid., pp. 56 f.

17. See ibid.; also Shostak, *Blue Collar Life*, and Howell, *Hard Living on Clay Street*.

18. See Rubin, *Worlds of Pain*; Shostak, *Blue Collar Life*; Sennett and Cobb, *The Hidden Injuries of Class*; and Terkel, *Working*.

19. Rubin, *Worlds of Pain*.

20. U.S. Bureau of Census, *Statistical Abstract of the U.S.*, 1974, 221 f.

21. Sylvia Junko Yanagisako, "Women-Centered Kin Networks in Urban, Bilateral Kinship," *American Ethnologist*, 4 (1977): 207–26. 1977.

22. This literature is reviewed in Yanagisako, "Women-Centered Networks." Further instances are found in the sources listed in note 6. The pattern is given much attention in Peter Wilmott and Michael Young, *Family and Kinship in East London* (London, 1957); and in Elizabeth Bott, *Family and Social Network* (New York, 1971).

23. Batya Weinbaum and Amy Bridges, "The Other Side of the Paycheck: Monopoly Capital and the Structure of Consumption," *Monthly Review* 28 (1976): 88–103.

24. Seifer, "Absent From the Majority; Working Class Women in America"; and Seifer, *Nobody Speaks For Me: Self-Portraits of American Working Class Women*.

25. Howell, *Hard Living on Clay Street*.

26. Throughout her work, Rubin (*Worlds of Pain*) is especially sensitive to this issue and provides an excellent discussion of individual life cyles in relation to domestic cycles. She explains why the labeling issue is such a critical one (p. 223, note 5).

27. Howell's study (*Hard Living on Clay Street*) provides important and sensitive insights into the domestic lives of poor and working white families, collected in the style of Oscar Lewis. Composite black family studies include Ulf Hannerz, *Soulside: Inquiries into Ghetto Culture and Community* (New York, 1969); Joyce Ladner, *Tomorrow's Tomorrow: The Black Woman* (New York, 1971); Elliot Liebow, *Tally's Corner* (Boston, 1967); Lee Rainwater, *Behind Ghetto Walls: Black Families in a Federal Slum* (Chicago, 1970); John Scanzoni, *The Black Family in Modern Society* (Rockleigh, N.J., 1971); Carol B. Stack, *All Our Kin: Strategies for Survival in a Black Community* (New York, 1974); Charles Valentine, *Culture and Poverty: Critique and Counter-Proposals* (Chicago, 1968); and Charles Valentine, "Black Studies and Anthropology: Scholarly and Political Interests in Afro-American Culture," *McCaleb Module in Anthropology*, no. 15.

28. Hannerz, *Soulside: Inquiries into Ghetto Culture and Community*.

29. Liebow, *Tally's Corner*.

30. Stack, *All Our Kin: Strategies for Survival in a Black Community*.

31. David Caplowitz, *The Poor Pay More* (New York, 1967).

32. Meyer Fortes, "Introduction," in *The Development Cycle in Domestic Groups*, ed. Jack Goody (Cambridge, 1972).

33. Ladner, *Tomorrow's Tomorrow: The Black Woman*; and Stack, *All Our Kin: Strategies for Survival in a Black Community*.

34. See especially Stack, *All Our Kin: Strategies for Survival in a Black Community*, chap. 7.

35. Ibid., p. 21.

36. Ibid., pp. 105–7.

37. Gans, *The Urban Villagers*.

38. It is easier to make this point given the consciousness-raising works of Alex Haley, *Roots* (New York, 1976); and Herbert Gutman, *The Black Family in Slavery and Freedom, 1750–1925* (New York, 1976). They point out—in popular

and scholarly language respectively—the historical depth and importance of this pattern.

39. Braverman, *Labor and Monopoly Capital*, chap. 18.

40. Vance Packard, "Mobility: Restless America," *Mainliner Magazine*, May 1977.

41. Schneider and Smith, *Class Differences and Sex Roles in American Kinship and Family Structure*, chap. 4.

42. Rubin, *Worlds of Pain*.

43. I know of no substantial work describing the uses of friendship versus kinship in the middle class. Ingelore Fritsch is currently conducting research on the networks of families in a suburban, middle-class, East Coast community; her results should add to this discussion.

44. William Hoffman, *David: Report on a Rockefeller* (Secaucus, N.J., 1971); E. Digby Baltzell, *Philadelphia Gentlemen: The Making of a National Upper Class* (New York, 1958).

45. Baltzell, *Philadelphia Gentlemen: The Making of a National Upper Class*.

46. G. William Domhoff, *The Higher Circles* (New York, 1971).

11

ELI ZARETSKY

The Place of the Family
in the Origins
of the Welfare State

*The abstraction of the state as such was not born until the modern
era, because the abstraction of private life was not created until the
modern era.*

—Marx, *"Critique of Hegel's Doctrine
of the State" (1843) in* EARLY WRITINGS

Posing the Problem

Women, the Family, and the Welfare State

The main strands of modern American social thought have tied the
decline of the family, or at least its narrowing, to the rise of the welfare
state, which, until recently, was supposed to remedy this decline. This
relation was anticipated by the many nineteenth-century reformers who
blamed the family's failings for the evils they sought to eliminate, and who
modeled orphan asylums, schools, prisons, and mental hospitals on the
well-run family. The full expression of this perspective occurred during
the "Progressive era" (1890–1920), when the essential structure of the
modern welfare state was put together. That period's reforms were generally defended with the argument that industry had obviated many of the

I wish to thank Ellen DuBois for reintroducing me to American history and for urging
me to "never forget the oppression of women," and to thank Carol Stack and Jim Gilbert for
support when I needed it. The American Council of Learned Societies made it financially
possible. I would also like to thank Mari Jo Buhle, Barbara Epstein, Eric Foner, Linda
Gordon, Karen Hansen, Michael Katz, Fred Konefsky, David Plotke, Anne Firor Scott,
Wally Seccombe, Kathryn Sklar, Martin Sklar, Judy Stacey, Jules Tygiel, Barrie Thorne,
and Kay Trimberger for reading an earlier draft.

traditional functions performed by the family, thereby requiring the creation of new institutions to perform tasks the family no longer could perform. For example, John Dewey explained the need for progressive education by arguing that children were no longer taught the necessary industrial skills within the home.[1]

During the 1940s and '50s the dominant school of American sociology, led by Talcott Parsons, hypothesized a process by which "functions" were "transferred" from families to specialized institutions such as schools, hospitals, and asylums. This process, Parsons and others argued, would leave the family better adapted to the specialized tasks left to it, especially child rearing. This perspective, with its implication of inevitable progressive development, was incorporated uncritically into the vast monographic literature produced by historians of reform schools, poorhouses, mental asylums, and the like, and broadly influenced historians of social reform. It also pervaded the training of social workers, child-care specialists, and other professionals.[2]

From the late nineteenth century until very recently, American socialists and communists shared the progressive/liberal faith in the growth of the state. During the 1930s an alternative view had developed in the work of the Frankfurt School theorists, several of whom migrated to the United States. Responding especially to the growth of fascism, Max Horkheimer and Theodor Adorno attacked the "rationalization" of modern society and extolled the family as the last repository of human ties being eroded by the state, but their highly abstract discussion had little resonance at a time when the Left was preoccupied with preserving New Deal programs against the Right.[3]

By the 1960s, however, both New Left and black radicals began to break with earlier ties to governmental liberalism. In 1971, David Rothman's influential synthesis, *The Discovery of the Asylum*, developed a leftist critique of governmental intervention into the lives of the poor. According to Rothman, the early mental hospitals, reformatories, poorhouses, and asylums were institutions of "social control" rather than benign aid. A few years after the furor raised over the Moynihan Report's attitudes toward black families, Rothman showed that the distinction between "normal" and "abnormal" or "pathological" families was not a scientific one but had arisen in the early nineteenth century. However, Rothman failed to explain the roots of this distinction in America's social structure and made no reference to the coercive pressures on those who remained within the norm.[4]

Anticipated by both the Frankfurt School and Rothman, Christopher Lasch's recent works, *Haven in a Heartless World* and *The Culture of Narcissism*, have established the outlines of a new synthesis. Lasch was more historically concrete than the Frankfurt theorists, and more theoretically coherent than Rothman. His work broke with Parsons' evolutionary model and sought to show that the contemporary family was "the product of human agency, not of abstract social 'forces.'" *Haven in a Heartless World* caustically argued that the modern liberal approach to the family, with all its apparent diversity, remains an apology for the special interests of middle-class professionals, behind which lies the need of twentieth-century capital to reorganize and socialize the sphere of private and familial life. *The Culture of Narcissism* pointed to the disintegrative effects that this reorganization has had on the character structure of men, women, and children.[5]

In particular, Lasch's Freudianism marked a new and positive development in the body of modern theory concerned with the welfare state. Previous socialist and liberal accounts had lacked any theoretical conception of the needs to be met or not met by the welfare state and therefore tended to be quantitative and empirical in content: Had the "standard of living" increased? Did "poverty" remain? Had "income redistribution" been fostered? Lasch rejected these economistic approaches and sought to show that the expansion of the welfare state had been an assault on primary human ties and on the instinctual roots of individuality.

But in one crucial respect Lasch remained within the functionalist paradigm he rejected. Lasch equated both primary ties and individuality with "the family" and, like Parsons, sought to conceptualize the impact of state intervention on the family. While Lasch judged state intervention negatively, he agreed with Parsons that it had occurred and that the modern welfare state had substantially displaced the family as the key agent of social reproduction. Hence, Lasch spoke of the state's "invasion of the private realm," described his subject as "the assertion of social control over activities once left to individuals or their families," and complained of the "proletarianization of parents" by the state.[6] Both Lasch and Parsons shared a unilinear model describing a flow of authority and purpose from the family to the experts, in one case encouraging a bland optimism and in the other a one-sided pessimism. Lasch's sweeping condemnation of the welfare state tended to blur the distinction between those whose autonomy has truly been undermined by the state—those in prison, on parole, or on welfare—and the rest of us, whose autonomy may well be strengthened by the army of professional therapists, planners, educators, pediatricians, and the like with whom we are surrounded.

Perhaps more significantly, Lasch mounted a general defense of "the family" without considering the ambivalent relation of women toward that insitution. Coming after a decade of feminist questioning of the traditional ideal of what is popularly termed the "nuclear family," Lasch's work was widely read as a rebuke to what he elsewhere called the family's "feminist-socialist-psychiatric critics."[7] A critique of the nuclear family model was important not only to feminists but to certain segments of the New Left and, in the debate over the Moynihan Report, to black and Third World opinion as well. Lasch's unilateral defense of the family contrasts strikingly with the place that a critique of the family has occupied in every modern revolution, from seventeenth-century England to contemporary China and Cuba, sometimes embodying a feminist point of view and sometimes not, but in either case forming an inescapable heritage for modern revolutionary thought.

Coincident with Lasch's work but independent of it, a feminist critique of the welfare state emerged; like Lasch's, it sought to break with the optimistic evolutionism of the earlier reform tradition. The "social feminists" of the Progressive era, such as Jane Addams, Florence Kelley, and even Charlotte Perkins Gilman, were leading advocates of the welfare state because they believed it would foster women's special contributions as mothers and as professionals. Barbara Ehrenreich and Deirdre English's *For Her Own Good* and Heidi Hartmann's "Capitalism, Patriarchy and Job Segregation by Sex," the most important contemporary feminist accounts, criticize the welfare state because they believe it was premised on women's special responsibility for the family, especially for children.[8] Far from finding that the welfare state had eroded the family, these works argued that it had promoted the particular "nuclear family" characterized by women's isolation within the home and subordinate position within the work force.

The account of progressive reform in *For Her Own Good* shares a good deal with Lasch's, the difference being that Ehrenreich and English seek to show that it was *women's* autonomy and the ties of a women's culture that were undermined by the rise of the professions. For example, Ehrenreich and English portray the experts as men "wooing their female constituency." Hartmann's account represents an even more decisive break with prevailing lines of thought. In her view, nothing in the nature of capitalism entailed the kind of welfare state that developed and, particularly, the role it fostered for women in an industrial society. Instead, taking protective legislation for women as a case in point, she seeks to show that the enactment of this reform depended upon the prior agreement of capitalist men and working-class men whose sexual and economic interests converged on the issue of excluding women from equal participation in wage labor.

If Lasch's work downplays the conflict between women and the family, Hartmann's ignores women's historic commitment to the family (i.e., to heterosexuality, men, and motherhood). In spite of their common emphasis on "agency," both Lasch and Hartmann privilege one group of historical actors. Lasch portrays the welfare state as the creation of middle-class reformers and professionals, ignoring the active initiative of the urban working class and the poor in bringing about reforms. Hartmann portrays it as the creation of men, ignoring the powerful drive of women, including feminists, for such reforms as protective legislation; and Ehrenreich and English ignore the fact that so many of the "masculinist" experts they condemn were women.

Lasch's Freudianism, the feminism of Hartmann, and Ehrenreich and English mark important advances in understanding the history of the welfare state. But the advances are never joined: Lasch does not grapple with the possibility that the family is intrinsically patriarchal, while Ehrenreich, English, and Hartmann write as if families were largely imposed on women, rather than arising in good part out of women's own needs and desires.

This essay is a reexamination of the origins of the welfare state in America that seeks to build on the advances made by these authors. While I ascribe an important place in the origins of the welfare state to both trade-union protectionism and middle-class reform, I make room for other movements: early twentieth-century urban liberalism and, especially, feminism. More important, I try to show that the class and sexual structure of American society, rather than the intentions of any single group, shaped the meaning of diverse reform efforts in unforeseen (and still untheorized) ways. While I agree with Lasch that the welfare state has had destructive effects on psychological bonds, I do not equate these bonds with the family but argue instead that "the family," in the conventional sense of a private, self-supporting nuclear unit, was to a large extent created, or at least reconstituted, by the modern state, first in the "liberal" or "laissez-faire" and then in the "welfare" phases of its history. While I agree with Ehrenreich, English, and Hartmann that the welfare state has had destructive effects on women, I also try to understand the reasons for the failure of the feminist movement to foresee the negative side of the reforms that it played such a role in sponsoring .

The History of the Welfare State Viewed in the Context of the History of the Family

I begin by distinguishing those aspects of the family that are historically specific—especially its emergence as a private economic unit and the domestic ideology that accompanies its economic role—from the more deeply rooted biological, psychological, and social necessities that the historically modern family now accommodates. The historic tendency in America—the result of the market (i.e., the frontier) and of industrialization—has been to weaken or destroy primary bonds of kinship and community and to make the economically independent individual or family responsible for his or her welfare and for the care of those (especially children) who cannot care for themselves. Changes in state policy and in the law have reflected this tendency. Such scholars as Nancy Cott and Carl Degler have traced the "birth" of the modern American ideal of the family as a private institution to the late eighteenth and early nineteenth centuries, and it is widely agreed that the nineteenth-century liberal state fostered and presupposed ideals of individual or familial autonomy.[9] I argue that this is also true of the welfare state; it fostered individualism and familial autonomy, but in a historically specific form that weakened the primary human ties of interdependence on which individualism and autonomy ultimately depend.

In a recent article on the psychological bases of the welfare state, psychoanalyst Willard Gaylin described some of the biological and psychological limits to the pursuit of individual independence.[10] At one end of life, human infancy, characterized by prolonged helplessness; at the other end, sickness, old age, and death. Both shadow the modern adult's insistence on independence, which often rides uncertainly on a denial of the realities of dependency. "All of us," Gaylin writes, "inevitably spend our lives evolving from an initial to a final stage of dependence. If we are fortunate enough to achieve power and relative independence along the way it is a transient and passing glory." Such a perspective on human biopsychology emphasizes that primary ties of dependence, nurturance, and mutual help are an inevitable part of the structure of any society, even one like our own, ostensibly organized around individualism and independence. Furthermore, Gaylin's perspective directly addresses the issue of sexual inequality, for, as contemporary feminists have argued, the unequal division of responsibility for nurturing the dependent, and above all children, is a key element in defining women's oppression. It is a tragic paradox that the bases of love, dependence, and altruism in human life and the historical oppression of women have been found within the same matrix.

Ties of sexuality, kinship, and biological and psychological dependence are inevitable; self-supporting nuclear families are not. The relevance of this distinction recurs throughout the history of the American family. Herbert Gutman's *The Black Family in Slavery and Freedom* demonstrates how the slave community built and maintained elaborate systems of kinship after the African systems were destroyed by the passage. Primary bonds between mothers and children, as well as between men and their families, were sustained through being imbedded in a larger kin-based community. The psychological effectiveness of these ties survived the physical disruption of the couple or the family unit. Of course, slaves could not maintain independent, self-supporting economic units; kinship, not the family, supplied the "normal idiom of social relations." [11] Even at present among the welfare mothers studied by Carol Stack, one of the groups least integrated into the labor force, family life is organized around kinship, reciprocity, and female networks rather than around an employed head of household.[12]

Similiar themes pervade the history of the working-class family. Social historians of immigration such as Rudolph Vecoli, Tamara Haraven, and Virginia Yans-McLaughlin have pointed to the importance of kinship ties and of the ethnic community among the immigrants, and in contrast to previous scholars, have argued that these survived the entry into an industrial society.[13] But there is a vast difference between a society *organized* around ties of kin and community and the *survival* of kin and community in a society organized around wage labor. The classic works in the history of immigration—William I. Thomas and Florian Znaniecki's *The Polish Peasant in Europe and America* and Oscar Handlin's *The Uprooted*—rightly argue that the kinship ties and communal obligations of traditional peasant society were giving way, even before immigration, to the individualizing pressures of a wage-labor-based economy. Thomas and Znaniecki contrast the peasant "the basis of [whose] existence is in the group" to "the man with a workman's psychology," driven by "a new idea which we may term the standard of living," the essence of which "lies in the power which the individual has over his economic environment by virtue of his income." [14] In this perspective, the panoply of "survivals" cited by the new social historians—grandparents living nearby, the persistence of rural values in the decision to buy homes rather than educate children, the role of kin in softening the blows of unemployment—need to be understood either as points of resistance against the imposition of wage labor or as aspects of their compliance with it.[15]

There was no need for the state to "impose" the family or sex roles on the immigrants, as Ehrenreich and English argue. Nothing so psychologically fundamental could have been imposed from without. On the other hand, private, self-supporting nuclear families were neither the legacy of slave or immigrant history nor intrinsic to human nature, as ties of sexuality, nurturance, and dependence are intrinsic. As slaves maintained families, so would the immigrants, but in neither case under conditions of their own choosing. The power of those conditions is indicated by an examination of the process by which, at the end of the nineteenth and beginning of the twentieth centuries, immigrants from throughout the world, representing a vast diversity of cultural, religious, and familial backgrounds, came within a generation or so to settle on a more or less common ideal: the nuclear family. While there may well have been some universal grammar of sexual/parental possibilities that underlay the apparent diversity of immigrant families, it was the attempt to survive in an industrializing society—to get a job, to support a family—that supplied the common historical ground upon which that diversity met and within which those possibilities could be realized.

The American political system, overall, has sought to foster independent, self-supporting units (individuals or families) rather than a particular family form. Social reformers and philanthropists throughout the nineteenth century took private property to be the basis of a "normal" (i.e., self-supporting) family, properly divided in role and function according to sex. When the rise of industry in the late nineteenth century threw the possibility of familial autonomy and self-sufficiency into question, many traditions and interests converged on a new solution during the Progressive years. Just as private property was assumed as the basis of the independent political or social individual, according to eighteenth- and nineteenth-century reformers, so a wage or salary was assumed to play that role by twentieth-century reformers; this assumption has been incorporated into the reforms of the welfare state. The fact that wage labor has made family life possible at all supplied the crucial mediation that made the middle-class preaching concerning the family and domesticity even plausible to working-class immigrants and led both the middle class and the working class to support a more active role for the state. Rather than the state undermining the family, it is difficult to imagine how any form of the family could have survived the enormously destructive uprooting that accompanied industrialization without some intervention from the state. The issue is not whether the welfare state eroded the family, but rather in what form it preserved it. My argument is that the family has been preserved as an economically private unit and that most of the normative aspects of state policy are based on that.

I make this argument in two parts. In the first, entitled "Origins of the Welfare State," I begin by briefly describing colonial New England as a point of contrast. Colonial families were to a great extent the agents of community functions; political authority was patriarchal, resting on what was termed "family government." As Gaylin suggests, the place of dependence in society and the place of women were inextricably linked. I then describe the nineteenth-century liberal prehistory of the welfare state. Women especially welcomed the development of a liberal polity in the nineteenth century, which promised to free them from the political control of men. At the same time there emerged new principles and techniques for caring for the poor and the insane that sought to foster independence and self-reliance rather than accept the inevitability of charity, dependence, and need. Only from an ahistorical perspective do the asylum reformers or the charity organization movement leaders appear paternalistic; their principles were primarily individualistic and laissez-faire. Nineteenth-century feminism and reform, however, were aimed not only at patriarchy and paternalism; insofar as they assumed market principles, they were often posed against the ties of human interdependence.

In "Progressivism and the Modern Family," I argue that the market-based principles of individualism and self-reliance were not repudiated by the emphasis on "altruism" and "interdependence" so often heard during the Progressive years but were incorporated into the sociological perspective that then took shape. The reforms of the Progressive era were premised on the perpetuation of the self-supporting family into the era of the large corporation. While new forms of collective organization were formed—trade unions, professions, reformed political organizations—market individualism permeated these new forms as well as permeating the welfare state.

Origins of the Welfare State

Colonial New England

According to Karl Polanyi, "the individual in primitive society is not threatened by starvation unless the community as a whole is in a like predicament. . . . The principle of freedom from want was equally acknowledged under almost every and any type of social organization up to about the beginning of sixteenth-century Europe, when the modern ideas on the poor put forth by the humanist Vives were argued before the Sorbonne." [16] Similarly, Ernst Troeltsch speaks of "the pleasure in giving away that which cannot be eaten, which is to be found in all social systems based upon a natural economy." [17] The decline of the feudal lord with his retainers and of the medieval Catholic emphasis on alms provides the backdrop for the modern state's responsibility for the poor. The earliest history of that responsibility is to be found in the series of sixteenth-century laws that sought to enforce a market in labor, culminating in the Elizabethan Poor Law of 1601. According to Christopher Hill, "the main problem was to transform the mental outlook of the lower orders so that they no longer waited at the rich man's gate for charity, but went out to offer their services on the labour market." [18]

Colonial New England, though it certainly relied on Protestant/ bourgeois principles of contractualism and labor, was still largely corporatist in its outlook, imbued with what Perry Miller called "an elemental sense of the organic body." [19] So much was this the case that our present practice of opposing the family to the state makes no sense when applied to colonial New England. Although using the Elizabethan Poor Law as the basis of a colonial welfare system—as did the other American colonies—the Puritans, relatively free from the market upheaval of seventeenth-century England, established a close continuity between families and local government. This continuity contrasts with the commitment to the private family unit that came to prevail later, along with the market system. Because of the overlap between colonial government and the colonial family, I will call New England "patriarchal" and reserve the term for that usage.

The partriarchal family, no more and no less than the rest of society, was thought by the Puritans to be a natural unit, created by God, imbued with possibilities for sin and redemption, and governed by natural law. The family generally consisted, wrote the English authority Richard Baxter in 1673, of a *"pater familias, mater familias, filius and servus,"* but the essentials were present as long as there was ruler and ruled.[20] Hence it was plausible for the challenged monarchs of seventeenth-century England to buttress their claims to absolutism and divine right by analogy to the position of fathers within the family. The king, proclaimed James I in 1609, is *"parens patriae, the politic father of his people."* [21]

The claim of the father to obedience was directly linked to his responsibilities as "family-governor" to provide for his subordinates and dependents. According to Edmund Morgan, the "chief problem for the [Puritan] state . . . was to see that family governors did their duty." [22] The colonial New England family was responsible for the care of the poor, the widowed, and the disabled—those who could not care for themselves. Similar principles prevailed regarding education. Fathers were obliged to teach their children certain skills and precepts. If they failed, the township intervened to place the child in another household. The Massachusetts Assembly of 1745 ordered all children over the age of six who were still ignorant of the alphabet removed to another family. Fathers were also responsible for training their children in useful occupations. The apprenticeship system contracted children—and not only orphans or the very poor—between families, with the new family being made responsible for education and upbringing.[23]

In all these ways colonial New England contrasts with the market-based system that followed. The protectionist principles it established— the poor law, *parens patriae*—have remained the legal basis of an ever expanding series of governmental interventions in regard to women, children, and the family ranging from reform schools and truant officers through protective legislation for women. But although the language of the law has been rooted in a corporatist era, its content and meaning have reflected the social changes that occurred with the growth of the market.

Liberalism and the Family

The modern English and American liberal tradition broke with the patriarchal assumption of continuity between families and the state. Already in 1685 Locke mocked Filmer's belief that authority was vested in a kind of transhistorical fatherhood: "a strange kind of domineering phantom," Locke called it, " a gigantic form." [24] In Locke's view it was property that gave the "political quality to personality."[25] In the development of the modern state the ownership of property was taken to establish a sphere of autonomy around the individual or family, into which the state could not intrude. "Property," over time, acquired many meanings, including labor and ultimately one's personhood.

Only with the attempt to establish the market as an autonomous sphere of society did the ideal of the family as a private (i.e., nongovernmental) unit take hold. Tocqueville in 1835 contrasted the father in an aristocratic family with his "political right to command" to the father in a democracy, "the legal part of parental authority vanish[ed]."[26] It was only after a boundary was drawn between civil or private society (individuals and their families) and the state that one can begin to speak of state intervention into the family, much less of the state replacing the family.

The various ways in which the state began to take over responsibilities from families in the early nineteenth century, or to intervene into the family, should not be understood solely in terms of the expansion of state authority. These new forms of intervention simultaneously involved a drastic limitation on the state when compared to the powers of seventeenth- and even eighteenth-century governments to intervene. The terms on which the laissez-faire state could intervene into the family were similar to those by which it could intervene into the economy. The liberal or laissez-faire state had the responsibility for establishing the arena and the formal rules within which private (i.e., economic or otherwise civil) activity proceeded (e.g., it was responsible for international relations or currency). The laissez-faire state was permitted to intervene into the economy where private means were inadequate, for example, in the building of canals or public education. Finally, the laissez-faire state was obliged to intervene where misbehavior had taken place, as in an obstruction of trade.

In order to lay the basis for an understanding of the individualistic character of the welfare state I now discuss three currents of nineteenth-century reform that, while based on laissez-faire or liberal principles, nonetheless called for governmental intervention into the family. The first, which was the most purely laissez-faire, was the feminist effort to establish a nonpatriarchal family by unblocking obstacles to equality and freedom of contract in the realms of marriage, divorce, custody law, and economic rights. The second, a more direct precursor to the welfare state, was the transfer of responsibility for the poor and the dependent from families and the community to what became state institutions. David Rothman has termed this process "the discovery of the asylum," and Michael Katz has called it "the rise of the institutional state." These phrases are misleading because these reforms were not meant to build institutions but rather to rehabilitate and perfect individuals, largely by encouraging a certain kind of private family, and in that way to ultimately eliminate the need for institutions. The third is the development of the principle of "scientific charity" in the late nineteenth century that, in my view, supplies a bridge between the early nineteenth-century emphasis on rehabilitation and the reforms of the Progressive era. By the end of the nineteenth century the idea that a living wage for individuals or families was a "right" rather than "charity" began to be accepted and is generally taken to mark the beginnings of the interventionist welfare state. I intend my examination of nineteenth-century reform to show the way in which the progressive principle of a "living wage" involved a rejection of the principle of personal or social interdependence, rather than its acceptance.

Feminism and Marital Reform

The antebellum feminist redefinition of individualism to include women was perhaps the most important, though also the most removed, contribution that laissez-faire thinking made to the welfare state. Morton Horowitz has described the general shift in the antebellum period from a "protective, regulative, paternalistic" conception of law to one "thought of as facilitative of individual desires." [27] Beginning in the 1840s, feminists sought to extend this conception of contract into the sphere of the family. They challenged the patriarchal common-law presumption of marital unity by which husband and wife were taken to be one person—and that one the husband, as Blackstone had put it. They sought to revoke the husband's legal right to sexual services from his wife, and the presumption that child custody should be inevitably awarded to the father in case of divorce. They achieved some success in the passage of the Married Women's Property Acts of the 1840s in New York, California, and other states, which gave women the right to trade and contract on the marketplace, to earn wages and to spend them.[28] The same period saw the beginnings of divorce reform. The general idea underlying these movements was expressed by Stanton: to make democracy "the law of the family as well as the state." [29]

After the Civil War and Reconstruction, the idea that government should intervene to protect individual rights gained much wider currency. During the late nineteenth century there was an upsurge in legislative and judicial action concerning the family, reflecting an ever-rising number of women (and children) who called on the state to protect their rights against patriarchal authority, as well as a rising number of fathers who called on the state to aid them in maintaining their authority. These laws and cases touched not only on property rights but on the nature and limits of parental authority and obligations. The most important issue was divorce, as the rate rose by more than 600 percent between 1860 and 1920.[30]

The relevance of these currents to the twentieth-century welfare state became clear during the Progressive era when judges, social workers, and government officials, who were at least influenced to think of the family in terms of individual rights for women and children, encountered the traditional, often preliberal families of the immigrants. As Thomas and Znaniecki then argued, the effect of government intervention on the traditional extended family (in that case, Polish-American) would inevitably be destructive since the modern state placed matters on the basis of individual rights and of a contest between individuals and denied the traditional subjection of the individual to the group.[31] As if anticipating this objection, nineteenth-century judges and legislatures sought to protect a special place for the family in the face of continuing, often feminist, efforts to establish the existence of individual rights in the domestic realm.

As Norma Basch and William Leach have recently shown, judges interpreted the Married Women's Property Acts as protecting women from dissolute husbands rather than as enabling them to trade on their own. Judge Joseph Story distinguished marriage from all other contracts since, as the "basis of the whole fabric of civilized society, it could not be dissolved at will." [32] The continued preservation of a foothold for the *parens patriae* tradition, even amid the high tide of laissez-faire, was significant. It indicates a recognition of the impossibility of ever organizing society on a completely individualistic basis, as well as the effort to make women pay the costs of that recognition. By the late nineteenth century, feminists became much less concerned with purely legal changes in the family and sought instead to establish social and economic equality between the sexes, both within the family and outside it. At that point they themselves called upon the *parens patriae* tradition to protect motherhood, which is not the same as "the family."

Economic Liberalism and "Moral Treatment"

The dramatic construction of nonfamilial institutions for the dependent poor, the orphaned, the sick, and the insane in the early nineteenth century is a more direct precursor of the twentieth-century welfare state. But the historical significance of these institutions is poorly described in terms of a transfer of functions from families to the state. The basic outlook of the asylums was as much rooted in early-nineteenth-century political economy, with its attack on patriarchal and community charity, and its aim of a society of self-supporting individual family units, as in religious forms of humanitarianism. As the spread of the market broke down older paternalistic and community traditions, such as apprenticeship, it created a new form of dependency largely unique to market societies: individuals outside families. At the same time, the market supplied a new model of social health: the self-supporting individual or family, which the nineteenth-century agencies of rehabilitation took as their goal.

The building of the asylums has been described well by David Rothman and Michael Katz. Except for prisons, these asylums began as private corporations that were increasingly taken over or supplemented by state governments. In the early 1820s, the famous reports of Josiah Quincey and John Yates encouraged the abolition of "outdoor relief"—aid given to the poor while they remained in their own (or others') families—and led to the construction of a network of poorhouses in New York and Massachusetts. The first state mental hospital was built at Worcester, Massachusetts, in 1835. The first orphan asylums were founded in the same period, and by 1850 had replaced apprenticeship as the main means of caring for orphaned children. The first state reform school was opened in 1848.[33]

The sense in which these new institutions severed the chains that united communities around a recognition of the need to give, and be given to, was captured in William Wordsworth's 1797 poem, "The Old Cumberland Beggar," inspired by similar developments in English history. Wordsworth's poem contrasts a society organized around mutual help and dependence with one in which the dependents have been isolated from the community. Wordsworth describes the beggar: [34]

> *Him from my childhood have I known; and then*
> *He was so old, he seems not older now.*

The beggar had a stated round; everyone knew him. At regular fixed days at different houses he received alms, sometimes food, more rarely money. Wordsworth lashes out at the building of the poorhouses:

> *Statesmen! ye deem not this man useless . . . ye*
> *Who have a broom still ready in your hands*
> *To rid the world of nuisances . . .*

and explains the value of the man to the community:

> *The villagers in him*
> *Behold a record which together binds*
> *Past deeds and offices of charity,*
> *Else unremembered . . .*

He calls the beggar "a silent monitor" with whom "the easy man who sits at his own door," "the robust and young, the prosperous and unthinking" can learn what the beggar himself also must learn, that we are all of us "the dealers-out of some small blessings . . . that we have all of us one human heart."

202 / ELI ZARETSKY

The concept of individual rehabilitation that these asylums were built to effect is much more important for understanding the nature of the welfare state than the fact that they ultimately expanded the domain of the state. The philanthropists and reformers who built these asylums rejected the idea that mental illness or poverty were inevitable in any community and instead tried to think through the causes of deviance and dependency and their cure. According to their conception, both the person's heredity and environmental history (particularly the family history) established the context within which his or her free will or moral faculty expressed itself. The asylums were a way of changing people's environment so that they became responsible for themselves once again. This principle of individual responsibility, not the growth of tutelary institutions, marks the early nineteenth century as the seedbed of what Lasch has called "the therapeutic state." [35] The doctors, penologists, reformers, neurologists, and philanthropists who built the early asylums shared an optimistic, perfectionist—and ultimately laissez-faire—outlook similar to the emphasis on self-reliance and self-help that characterized other reformers and radicals during the antebellum period.

In his book David Rothman gave a typical case history of a prisoner, convicted of forgery at the age of fifty-five and discharged from prison in 1829:

> No. 315—A.N., born in Massachusetts; father was killed at Quebec when he was very young; family soon after scattered and he was bound out to a farmer, with whom he lived till of age; was a wild, rude boy, and early addicted to some bad habits, drinking, swearing, etc.

The man who wrote this case history seems to have believed that the boy had inborn traits (wildness, rudeness) and an unfortunate family situation but that in a new environment—isolated or socialized, treated harshly or benevolently, indoors or outdoors—he had a chance to reform. "What we want," wrote prison reformers Theodore Dwight and Enoch Wines, "is to gain the will, the consent, the cooperation of these men, not to mold them into so many pieces of machinery." [36]

Orphan asylums and reform schools did abrogate the rights of parents and others from the "abnormal" (i.e., broken or non-self-supporting) families they sought to help. Many nineteenth-century Americans believed that the children of the poor were better off in institutions. In 1838, in an important case, a Pennsylvania court upheld the right of magistrates to commit children to a house of refuge over parental opposition. [37] These tendencies are important. But there is a difference between the state's weakening or restriction of parental authority and the state's weakening of the family. The threat to working-class parents had a reconstitutive dimension to which the Lasch/Rothman perspective has not given much weight. The same institutions that threatened the parental authority of the poor also valorized family life in general, as in the case of the director who sought to model his asylum after the "well-regulated family" or the orphan asylum that sought to cultivate a "home feeling." The emphasis of these institutions on individual treatment through the reform of character both encouraged and embodied the same ethical principles and scientific theories that reformers were then urging upon the family, suggesting that the causal element does not rest with the asylums.[38]

David Rothman and other historians have stressed the extent to which the new institutions were directed at the poor, especially immigrants. Henry James' description of an early-nineteenth-century prison "sprawling over the whole neighborhood, with brown, bare windowless walls, ugly truncated pinnacles and a character unspeakably sad and stern" vividly evokes their oppressive character.[39] No one would deny the vast difference in treatment and condition between those who care for themselves and those who are "cared for" in state institutions. But this emphasis on the imposition of morality by one class on another tends to ignore the development of an internalized family-centered morality in all classes. As Paul Faler showed in his study of Lynn, Massachusetts, the heightened nineteenth-century emphasis on discipline, order, hard work, and temperance was not necessarily imposed by the upper classes on the lower, but was also a demand the working classes made upon themselves.[40] In those famous passages in which he evoked the "tyranny of the majority," which "acts upon the will as much as upon the actions," Tocqueville partly grasped that modern liberal capitalism had developed a new form of ideology, secular and personal in nature, rooted in the individualistic structure of society, and reflected in the forms of political democracy and public opinion characteristic of that structure.[41]

The schematic model of the state replacing the family obscures the sense in which government intervention, as it developed, was accompanied by an increasingly sharp delineation of the "normal" family as a private and autonomous (i.e., self-supporting) institution. The transfer of responsibility for the poor and other dependent groups from the family and community to asylums and state institutions was accompanied by an intensified emphasis on the role of the family in educating both men and women for their different places in a market-based society, a role for which women were held responsible. While economic independence was highly prized in society as a whole, within family units the theme was self-sacrifice for women, and a new level of attention was paid to the nurturant role of mothers and the special needs of children.

The Late-Nineteenth-Century Critique of Charity

If the building of asylums in the early nineteenth century expressed the outlook of political-economic individualism more than of paternalism, this was no less true of the spread of principles of rationalization and scientific management among charity workers in the late nineteenth century, principles that clearly anticipate the outlook of Progressive era reform.

Beginning with the Civil War, "business principles"—strict administration, careful control of funds, and, closely related, a faith in social science—became the leading principles governing work with the poor. The Sanitary Commission, formed during the Civil War, led the way in the attack on spontaneous generosity. The purpose of the commission, according to its own statement, was "neither humanity nor charity. It [was] to economize for the national service the life and strength of the National Soldier." The commissioners were contemptuous of the sentimental outpourings of humanitarianism that the war occasioned, asking, "How shall this rising tide of popular sympathy . . . be rendered least hurtful to the army system?" Rather, they stressed the need for hardheaded acceptance of suffering, planning, and rationalization. They used paid agents rather than volunteers, avoided all interference with doctors, and instituted a board of experts between donors and recipients who made "scientific" decisions on how aid would be used.[42]

By the time of the Civil War, many of the earlier asylums had been taken over by state governments and the scale of public welfare had widened considerably, mostly as a result of immigration. Massachusetts, always the forerunner in public welfare, found itself in the 1850s with three mental hospitals, two reform schools, one hospital, four other charitable institutions, and a budget that had quintupled in two decades. These developments led to the founding of State Boards of Charity and the growth of a sector of public administrators. Their claim was to represent society as a whole, rather than any particular group of dependents. In 1865, the American Social Science Association was founded with, among other goals, that of making "useful inquiries into the causes of Human Failure." The National Conference of Charities and Correction, founded in 1874 by the State Boards of Charity and the ASSA, was the leading organization concerned with questions of public policy regarding the poor until well into the Progressive era. It was one arena in which the settlement house movement arose, and in 1904 Jane Addams became its president.[43]

Concurrently, principles of scientific management came to dominate private philanthropy. In 1877, the Reverend Humphrey S. Gurteen, drawing, as usual, on British precedent, founded the Charity Organization Societies (COS) in Buffalo, New York. The COS sought to replace the old philanthropy that fostered dependence by "intelligence," which would foster independence. Responding to the depression of the 1870s, they recognized that poverty was systematic and social but held to a faith in the personal rehabilitation of the poor. The COS sought to turn themselves into a "machine" of rehabilitation, "to do in charity what is done in commerce and industry—so to arrange its different agencies, and so to coordinate its different forces as to attain a certain end with the least possible waste of energy." Encouraging city-wide organizations, dividing the city into districts, and keeping careful records on those seeking relief, the COS sent forth thousands of volunteers into the poorer districts of the city with the hope that individual contact would encourage the rehabilitation of the poor.[44]

The purpose of the movement was to turn the poor into self-supporting citizens. "Not alms but a friend" was its well-known slogan. H. L. Wayland, one of its leaders, wrote in 1887 that "next to alcohol . . . the most pernicious fluid is indiscriminate soup." "Let me have one cord of wood to do it with, and I can ruin the best family in Boston," wrote another philanthropist. "It is still in our midst," wrote Mary Richmond, later the founder of professional case work, in 1890: "the old charity . . . regarding pauperism as a divine spirit in the poor, and reducing the current rate of wages by supplementing the earnings of the underpaid." Edward Everett Hale saw the charity organizations as "giving form to the chaotic charitable sentiments sometimes floating in the minds of women," and the Reverend Mr. Hayland saw them as a needed corrective to the "tender-hearted, sweet-voiced criminals." Human nature, wrote Josephine Shaw Lowell, "is so constituted that no man can receive as a gift what he should earn by his own labor without a moral deterioration." Only a society organized around independent, self-supporting individuals and families could effect the "reunion between the classes" that Lowell saw as the point of the new philanthropy.[45]

The "scientific charity" movement of Gilded Age America was the direct descendant of the antebellum humanitarianism it attacked, as well as the progenitor of the settlement house and social work movements of the Progressive era that attacked it. All three movements were organized around an attack on charity on the grounds that charity fosters dependence. The proponents of "scientific charity" accepted governmental action or social reform so long as it was not "charity" (i.e., handouts). Early Progressive thinking, as expressed by the settlement house workers, continued to look toward regeneration through personal relationships, although this became less and less important with the development of professional social work. At the same time, the reformers of the Progressive era developed the idea that independence was a social right—not a charitable gift—and that government was responsible for guaranteeing that right.

In 1891 John Dewey, in his *Outlines of a Critical Theory of Ethics*, attacked charity as an effort to control the character of the recipient and urged instead a change of conditions to make possible self-support. Dewey, in common with many other thinkers of his epoch, used Darwinian premises to redefine character as "the organized capacity for social functioning." [46] George Herbert Mead supplied the deepest Progressive era critique of charity in his 1918 "Psychology of Punitive Justice" and later in his contribution to Ellsworth Faris's *Intelligent Philanthropy*. Giving, Mead wrote, is a primitive impulse. Its ultimate basis is narcissistic: We cannot help but see ourselves in another's plight, and charity thereby justifies itself through the giver's satisfaction. (Mead did not understand that the traditional understanding that charity benefited the donor also protected the recipient.) The impulse to give, Mead argued, must be socialized. Charity should be replaced by social service and social work. This was a task of social organization, of reform, of politics; it was the achievement of civilization, of "social order," to replace the voluntary character of charity with an obligation. "Social service," Mead wrote, was "still in some communities hardly more than an artificial island, scientifically fabricated, as it were, in an ocean of primitive impulsiveness." [47] By the early years of the twentieth century even the word charity had come into disfavor to be replaced by a series of euphemisms: first, social work, and later, aid, pensions, welfare, and human resources.

Christopher Lasch has shown that the rise of the state in the Progressive era was linked to the development of desexualized and depsychologized conceptions of human nature on the part of such thinkers as Mead and Dewey. But the thinkers of that era—including even the most statist, such as Herbert Croly or Ellen Richards—did not wish the state to supplant the individual. They believed that the rational, economically self-supporting person (or family) they had in mind needed rational, limited reforms to protect his or her family's rights. Although paternalistic thinking continued to prevail in many areas (e.g., juvenile courts and, arguably, protective legislation for women), the main thrust of Progressive era thought and practice was toward minimizing all forms of interpersonal dependence among adults. In this sense we can say that it weakened the family, and not because it weakened the family's independence or autonomy. The best proof of this lies in an examination of the characteristic forms of social organization that developed during the first two decades of the twentieth century. These new groupings—the AFL, the reorganized suffrage movement, the reformed political organizations, the professions—can be called "collective" but not "communal." In them, individuals were brought together according to their "rational" (i.e., economic) interests, or their function in society, at the same time as they were "serialized"; all personal—emotional, dependent—ties among them tended to be eliminated.

Progressivism and The Modern Family

The Rationale of Progressive Reform

The vast transformation of American life wrought by late-nineteenth-century industrialization led to the great expansion of the state that we identify with Progressivism. The principle that government should intervene into social and economic conditions on behalf of "the public" existed in the nineteenth century, but the Progressive era marked a shift, above all in the extended regulation of business, protection for consumers and, beginning during World War I, protection of the collective bargaining process. Within this context, urban and state governments enacted a series of measures aimed at protecting the health, housing and neighborhood conditions, and educational opportunities of working-class and immigrant families. The most important new forms of "intervention" into the family were the abolition of child labor and the enactment of protective legislation for women. In contrast to the reform tradition of the nineteenth century, progressive reforms were not directed at the "poor" but sought to shore up the "normal," self-supporting family as well. In this sense, Progressive reforms anticipated and laid the basis for the comprehensive governmental intervention of the twentieth century as expressed during the New Deal and post–New Deal eras in such areas as social security, housing, and education reform.

Beneath the diversity of thought of that era lay a common grid of assumptions shared by most thinkers and made explicit among those at Hull House and the University of Chicago, such as Jane Addams, William I. Thomas, and John Dewey. These Progressives relied on a Darwinian model of social interdependence to repudiate the individualistic political economy that underlay so much nineteenth-century thought. In their view, the rise of industry had destroyed the self-sufficiency of the old, petit bourgeois family, making it necessary to develop other institutions, particularly schools and neighborhoods, to perform many tasks once performed by the family. They hoped that any such new institutions would reflect the general evolutionary tendency toward a more specialized and interdependent division of labor.

While fostering governmental intervention, their key concept was that of the "social," and they drew upon the contemporaneous development of sociology for such notions as custom, mores, and folkways. According to George Herbert Mead, "we must recognize that the most concrete and most fully realized society is not that which is presented in institutions but that which is found in the interplay of social habits and customs, in the readjustments of personal interests that have come into conflict, and which takes place outside of court, in the change of social attitude that is not dependent upon an act of legislature." [48] *The Polish Peasant in Europe and America*, arguably the culmination of Progressive era social thought, is a critique of those reformers who ascribe an "exaggerated importance . . . to changes of material environment," or who assume "that good housing conditions will create a good family life [or] that the abolition of the saloon will stop drinking." [49]

Using the concept of the social, Progressive thinkers sought to redefine individualism in order to free it from its political-economic and masculinist integument. As we have seen, their view of people as intrinsically social was based on a denial of the aggressive and sexual bases of the individual. Their critiques of political-economic individualism and war tended to ignore the aggressiveness taken for granted by most previous thinkers. Progressive reform looked to pragmatic regulation, compromise, "balancing acts," and "rules of reason." The spirit of adjustment and compromise can be seen in the vast extension of discretionary powers granted to the juvenile courts and in the creation of regulatory agencies; ironically, both reforms tended to intensify the process of corruption, manipulation, and special pleading they were in part designed to eliminate.

Similarly, the attempt to redefine individualism to include women minimized the importance of biological differences between the sexes, when compared to the central place that these differences held for nineteenth-century thinkers. The reform of society, they expected, would lead to the reform of the family as well. Through a recognition of its place in a democratic, interdependent, and functionally divided society, it would become more sociable, more democratic and cooperative, more personal and informal, and less private and self-contained. "Industrialization," wrote the evolutionary socialist and family historian Arthur Calhoun in 1919, has led to the "general democratization of society" and the "waning of domestic monarchy." As women gained "economic opportunity outside of marriage," they would become more independent within the home. The modern family would be based on a recognition of the individual rights of its members, especially women and children. [50]

At this point we can see the extent to which the general attack on dependence converged with the history of feminism. Jane Addams was one of the thinkers of the period most sensitive to the contradictions involved in the critique of paternalism; nevertheless, that critique was the central theme of her early work. In 1902 she put *Democracy and Social Ethics* together out of a series of magazine articles she had written during the

1890s that contains six critical discussions of paternalistic relationships: father/daughter, mistress/maid, ward boss/immigrant, teacher/student, charity worker/recipient, and company town boss/worker. She offered a parable of the welfare state in contrasting a good-natured but poor landlord and a hard-hearted but rich landlord. The rich landlord "collects with sternness . . . accepts no excuse, and will have his own," while the good-natured landlord "pities and spares his poverty pressed tenants." Though the rich landlord is unloved, he commands admiration; the good-natured landlord is treated with a "certain lack of respect. In one sense he is a failure." Intermingled with the love his tenants bear him, there is contempt. Quite properly, they suspect that his behavior is weak at its root, that it is not based upon reality, and that it hides unacknowledged motives, perhaps a fear of standing one's ground or an excessive need to be loved. For Addams, the development of relations of individual integrity among people depended on their recognition of their real economic position. A society organized around wage labor, she believed, made possible a kind of equality and independence that paternalism foreclosed.[51]

In her very way of telling the story Addams expressed her ambivalence. She put her own critique of the "cold and calculating" charity worker into the mouth of the immigrant: "If the charity visitor is such a person, why does she pretend to like the poor? Why does she not go into business at once?" Similarly she explained the power of the ward bosses by people's continued need to be childish and dependent and likened Johnny Powers, the ward boss against whom she campaigned vigorously but without success in 1896, to a "friendly visitor" (i.e., a parent).[52] Addams hoped that the need for human ties would prevail in the social sphere—in such forms as the settlement house, the park, the neighborhood—though the economic sphere might continue on a "cold and calculating" basis.

Similar themes underlay the development of professional social work. Mary Richmond drew upon the Darwinian/Hegelian social psychologies of Charles Horton Cooley and James Mark Baldwin to criticize "solitary horseman" conceptions of the individual and "isolated-and-in-his-body-alone" theories of the self. She lamented the fact that nineteenth-century charity work had been dominated by the outlook of political economy and expected that social work would be based on sociology with the great value that discipline placed on social ties. She sought to replace the emphasis on rational self interest with an emphasis on social obligation and responsibility, not by dissolving the individual into society but through a "development of personality through the . . . adjustment of social relationships," which she defined as the goal of case work. She even expected that the social worker would be a reformer concerned with industrial conditions. But, of course, she anticipated that the sphere of the social would more or less fade away at the boundaries of the economy itself, where individual competition and the purchase of labor as a commodity were still primary.[53]

Political economic theories that had been explicit in social thought and practice a century earlier became implicit assumptions in the thought and practice of the Progressive era. The reconciliation of market individualist principles with the development of an industrial society was accompanied by a process of abstraction in legal and social thought, exemplified by the development of the corporate form of economic organization. According to John Commons, the legal history of the early twentieth century had been marked by an "enlargement of the idea of property . . . from that of ownership of tangible objects to that of ownership of an occupation, a calling, a trade, and even the ownership of one's labor; and the enlargement of liberty from personal liberty to economic liberty." [54] In 1888, Carroll D. Wright, chief of the Massachussetts Bureau of the Statistics of Labor, used the term "unemployment" for the first time in English. His investigations marked the public recognition of the fact that poverty might be involuntary.[55] The crucial idea shared by so many proponents of government action but never incorporated into an act of legislation or administrative policy was that it was the responsibility of society to provide every family with the means necessary to support itself, essentially by earning a living. But as the most advanced Progressives sought to redefine a livelihood as a social and political right, they cut themselves off from an understanding of the continued autonomy of market forces.

One of the clearest ways in which economic individualism was preserved in the form of social collectivism was the workmen's compensation system. Workmen's compensation was the only form of social insurance successfully enacted during the Progressive era, and foreshadows the development of an enlarged "social wage" during and after the New Deal. The nineteenth-century predecessors of workmen's compensation had been forms of mutual aid such as friendly societies, fraternal orders, unions, secret societies like the Masons, and, especially, immigrant organizations for whom insurance was often both inspiration and mainstay. These forms of insurance were themselves collective, either rooted directly in a community or, as in the case of funeral insurance, in the need to meet one's emotional and practical obligations to a community. These forms proved inadequate to both workers and their employers with the development of large-scale corporations. The workers faced the erosion of sustaining communities, while employers faced a welter of ersatz arrangements leading to many lawsuits and unpredictable costs. Workmen's compensation legislation tied insurance to the wage contract, as well as protecting the insurance companies that served as private carriers. Its supporters argued that it would replace "paternalism" and ensure a "democratic discipline" based on the worker's individual foresight and initiative. As I. M. Rubinow later argued for social security, it was made necessary by the decline of the extended family and the "increasing dependence of the majority of mankind . . . upon a wage-contract for their means of existence." Although often portrayed as a victory for collective over individual solutions, the history of workmen's compensation actually reveals the reverse: the decline of community and the confirmation of individual responsibility by the state.[56]

The shift the Progressives helped accomplish from a laissez-faire outlook to one appropriate to a highly integrated corporate capitalist welfare state masked the continuity of market relations both in society and as incorporated into governmental reforms. The idea that government should guarantee a job was different from the laissez-faire state's responsibility for guaranteeing the market but, like it, was based on the accommodation of collectivist arrangements to the capitalist property system. As with government intervention into business, government intervention into social life presupposed wage labor and private property. The paradox is that the Progressive attempt to reshape the family and individualism in line with increasing social cooperation and interdependence not only preserved the economic individualism of the nineteenth-century marketplace but intensified it. That this was the result of the structure of society rather than the intent of any single group can be seen by examining two different groups whose efforts contributed to twentieth-century reform: the feminist and labor movements.

Feminism and Progressivism

A key source for Addams's attack on paternalism was her immersion in the politics of the late-nineteenth and early-twentieth-century women's movement. When that movement is remembered in all its diversity, to include not only suffrage but temperance, the social purity movement, women's labor organizations, and women's clubs, it can be ranked with labor, populism, and urban reform (with all of which it overlapped) as among the largest and most influential social movements of the period. The central problem that all tendencies of the women's movement faced was that of reconciling the spread of the marketplace, with its emphasis on individualism and competition, with the traditional values of "women's sphere"—benevolence and selfless nurturance. The spread of market relations promised to free women from the backwardness of the patriarchal family but at the same time threatened to corrode and undermine family life and the values it embodied. For the first generation of college-educated women, entering the labor force in the 1890s, the contradictions between the family and the market or, put psychologically, between dependence and autonomy, were particularly acute. One expression of this was the search for a politics that could combine wage labor and economic independence, especially for middle-class women, with state protection of the family, especially among the poor.

Jane Addams, one of the most important feminists of the period, as well as a leader of Progressivism, spoke to this issue. Government, she wrote, was simply "enlarged housekeeping":

> From the beginning of tribal life women have been held responsible for the health of the community, a function which is now represented by the health department; from the days of the cave dwellers, so far as their home was clean and wholesome, it was due to their efforts, which are now represented by the bureau of tenement-house inspection. Most of the departments in a modern city can be traced to woman's traditional activity, but in spite of this, so soon as these old affairs were turned over to the care of the city, they slipped from woman's hands.[57]

In a single metaphor, Addams combined the Progressive view that society was moving toward increasing interdependence and a more socially oriented ethics with the feminist view that women, who once took private responsibility for nurturance, would carry this value into the world of work and government. In this way, she brought the "separate sphere" ideology of feminism into the corporate era. She was able to defend both the entry of women as individuals into the world of work and the obligation of the new government services to protect the family (particularly its most dependent members, women and children) and particularly the families of the poor.

As early as 1880, Lester F. Ward, a prophet of the welfare state and a favorite author among feminists, had described the ideal outlook of the future state as "maternalism." In fact, almost every Progressive reform directed at the family was first anticipated and fought for by the women's movement. These reforms included laws to protect the mother's place within the family, protective labor legislation being the most important. Such legislation, regulating the hours and working conditions of women, was based on the feminist program that women who were wage earners must be protected in their eventual role as mothers and housekeepers. A second set of reforms gave an ethical basis to the modern family and aimed at eliminating the sexual double standard. These included censorship, social purity, and the crusade against prostitution. A third set protected the special character of childhood by attempting to abolish child labor, by extending the school day and the school year, and by raising the age of sexual consent for teen-agers. As the movement to abolish child labor came into conflict with what one observer termed the "rigid system of household economics . . . needed for mere preservation,"[58] which was characteristic of immigrant and working-class families, many feminists were led to support higher wages and trade unionism. By 1900, thirty states had adopted some form of child labor regulations.[59] The ideological and political leadership that feminists gave to Progressive reform is ignored by Ehrenreich and English in their portrayal of Progressivism as a movement of male experts who expropriated women's traditional skills and used those skills against them.

Besides justifying the focus on the family, feminism supplied a crucial bridge between classes that was an essential component of Progressive reform. While middle-class feminists certainly condescended to working-class men and women, they also expressed an important sisterly identification with working-class mothers, which can be seen in the writings of Addams, Florence Kelley, and the women associated with the Children's Bureau. This cross-class feminism provided a crucial element of respect for the working-class family that infused Progressive reform and distinguished it from the reforms of the early nineteenth century. The feminist-led Home Economics Movement and the Congress of Mothers, forerunners of the PTA, supplemented "friendly visitor" moralism with the propagation of home management, hygiene, dietetics, and child psychology among the poor. By 1896 welfare reformers and child advocates came to accept the principle that a needy child was better off in a private home than in an institution. This led to a great growth in foster care, and even in day care, to allow working mothers to keep their children. By 1909, after great debate, "mothers' pensions" were enacted in several states. These public cash grants, generally to widows with children, foreshadowed the AFDC program. Private agencies and the charity organization movements opposed mothers' pensions because they believed that an impersonal state bureaucracy could not accomplish the task of personal rehabilitation. In the compromise program that passed, state officials took on the task of enforcing behavioral norms among recipients. The reformed juvenile courts, which often administered the mothers' pensions, depended on the new profession of probation officer to return delinquents to their family rather than to an institution. As Carl Kelsey wrote of the Chicago juvenile court in 1901, "lessons of home life and individual responsibility cannot well be taught to children en masse."[60] Far from "replacing the family," these reforms all had the aim of protecting and extending it among the poor.

Progressive era feminists, therefore, sought to combine greater individual opportunities for women with protection of the family. Both goals involved governmental action, and in both cases, whether for individual women or families, they took for granted that the basis for independence would be a wage or salary. Charlotte Perkins Gilman was almost alone in her critique of this position. Gilman believed that the payment of wages for work outside the home, and not for work within the home, would keep the family as isolated, as inward-turning, and as male-dominated as it had been in the nineteenth century. She called the private economic basis of the family the "hidden spring" through which the antisocial and antifemale biases of the nineteenth century would flow into the twentieth. But Gilman never thought in terms of an end to wages and sought instead to extend wages to housewives. The critical difference between Addams and Gilman is that Addams was ambivalent about the development of a modern industrial society; Gilman, although she was a socialist, welcomed it.[61]

The Role of the Trade-Union Movement

The continued centrality of political economy in twentieth-century society has been well recognized by the trade-union movement in a way that contrasts with the sociological emphasis of other reformers and feminists. But if the latter have tended to "bracket" the economy, the labor movement has often done the same with society when economic issues were at stake.

The central goal of the AFL and other labor organizations by the 1890s was to control the supply of labor as fully as possible. The connections of this effort to the feminist program toward the family may be difficult to grasp within a pluralist/interest-group perspective, but the links were historically critical. Craft control would enable union members—mostly male—to maintain leverage over wages and hours and to sustain their unions, especially at a time when the market value of many of the older skills was being eroded. Historians' emphasis on the nonpartisan character of trade unions in this period has often led them to underestimate labor's intense political activity in support of any legislation that promised to lessen the effects of what was called "cheap labor." This included protective legislation for women, the abolition of child labor, immigration restriction, the control of the apprenticeship system, and the eight-hour day. In these efforts, particularly those associated with the restriction of child labor, trade unions cooperated with women's clubs, consumer leagues, and charity aid associations. Adolph Strasser, president of the Cigar-Maker's International Union, stated in 1879: "We cannot drive the females out of the trades, but we can restrict their daily quota of labor through factory laws." [62] Samuel Gompers in 1906 boasted, "There is not a child labor law on the statute books of the United States but has been put there by the efforts of the trade-union movement." [63]

Where the trade-union movement resisted government intervention, however, was in the wage relationship. In part, this was because business had much more influence over government than labor and had been able to use police, the military, legislation, and the courts to break strikes. Trade unionists also held to an ideology of independence and self-reliance associated with the term "free labor." The founders of modern American trade unionism, like their Progressive and feminist contemporaries, were opponents of paternalism. Samuel Gompers' famous definition of the goals of trade unionism—"More, more and more"—is rarely quoted in full. He went on to say, "We shall want more and more. . . . Then I think you will find your eleemosynary occupations will be gone." And in another speech: "What the working-men want is less charity and more rights." [64] By this, Gompers meant that he expected the labor market itself, through the collective bargaining process, ultimately guaranteed by the state, to supply the necessities of life. According to labor historian Irwin Yellowitz, "It was a generally accepted principle that the working conditions of adult men were not subject to legislation." [65] The consequences of this consensus in the realm of social welfare have been vast. Mark Leff, a historian of the mothers' pension movement, notes one: "No other major industrial nation had such a special concern for its children and such a fear of providing assistance to indigent men." [66] More broadly, twentieth-century trade unionism, like other interest groups, failed to develop a conception of the common good but assumed this would emerge out of the play of special interests.

The Family Wage

In retrospect, we can see how the politics of feminism converged with those of the labor movement of the same period. Unlike feminists, the labor movement had no "program" for the family, any more than the feminists had a "program" for the economy. In both cases, however, it was the element left unexamined—the wage basis of familial existence—that proved critical. This established a generally unremarked basis of agreement between the politics of working-class men and those of middle-class women, a much more important agreement than their explicit, limited cooperation in such campaigns as child labor. Their shared and unexamined assumptions allowed the deep structure of society—its organization around the capital/labor relationship on the one hand and around the inherited, largely unconscious structure of relations between the sexes on the other—to mediate between a series of disparate reforms and to establish their long-run meaning and relationship. The institution that has integrated historically specific economic factors with more general structures of sexuality is the modern family, in which men have the task of primary breadwinner while women are primarily responsible for rearing children and keeping the home—and increasingly are assumed to work outside the home as well.

In the Progressive period, as earlier, government policies continued to respond to pressures to protect both the individual man or woman and the family. However, the great expansion of government intervention in this period coincided with the vast and unremitting growth in women working, and the beginning of the elimination of children and young people from the labor force. This posed in graphic terms the contradiction between women as individuals (i.e., wage earners) and women as the radiating core of the family. The most important recognition of this contradiction in government policy was protective labor legislation for working women, upheld after a series of efforts by the U.S. Supreme Court in the case of *Muller* v. *Oregon* in 1908. Supported for different reasons by labor and by the women's movement, protective labor legislation sought to reconcile women's wage labor, especially before marriage, with their traditional responsibilities within the home.

Heidi Hartmann's "Capitalism, Patriarchy and Job Segregation by Sex" puts the issue of protective legislation at the center of a critique of the welfare state. According to Hartmann, men, acting as a gender (specifically, working-class men coopted by employers) excluded women from the trade-union movement during the late nineteenth century and supported protective legislation to enforce occupational segregation by sex.[67] Hartmann convincingly demonstrates that there were major conflicts between male and female trade unionists during the late nineteenth century. I would add to her evidence an example from the Progressive era: Trade unions composed of men either stood aloof from or opposed the powerful movement for a minimum wage for women, which reached its highest point in the years 1909–12.[68] But these conflicts must be understood alongside the simultaneous struggle shared by working-class women and men for a decent family life. At a time when it required everyone within the household to support a family, the idea of a single wage for a single breadwinner was viewed as extremely desirable. At a time when most of a woman's adult life span corresponded to the years of pregnancy and child rearing, many if not most women shared the idea that this breadwinner should be the man. The growth in women working during the early twentieth century, insofar as it was a necessity imposed on working-class women, was viewed as a social evil by every feminist organization of the period, as well as by a great many working-class women themselves, as Leslie Tentler's work has shown.[69] The slogan of the Women's Trade Union League, the primary organization of working women, was "The eight-hour day; a living wage; to guard the home."

One indication of the importance of this popular struggle for a family life in the Progressive era was the prevalence of the idea of a "living" or "family" wage. This idea, which became an explicit part of state policy in Australia and elsewhere in the early twentieth century, may have received its most important public impetus from Pope Leo XIII's 1891 encyclical "On the Condition of Labor," which called for a wage "sufficient to support the worker in reasonable comfort" and was followed by a debate among Catholic trade unionists and reformers over whether the encyclical referred to the individual worker or his family.[70] This discussion overlapped with the concern of late-nineteenth-century social workers and charity officials with determining the "subsistence minimum" of a family. In 1907, Louise Bolard More's *Wage Earner's Budgets* argued that the wage should provide more than "physical efficiency"; ten years later, economists at the Universities of Washington and California argued against the "subsistence" concept and in favor of a culturally determined standard, meant to include vacations, movies, candy, tobacco, and other such items. There was scarcely an industrial commission of the time that did not study the issue. From 1910 to 1915, the family wage principle was at the center of a series of federally supervised wage arbitrations between the railroads and their crews. In 1917, President Woodrow Wilson procaimed it a guiding principle for wage determination in industries involved in war production.[71]

More important than the history of the family wage issue is the history of working people's aspirations for a family. The goal of the family wage combined the feminist emphasis on the importance of motherhood and the family with the trade-union emphasis on the dignity and self-reliance of the male breadwinner. Its ethical and social origins certainly included traditions of community more characteristic of working-class than middle-class life, and probably also drew upon expectations of cooperation and sharing between the sexes. In the 1880s, when the first modern investigations of working-class family life were undertaken by the Massachusetts Bureau of Labor Statistics, one of the findings that most shocked and dismayed the middle-class male investigators was that working-class men would cook, clean, and care for the children while their wives were at work and they were not.[72]

Hartmann's account essentially remains on an empirical level. She equates capitalism with employers and patriarchy with men and then shows that men did as much as employers (who were anyway men) to relegate women to a secondary status in the workforce. In my view, both "capitalism" and "patriarchy" should be used as theoretical concepts, valuable only insofar as they relate to other concepts and insofar as they explain empirical material. That men oppress women is an empirical observation that needs to be explained. Giving it a name—"patriarchy," "male supremacy," the "sex-gender system"—may be temporarily useful, but it is no substitute for an explanation.[73]

Explaining the modern family as the result of "capitalism" is no more adequate. Many scholars have observed that the organization of modern family life around wage labor conformed to the needs of an ascendant capitalist class and a new imperialist state that proclaimed children as its most important national resource and that considered education and population policy as essential props of national strength.[74] But state policy toward the family was not dictated by any capitalist conspiracy. Rather, it was the outcome of a series of single-issue reform movements, each one of which was "realistic" enough and "pragmatic" enough to take the rise of corporate capitalism and the accompanying individualistic structure of family life for granted and to seek to attain a specific goal—even goals that had major impact, such as the abolition of child labor—within its confines. A common historical process shaped the acquiescence of feminists in the domination of capital at the workplace and the acquiescence of labor in the domination of men within the home, but neither of these was an inevitable outcome.

Conclusion

Far from the state "invading" or "replacing" the family, a certain kind of alienated public life and a certain kind of alienated private life have expanded together. The form in which the welfare state expanded was public, the content private. The vast expansion of government spending that marked the New Deal and post-New Deal eras has scarcely eliminated the strength of market forces in our society, and in many ways has strengthened them.

While the basic ideas that underlay this expansion were already foretold during the Progressive era, the New Deal era did mark a qualitative shift. The responsibility that the federal government took for the economy during the 1930s signified the extent to which we had become a nation of wage earners rather than a nation of citizens. The logic of Keynesianism was that through the mediation of government spending, an increase in wages could increase profits, investment, and economic growth rather than, as previously thought, retard them. The vast Keynesian spending that fueled the postwar boom brought about the development of the suburbs, the spread of home ownership, the automobile, upward mobility through higher education—the extension of the family romance to the furthest reaches of the working class. It is against this background that the current debate over the family has taken shape.

The spread of a society organized around self-reliance, the market, and wage labor marked a great advance, perhaps especially for women, but we should also mark its costs and limits. By the time our nation reached the early twentieth century the attempt to shore up independence through economic means had become largely defensive,[75] and in our own time economic individualism largely betrays the promise it once held out. Neither the attempt to extend the traditionally male ideal of individual independence to women nor the attempt to extend the traditionally female ideal of nurturance to men can be based on an economic system that fosters a one-sided ideal of economic independence and a correspondingly hollow collectivity. True independence, for both sexes, is based on an acceptance of our dependence on others and is realized through our ability to nurture and give to others without conflict within ourselves.

Notes

1. John Dewey, *The School and Society* (rev. ed. 1943, 1969; Chicago: University of Chicago, 1900).

2. Talcott Parsons, Robert F. Bales, et al., *Family, Socialization and Interaction Process* (Glencoe, Ill.: Free Press, 1955); and Neil Smelser, *Social Change in the Industrial Revolution* (Chicago, 1965).

3. Max Horkheimer, "Authority and the Family" (1936), reprinted in Horkheimer, *Critical Theory: Selected Essays*, trans. Matthew J. O'Connell et al. (New York, 1972); and Max Horkheimer and Theodore Adorno, *Dialectic of Enlightenment* (New York: Herder and Herder, 1972).

4. David Rothman, *The Discovery of the Asylum: Social Order and Disorder in the New Republic* (Boston: Little, Brown, 1971). See also Michael Katz, "Origin of the Institutional State," *Marxist Perspectives* 1, no. 4 (Winter 1978).

5. Christopher Lasch, *Haven in a Heartless World* (New York: Basic, 1977); and idem, *The Culture of Narcissism* (New York: Norton, 1979).

6. Lasch, *Haven in a Heartless World*, pp. xiv, xvii.

7. This phrase is used in Lasch's endorsement of Jacques Donzelot's *The Policing of Families* (New York: Pantheon, 1979). Donzelot's work appeared too late for discussion here.

8. Barbara Ehrenreich and Deirdre English, *For Her Own Good: 150 Years of the Experts' Advice to Women* (Garden City, N.Y.: Doubleday Anchor, 1978). See esp. chaps. 5, 6, and 7. Also, Heidi Hartmann, "Capitalism, Patriarchy and Job Segregation by Sex" in *Capitalist Patriarchy and the Case for Socialist Feminism*, ed. Zillah Eisenstein (New York: Monthly Review Press, 1979).

9. Nancy F. Cott, *The Bonds of Womanhood: "Womans' Sphere" in New England, 1780–1835* (New Haven, Yale University Press, 1977); and Carl N. Degler, *At Odds: Women and the Family in America from the Revolution to the Present* (New York: Oxford, 1980).

10. Willard Gaylin, "In the Beginning: Helpless and Dependent," in *Doing Good: The Limits of Benevolence*, ed. Willard Gaylin, et al. (New York: Pantheon, 1978).

11. Herbert Gutman, *The Black Family in Slavery and Freedom, 1750–1925* (New York: Pantheon, 1978). The quote is on Gutman's p. 217 from Sidney W. Mintz and Richard Price, "An Anthropological Approach to the Study of Afro-American History" (unpublished paper, February 1974).

12. Carol Stack, *All Our Kin* (New York: Harper & Row, 1974).

13. Rudolph Vecoli, "Contadini in Chicago: A Critique of the Uprooted," *Journal of American History*, December 1964; Tamara Haraven, "The Laborers of Manchester, New Hampshire, 1912–1922," *Labor History* 16 (Spring 1975): 249–65; and Virginia Yans-McLaughlin, *Family and Community: Italian Immigrants in Buffalo, 1880–1930* (Ithaca: Cornell University Press, 1977).

14. William I. Thomas and Florian Znaniecki, *The Polish Peasant in Europe and America* (Chicago: University of Chicago, 1918; and Badger Press, Boston, 1920), 1: 197, 509. See forthcoming abridgement of all five volumes, ed. Eli Zaretsky (Carbondale, Ill.: University of Illinois Press, 1980); and Oscar Handlin, *The Uprooted: The Epic Story of the Great Migrations That Made the American People* (Boston: Little, Brown, 1951).

15. As in Herbert Gutman, *Work, Culture and Society in Industrializing America* (New York: Knopf, 1976); and, especially, Victor Greene, *The Slavic Community on Strike: Immigrant Labor in Pennsylvania Anthracite* (Notre Dame: University of Notre Dame Press, 1968).

16. Karl Polanyi, *The Great Transformation* (Boston: Beacon, 1944, 1957), pp. 163–64. Also see Hace Sorel Tishler, *Self-Reliance and Social Security 1870–1917* (Port Washington, N.Y.: Kennikat, 1971), pp. 4–5.

17. Ernst Troeltsch, *The Social Teaching of the Christian Churches* (New York: Macmillan, 1931, 1949), p. 166.

18. Christopher Hill, "The Puritans and the Poor," *Past and Present* 2 (1952): 36.

19. Perry Miller, *The Seventeenth Century* (Boston: Beacon, 1953), p. 416. For a somewhat opposed viewpoint, see Michael Walzer, *The Revolution of the Saints* (New York: Atheneum, 1974), p. 151n.

20. Richard Baxter, *A Christian Directory: or, a Summ of Practical Theologie and Cases of Conscience* (1673) pt. ii, p. 194, quoted in Richard B. Schlatter, *The Social Ideas of Religious Leaders 1660–1688* (London: Oxford, 1940), p. 3.

21. Quoted in Lawrence Stone, *The Family, Sex and Marriage in England, 1500–1800* (New York: Harper & Row, 1977), p. 152.

22. Edmund Morgan, *The Puritan Family* (New York: Harper & Row, 1966), pp. 142–43.

23. Rothman, *Discovery of the Asylum*, chap. 1; Willystine Goodsell, *A History of the Family as a Social and Educational Institution* (New York: Macmillan, 1915), p. 355, quotes from Plymouth Laws: "No single person be suffered to live by himself or in any family but such as the selection of the town shall approve of. . . ." Robert Bremner, ed., *Children and Youth in America: A Documentary History, Vol. I, 1600–1865* (Cambridge, Mass.: Harvard University Press, 1970): 103–4; and Bernard Bailyn, *Forming of American Society* (Chapel Hill: University of North Carolina Press, 1960), p. 17.

24. John Locke, *Two Treatises of Government*, ed. Thomas I. Cook (New York: Hafner, 1966), p. 11.

25. Peter Laslett, "Introduction," in Locke, *Two Treatises of Government*.

26. Alexis De Tocqueville, *Democracy in America* (New York: Vintage, 1954), 2:203.

27. Morton J. Horwitz, *The Transformation of American Law 1780–1860* (Cambridge, Mass.: Harvard University Press, 1977) p. 253.

28. Norma Basch, "Invisible Women: The Legal Fiction of Marital Unity in Nineteenth Century America." *Feminist Studies* 5, no. 2 (Summer 1979); and Jacobus tenBroek, "California's Dual System of Family Law: Its Origin, Development and Present Status," *Stanford Law Review* 16, no. 2 (March 1964): 297n.

29. Quoted in Ellen DuBois, "The Radicalism of the Woman Suffrage Movement: Notes Toward the Reconstruction of Nineteenth-Century Feminism," *Feminist Studies* 3, no.1/2 (Fall 1975): 66–68.

30. William O'Neill, *Divorce in the Progressive Era* (New Haven: Yale University Press, 1967); and Morton Keller, *Affairs of State: Public Life in Late Nineteenth Century America* (Cambridge, Mass.: Harvard University Press, 1977), pp. 461–72.

31. Thomas and Znaniecki, *Polish Peasant*, 5:265–68.

32. Basch, "Invisible Women"; and William Leach, *True Love and Perfect Union* (New York: Basic, 1980), pp. 175–79.

33. Rothman, *Discovery of the Asylum;* and Katz, "Origin of Institutional State," *passim*.

34. William Wordsworth, "The Old Cumberland Beggar," in Wordsworth, *Selected Poetry and Prose*, ed. John Butt (London: Oxford University Press, 1964), pp. 76–82. See the discussion of this poem by Steven Marcus, "Their Brothers' Keepers: An Episode from English History" in Gaylin, *Doing Good*, pp. 39–68.

35. Christopher Lasch, "Life in the Therapeutic State," *New York Review of Books*, June 1980.

36. Norman Dain, *Concepts of Insanity in the United States, 1789–1865* (New Brunswick, N.J.: Rutgers University Press, 1964), p. 110; Rothman, *Discovery of the Asylum*, pp. 65, 243–44; and Henri Ellenberger, *The Discovery of the Unconscious: The History And Evolution of Dynamic Psychiatry* (New York: Basic, 1970), p. 197. On ante-bellum environmentalism, see Winthrop Jordan, *White Over Black: American Attitudes Toward the Negro 1550–1812* (New York: Norton, 1968, 1977), pp. 308–10.

37. *Ex parte Crouse*, 4, Wharton 9.

38. Michael Rogin, *Fathers and Children: Andrew Jackson and the Subjugation of the American Indian* (New York: Knopf, 1975), p. 274; Rothman, *Discovery of the Asylum*, pp. 105–8, 151–52, 230–35; and Michael Katz, *The Irony of Early School Reform* (Cambridge, Mass.: Harvard University Press, 1968), pp. 43–51, 187–89.

39. Henry James, *The Princess Casamassima*, quoted in Chrostopher Lasch, *The World of Nations: Reflections on American History, Politics and Culture* (New York: Knopf, 1973), p. 3.

40. Paul Faler, "Cultural Aspects of the Industrial Revolution: Lynn, Massachusetts Shoemakers and Industrial Morality, 1826–1860," *Labor History* 15 (Summer 1974): 381–91.

41. Tocqueville, *Democracy in America*, 1:264–81.

42. George Frederickson, *The Inner Civil War: Northern Intellectuals and the Crisis of the Union* (New York: Harper & Row, 1965), pp. 98–112.

43. Thomas I. Haskell, *The Emergence of Professional Social Science: The American Social Science Association and the Nineteenth Century Crisis of Authority* (Urbana, Ill: University of Illinois Press, 1977), p. 105; Robert W. Kelso, *The History of Public Poor Relief in Massachusetts, 1620–1920* (Boston: Houghton Mifflin, 1922), p. 143; and Gerald Grob, *Mental Institutions in American Social Policy to 1875* (New York: Free Press, 1973), p. 257.

44. Paul Boyer, *Urban Masses and Moral Order in America* (Cambridge, Mass.: Harvard University Press, 1978), pp. 144–50; and Kenneth Kusmer, "The Functions of Organized Charity in the Progressive Era: Chicago as a Case Study," *Journal of American History*, December 1973.

45. Josephine Shaw Lowell, *Public Relief and Private Charity* (New York, 1884), p. 66; and Marion E. Gettleman, "Charity and Social Classes in the United States, 1874–1900," *American Journal of Economics and Sociology* 22 (April 1963): 313–30; 22 (July 1963): 417–26.

46. John Dewey, *Outlines of a Critical Theory of Ethics* (New York: Greenwood, 1969); and Merle Curti, *Social Ideas of American Educators* (New York: Scribner's, 1935), p. 523.

47. George Herbert Mead, "Philanthropy from the Point of View of Ethics," in Ellsworth Faris, Fern Laune, and Arthur J. Todd, eds., *Intelligent Philanthropy* (Chicago: University of Chicago, 1930), pp. 133–48. George Herbert Mead, "The Psychology of Punitive Justice," *American Journal of Sociology* 23 (March 1918): 5; and T. V. Smith, "George Herbert Mead and the Philosophy of Philanthropy," *Social Service Review*, March 1932.

48. George Herbert Mead, "Natural Rights and the Theory of the Political Institution," *Journal of Philosophy* 12 (1915): 152.

49. Thomas and Znaniecki, *Polish Peasant*, 1:13.

50. W. Arthur Calhoun, *A Social History of the American Family* (Cleveland, 1919), 3:157–58; cf. Eli Zaretsky, "Progressive Thought on the Impact of Industrialization on the Family and Its Relation to the Emergence of the Welfare State, 1890–1920" (Ph.D. dissertation, University of Maryland, 1979).

51. Jane Addams, *Democracy and Social Ethics* (New York: Macmillan, 1901), pp. 24–25.

52. Allen F. Davis, *American Heroine: The Life and Legend of Jane Addams* (New York: Oxford, 1973).

53. Mary Richmond, *What Is Social Case Work?: An Introductory Description* (New York: Russell Sage Foundation, 1922), pp. 128–98; and James Mark Baldwin, *Social and Ethical Interpretations in Mental Development* (New York: Macmillan, 1902), p. 508. See also Samuel Mencher, "The Influence of Romanticism on Nineteenth Century British Social Work," *Social Science Review*, 28 (June 1964): 175–76.

54. John Commons, *The Legal Foundations of Capitalism* (New York: Macmillan, 1924), p. 153.

55. James Leiby, *Carroll Wright and Labor Reform: The Origin of Labor Statistics* (Cambridge, Mass.: Harvard University Press, 1960).

56. Roy Lubove, *The Struggle for Social Security, 1900–1935* (Cambridge, Mass.: Harvard University Press, 1968), pp. 4, 52, 82, 115, 314–15; and James Leiby, *A History of Social Welfare and Social Work in the United States* (New York: Columbia University Press, 1978), pp. 191–216.

57. Jane Addams, *New Ideals of Peace* (New York, 1970), p. 202.

58. Ruth True, *The Neglected Girl* (New York: Survey Associates, 1914), p. 48.

59. David J. Pivar, *Purity Crusade: Sexual Morality and Social Control, 1868–1900* (Westport, Conn.: Greenwood, 1973), pp. 104–5, 139–46.

60. Mark Leff, "Consensus for Reform: The Mothers' Pension Movement in the Progressive Era," *Social Service Review* 47, no. 3 (September 1973). Carl Kelsey, "The Juvenile Court of Chicago and Its Work," *Annals of the American Academy of Political and Social Science* 17 (March 1901).

61. Charlotte Perkins Gilman, *Women and Economics* (New York: Harper & Row, 1898, 1966).

62. Quoted in Hartmann, "Capitalism," p. 226.

63. Samuel Gompers, "Organized Labor's Attitude Toward Child Labor," *Annals of the American Academy of Political and Social Science* 27 (1906): 339.

64. Quoted in Tishler, *Self-Reliance*, pp. 64–65.

65. Irwin Yellowitz, *Industrialization and the American Labor Movement, 1850–1900* (Port Washington, New York: Kennikat Press, 1977), p. 104.

66. Leff, "Consensus for Reform," p. 415.

67. Hartmann, "Capitalism."

68. Robert Bremner, *From the Depths: The Discovery of Poverty in the United States* (New York: New York University Press, 1956), pp. 230–243.

69. Leslie Woodcock Tentler, *Wage-Earning Women: Industrial Work and Family Life in the United States, 1900–1930* (New York: Oxford, 1979). Hartmann, agreeing with William O'Neill, dismisses the "social feminists" as "not primarily interested in advancing the cause of women's rights."

70. The influence of Catholic social thought in pressing familial as opposed to individual considerations in government policy has been little studied. This is an important influence on Daniel Moynihan, for one.

71. W. Jett Lauck, *The New Industrial Revolution and Wages* (New York and London: Funk & Wagnalls, 1929), p. 19; J. Noble Stockett, *Arbitral Determination of Railway Wages* (Boston: Houghton Mifflin, 1918), chap. iii; Herbert Feis, *Principles of Wage Settlement* (New York: Wilson, 1924); Bureau of Applied Economics, *Standards of Living: A Compilation of Budgetary Studies* (Washington, D.C., 1920), pp. 96–101; and Bremner, *From the Depths*, p. 86.

72. Quoted from the Massachusetts Bureau of Labor Statistics in a speech by Herbert Gutman, Irvine, California, April 1979.

73. For "Sex-gender system," see Gayle Rubin, "The Traffic in Women: Notes on the Political 'Economy' of Sex," in *Toward an Anthropology of Women*, ed. Rayna Reiter (New York: Monthly Review Press, 1975).

74. For an English account, see Anna Davin, "Imperialism and Motherhood," *History Workshop*, no. 5, p. 49.

75. Robert Frost evoked the seamy side of the modern ideal of independence when he wrote:

> *No memory of having starred*
> *Atones for later disregard,*
> *Or keeps the end from being hard*
> *Better to go down dignified*
> *With boughten friendship at your side*
> *Than none at all. Provide, provide!*

From "Provide, Provide" from *The Poetry of Robert Frost*, edited by Edward Connery Lathem. Copyright 1936 by Robert Frost. Copyright © 1964 by Lesley Frost Ballantine. Copyright © 1969 by Holt, Rinehart and Winston. Reprinted by permission of Holt, Rinehart and Winston, Publishers.

The Family:
The View
From a Room of Her Own

Rethinking the family is more than a challenge; it is a threat. The family, as one author has pointed out, is expected to be "a haven in a heartless world."[1] And feminism has shaken us up; most of us positively, but the shaking up that goes with creativity is not always welcome. Life is scary, the world is scary, and we do not give up our "havens" easily, even when they don't seem to be working well and may never have been havens at all. Rethinking anything means taking risks: the risk of making mistakes, the risk of angering people, the risk of failing to have any impact. But rethinking is also a "high": the experience of being in a new space while old habits of thought and feeling are at least temporarily shed.

No one is neutral about a subject like "the family." We have all been raised in families and have strong feelings about the people we are related to and the institution that binds us to them. Here is where we experienced our first emotions and ambivalences: love and hate, joy and pain, giving and taking. Family is where people touch, physically and in their total being. Here we learned to hope, to suffer disappointment, to trust, and to be wary. Above all, family is where people get their start in life, where they experienced the most sharing and where they expect to be able to return in need. Expectation is, in fact, the key: People *expect* families to provide "togetherness" for better or for worse, in sickness and in health, etc., as the marriage vow sets it up. And most seemingly objective observations of reality are measured against such expectations to gauge the health of the institution of family. From such expectations, we frame questions like "Is the family falling apart?" and call state and national conferences about the matter. In other words, our feelings about the family strongly affect our thinking about it.

What *have* we been thinking about the family? What *would* rethinking

225

involve? A brief retrospective for the first question may clarify the answer to the second.

The study of the family as a formal academic subject is relatively recent. It emerged in Europe in the nineteenth century at a time when many families seemed to be disintegrating and the social fabric seemed about to unravel. The family became a "problem" that needed study for a "solution." Specifically, rapid industrialization in Europe, particularly and at first in England, was driving out small producers while better capitalized ones invested in mass production machinery. The result was the creation of a wage-earning or working class totally dependent on jobs that were subject to the booms and busts of the economy and having no other mainstay for survival. Faced with recurrent crises over which they had no control, working people resorted to a variety of strategies: sharing slim resources with one another, organizing for improved wages and working conditions, trying to redistribute wealth legally through taxes and illegally through crime, and organizing for more profound social change.

Finding themselves in an urban environment, far from the responsible ties of rural communities where social pressure was strong for mutual aid, families felt contradictory pressures. On the one hand, family members pulled closer together, having mainly one another on whom to rely and lacking the security of the small community. Many new in-migrants to cities came "sponsored" by family members who had gone before and were helped to get on their feet when they arrived. "Fictive kin"—make-believe relatives or valued friends who became honorary family members—also were admitted to this security network. In other words, family became more important, even as a *concept* to be applied to nonfamily.[2] On the other hand, lacking a clear shared enterprise, such as a family farm or shop or craft, families lost their positive core: a common creative project. Rather, while individuals in the family still contributed to its survival, increasingly they did so separately: They did different things in different enterprises, for different employers, at different hours, and for different wages. The labor market created by industrial capitalism tended to drive the family apart and make the individuals in it separate entities in that labor market. These opposing pulls sometimes wrenched those families out of shape. Parents were separated from children. Distant kin or nonrelated persons participated in networks of mutual aid and child care, much as poor people do now.[3] Some families broke apart completely under the strain, releasing uncared-for individuals into an uncaring society. Other families suffered temporary separation when individuals were forced into workhouses or poorhouses or when other individuals pioneered new places in which to work and live.

This did not happen all at once. In the first few decades of the English industrial revolution whole families entered a factory, to maintain family cohesion and out of the habit of working together.[4] Since workers no longer controlled the conditions of their work, however, the entire family of children, women, and men experienced long hours and brutal discipline at low pay. By the second third of the nineteenth century, the social consequences of this change became noticeable, and parlimentary investigations were undertaken. They revealed personal results such as ill health, shortened lives, and stunted intellectual development. Among the social results were crime and widespread addiction to alcohol and other drugs. Among the political results were radical movements for drastic social change and reformist movements for amelioration. Among the temporarily expedient solutions was the removal of women from the labor force through "protective" legislation. By reducing competition in the labor market, this pushed male wages up to the level of a "family wage."[5] It also restricted women to the home, where presumably they would anchor and restabilize the family, that is, make it look more like the family of the middle class, which defined the norm through its ideological hegemony.

In short, the context of the first European studies of the family was failure—failure to measure up to an imposed norm, failure to reproduce a smoothly functioning society. A major question thus raised for study was: How is the microcosm of survival and of reproduction affected by the macrocosm of survival and of reproduction? Or, how is family affected by the economic system? Or, to put it still differently, how does the way in which the *whole* social structure is organized to live affect the way its *units* are organized to live?

Karl Marx and Friedrich Engels asked these questions when they saw pauperism and family dissolution around them in England and when they studied reports of factory inspectors and studies by the Royal Commissions of working-class life. Engels, in particular, took an interest in family life and noted changes in its functions and in authority relations within it over time in his *The Condition of the Working Class in England in 1844* and in his *Origin of the Family, Private Property and the State* of 1884. Marx noted the effects of women's employment on family life in various places in *Capital* (1867) and contrasted bourgeois and proletarian families in *The Communist Manifesto* (1848). Together, the two men approached the subject historically, that is, with an eye to noting change over time in this particular social institution, and they rooted the change they observed in larger changes in society, specifically in the development of capitalist industralization as a way of organizing economic life. Such a view suggested continuing change as capitalism advanced further and developed still newer forms of social organization. Like all progress, according to Marx and Engels, new forms of family would ultimately liberate the individuals in it, though they might first pass through stages in which family life was disrupted or oppressive, in view of the context of capitalist exploitation.

Less accepting of continuing change in the nineteenth century, Frédéric Le Play, in his *Les ouvriers européens: Études sur les traveaux, la vie domestique et la condition morale des populations ouvrières de l'Europe* of 1855, closely studied thrity-six French families through interviews and budget analyses. Le Play is sometimes regarded as the founder of empirical family sociology for his method. His motivation, however, was to locate an ideal family form with stability as the major criterion, again, reflecting the major concern of his time. Defining three major types of family—traditional, stem, and modern—Le Play settled on the stem family as the most desirable. It was large, multi-generational, included non-kin like servants, was headed by a powerful patriarch, and held the family property intact through inheritance by a single male heir, the future patriarch. Other family members could seek their self-interest elsewhere, for example in the new cities, with cash bequests. The stem family achieved a balance between group interest (which was overriding in the older, traditional family) and individual interest (which threatened to dissolve the modern family), and between stability and flexibility. However, the dynamic of European capitalism continued to disequilibrate this "ideal" form. Le Play deplored the vulnerable, unstable "modern" family of only two generations (parents and children) with divisible property and declining group loyalty.[6]

All over Europe, the newer industrial cities manifested changes in family life that often shocked middle-class reformers and doctors, whose "medical geographies" recording class differentials in mortality still remain an important historical source.[7] Besides reformers' and revolutionaries' outrage against the social results of economic exploitation, the demands of the first women's movement also motivated analyses of family life. By the turn of the century, feminists recognized that the "woman question" was at bottom the question of woman's place in the family. This perspective allowed a closer look at individuals and their legal and customary rights and constraints within the family.[8] By the 1920s and 30s, however, reaction set in. A new psychoanalytic emphasis best represented by the *Institut für Sozialforschung* in Frankfurt, Germany, presented the diminishing authority of the father, that is, declining patriarchy, as the source of social problems including fascistic tendencies.[9]

The great Depression of the 1930s, which pitted women and men against one another for employment, reinforced antifeminist positions arguing that woman's place was in the home. Empirical studies of the family abounded, but new thinking emerged only after World War II and its locus shifted from Europe to the United States. Then North American sociologists such as William Ogburn and Talcott Parsons followed the

earlier hints of European thinkers like Georg Simmel and Emile Durk-
heim in viewing the family as one small social group among several, with
similar interpersonal relations among its members, apart from any joint
economic enterprise. The 1950s American school of family sociology
tended to view family relationships as reflecting the economic individuation of its members and as focusing now mainly on emotional needs. They
saw individuals within the family assuming certain modern specialized
functions: The father took an "instrumental" role, interfacing with the
larger society and becoming therefore "rational"; the mother took an "affective" role, mediating emotional relationships inside the family and becoming therefore "sensitive." The nuclear household produced only
enough children for simple generational replacement and included no
other kin or unrelated persons. Function dictated structure and pointed to
a new "norm"; as before, it was that of the middle-class family, now
modernized. Variations were considered deviant or pathological, and
"correctable" through social policy, indicating acknowledgement that the
contemporary family had been found vulnerable.[10]

In our own times, the arguments have become still more refined on
both sides of the Atlantic.[11] The structuralist-functionalist heritage, however, continues to predominate, though it has its critics. Scholars disagree
about family structure, indicating a search for a definition of "family." At
least one has proposed the mother-child dyad as the ultimately irreducible
core, whose articulation with other kin structures vary with circumstance.[12] Others see the nuclear family of mother, father, and children as basic.[13] Still others regard the nuclear family as a modern form,
evolving out of a preindustrial extended form, which had included distant
kin, and they either celebrate that trend as liberating or deplore it as
atomizing.[14] The debate is intensely political. To some, it means cham-
pioning or repudiating industrial capitalism, if its effects on family are
acknowledged; to others, it means not acknowledging such effects and
seeing the family as a separate structure, either unaffected by larger social
changes or even perhaps having effect on them.[15]

More recently, scholars have moved the question to a different plane,
showing that Western families have life cycles of their own in which
periods of extended family precede fission into new conjugal units or into a
premarital single or cohabitation phase. This interpretation allows the
presence of various forms simultaneously. Nor is this the only flexibility
to keep in mind. Family boundaries, it has been pointed out, expand and
contract according to changing historical need. Thus, individuals with
property to transmit may cut out lateral kin in favor of vertical lineage, to
maintain an inheritance intact and thus assure the family's continuing
power. In such a case, "family" comes to mean direct descendants rather
than distant cousins. This seems to have been the case for the rising

European bourgeoisie as it accumulated capital, and for the aristocracy once its wealth in land ceased to expand. On the other hand, those who need a large network to survive may count more distant relatives as important family members, as tends to be the case for a new urban proletariat, or even an older one, when economic crises occur.

Indeed, social class is a major factor determining family organization. Nevertheless, our understanding of changes in families by class is hampered by skewed evidence. An interesting but frustrating reversal occurs between studies of the family past and present. Most of our materials from the past are written sources, recorded by the literate, that is, by the aristocracy and bourgeoisie. The peasantry and wage earners left few written documents. Therefore, we know much more today about the experience of the upper strata of past societies than about the experience of their lower strata. By contrast, contemporary families are studied by sociologists who have access to "subjects." These are drawn from a pool of willing and unwilling people. The most unwilling to be studied are the very rich, especially those with a long ancestry of wealth who consider themselves upper class. One of the prerogatives of wealth and distinction is privacy; hence the outcry when the public media violate it.

In contrast with our scanty information about the contemporary upper class, we know a lot about the middle class, which seems to enjoy being studied, probably because its own members, professionals, are doing the studying. Self-studies seem less threatening. We also know a fair amount about the needy strata of the working class, which cannot avoid being studied by social agencies that claim the right to invade privacy as a condition of giving aid. The self-sufficient stratum of the working class protects its privacy and resists being studied, probably out of fear of losing further control over the conditions of its life. So we are in the curious position of lacking a continuous thread in family studies: We lose it for the upper class and pick it up late for sections of the working class. The most continuous evidence exists for the middle class, but reliance on this tends to reinforce the notion that the bourgeois family represents the "norm," even when it is far from the numerical majority.

To conclude this answer to the first question—What has been the thinking about the family?—it may be said that it has often been politically motivated, biased through its evidence, and practiced mostly by men, though, as noted, partly under the impetus of and in reaction to the women's movement of the nineteenth and early twentieth centuries. At the same time, family studies have become increasingly refined in method and more complex in theory, producing the paradoxical effect of both enriching debate and coming dangerously close to an arid scholasticism.

Rethinking has been spurred by noticeable social changes. Today, as in the nineteenth century, strains in and on the family draw public attention. Concerned observers point to the rising divorce rate, the rising rate of illegitimacy, the rising incidence of reported violence within the family, and the increase of preferred alternatives such as both hetero- and homosexual cohabitation and communal and single households. Some link the rise in married women's paid employment to these changes. While it has been shown repeatedly that married women take jobs either to improve their family's living standard or to keep it from falling, the interpretation persists that such work *for* the family is actually destroying it.[16] This opinion is possible only if one sees women as *the core* of the family, rather than as *one member* of the family. It also suggests that only a permanent presence in the *household* makes *family* possible, an unwarranted assumption at best. It has also been argued that the contemporary women's movement is destroying the family, a chronological absurdity, since the noted trends are at least twice as old as the women's movement. To the contrary, the increase in women's employment and in women's felt double burden of paid and unpaid labor (in the home) has helped create a *mass* women's movement, much broader than the socially narrow one of the nineteenth century.

One result is that women have begun studying the family. Feminist scholars have accrued substantial new research, informed by urgent new questions derived directly from women's experience. This work provides a corrective to earlier efforts, allowing a multidimensional view. For one thing, methods of research have been affected: Female informants are included in surveys of their own and alien cultures, where previously male anthropologists and sociologists had relied mainly on male informants; subjective experiences of power relations are weighed against objective measures of relative power; and women's contributions to and consumption in the family economy are individually factored out. In short, the sociology of knowledge has been refined to include gender perspectives.

But method is merely a way of gaining information. Behind it lie new questions in search of such information. And so the second question: What has feminist rethinking been about? demands its answer.

The major feminist contribution has been to view women as individuals within the family, rather than as mere components of it or anchors to it; that is, to view women as persons involved in familial and nonfamilial activities, as men routinely have been perceived. From that vantage point, everything looks different: the activities of other family members, their relationships to one another, the distribution of goods and power and the struggles over both, the socialization that reproduces gender-specific behavior and also changes it over time, and the interaction of family *members* (not just the family *unit*) with nonfamilial social groups. Put another way, feminists have opened a whole new vista by asking, *not what do women do for the family* (an older question), *but what does the family do for women?* What does it do *to* women? Whom does family organization serve best, and how? How does it reproduce these services historically? What changes occur in family form and function? In short, feminist rethinking takes us back to basics: What *is* a family and what does it *do?*

A major challenge has been posed by Rayna Rapp, an anthropologist. Noting the great variety of recognized kin and household organization in human societies, she considers that we have overly reified "the family," making of it a "thing," a biological given, and thus confusing ourselves about "its" norms and deviations, "its" changing structures and functions. Instead, she proposed that we more carefully distinguish households from families, since it is the former within which people pool resources, perform certain tasks, exhibit links to larger domains, and effectively reproduce society, especially class-stratified society. Family, Rapp argues, might be more usefuly understood as a mere *concept,* a social definition of who *should* be living together inside of households. Seen thus, "family" becomes an aspect of ideology, or normative thinking, which better explains its great variety. In Western civilization, "family" thus becomes a form of recruitment into households, which themselves are organized according to social class. Thus, peasant families are different from those of urban wage earners or the aristocracy or capitalist bourgeoisie because their households demand different kinds of social participation. People are born into a household of a certain type and thus find themselves in different "families"—dyadic, nuclear, extended laterally, extended longitudinally, inclusive of nonkin, and so on.[17]

Another apparent universal now under question is the activity of mothering. Seemingly biologically based in childbearing and lactation, even this phenomenon has been unveiled as temporally and geographically variable.[18] The questions that arise here are who raises children, how, and with what results? It is now clear that our form of raising children is historically specific, a product of advanced capitalist society, which idealizes mother*hood* while isolating and marginalizing mother*ing,* in a classic demonstration of the mystifying function of ideology. This occurred with the separation of home and work at the time of industrialization, which created two separate spheres: a private sphere inhabited by women and children subject to the vicissitudes of the public sphere of economics and politics ruled by men. Social infancy was prolonged into a world of "childhood," while the accompanying construct of "motherhood" presumed innate and therefore universal qualities of nurturance, self-sacrifice, and narrowness of focus.[19] This constellation of attributes was appropriate mainly to the European and American bourgeoisie in its two hundred years of dominance—a narrow social base for a "norm," as noted above.[20] In the last two decades, however, as married women and mothers increasingly gravitate toward the labor force, the public/private division translates for them into a "double burden" of paid and unpaid work and points to the erosion of "motherhood" as a full-time, undiluted, "natural" vocation.

In response to this historical change, feminists have questioned the entire concept of mothering and found that, indeed, other forms of parenting exist, appropriate to other material conditions. Thus, non-Western, noncapitalist societies make child rearing central rather than marginal, and share it with kin other than the biological mother and with nonkin, either by custom, as in preindustrial societies, or through planning, as in socialist countries and in those with a mixed economy.[21] In such societies women may be mothers without falling into "motherhood" and may more readily participate in society in other ways as well without guilt. Other aspects of women's potential become realizable when they are less defined by their purely reproductive capacities. In fact, feminist thinking has allowed scholars to take a step back and look at reproduction differently. In other places I have suggested the concept of social reproduction, which would include socializing agencies other than the family, such as schools, health services, work relations, the media, and so on. This notion, by including and transcending that of the family, would move the discussion to a different level.[22]

Feminist questions have focused not only on different modes of reproduction but also on its content, on what is being reproduced. They include: How is gender-specific behavior re-created? How are individuals daily reproduced through services such as housework? What has been the affective experience of women in households?

Interesting work has been done on the social construction of gender, as distinct from the biological determination of sex. Several feminist thinkers have challenged Freud's theories, which implied that anatomy was destiny. Gayle Rubin has analyzed the enormous social effort and motivation that goes into the creation and enforcement of gender distinctions.[23] Nancy Chodorow and Dorothy Dinnerstein also criticize the genital focus of Freud's oedipal situation, as well as its assumptions of patriarchal authority as normal. These assumptions underlie the identification of male psychological development with that of general human maturation, thus consigning adult females to permanent immaturity or a pathology of narcissism.[24] At the point of greatest concession, Juliet Mitchell and Jessica Benjamin have argued that the patriarchal, oedipal family may have had its necessary day but may be becoming obsolete.[25]

The lowly subject of housework, too "trivial" for most male scholars, has also been raised by feminist scholars to a new level of theoretical analysis. Questions have been raised about its economic value within the larger economy, the social meaning of its changing technology, its relationship to other family work such as child care, and its psychological effect on the homemaker.

Among Marxists, feminists have created a lively discussion about the economic meaning of unpaid housework in the creation and re-creation of a paid labor force.[26] Among non-Marxists, the value of housework has been computed in dollars; its work load has been measured against the expansions and contractions of the larger economy; and its role as a reserve pool for paid labor has been identified, as has its role as a market for the consumption of durable and perishable commodities.[27] As a workshop for reproduction, the household has seen greatly changing technology, from the open hearth to the microwave oven, from the broom and brush to the vacuum cleaner, and so on. But studies show that labor-easing devices have not become labor-saving ones. The housewife has not been liberated from janitorial work; she has been bonded more firmly by invisible links of hygienic and aesthetic standards that demand gleaming surfaces.[28] Technology, a closer look informs, was a mere reform, not a revolution in the life of homemakers. It simply allowed more women to do their *own* housework; former domestics could do their own instead of somebody else's, and former employers of domestics now also did their own housework. Child care, far from being a neatly meshing activity, frequently runs competition to housework for time and opposition to it for goals; a neat home and a happy child may be a contradiction in terms.[29] No wonder the happy homemaker has been subject to depression, alcoholism, and drug abuse.

Feminist rethinking has not only demystified the home as a workplace but as a locale of intense intimacy, of close encounters not always of the loving kind. It has x-rayed the greeting-card image of the smiling family to reveal the bared teeth of rage and pain: cases of incest, rape, battering, murder of the soul—not isolated, but remarkably widespread. The family has been unmasked in its oppressive relations, besides the more clichéd supportive ones. It has been revealed, among other things, as a political arena in which individuals compete and form alliances, in which their bargaining power fluctuates, and also their gains and losses. Historical struggles within the family can be discerned over unequal distribution of resources; over control over women's reproductive capacities; over life-affecting decisions, such as migration; and over the apportionment of space and leisure, still best articulated by Virginia Woolf in *A Room of One's Own*. Family harmony exists, but it is an achievement, not an omnipresent, given, natural condition.[30]

To conclude: The feminist perspective, by perceiving women as subjects, as individuals disembedded at least conceptually from the family, has reopened the questions of what a family is, what its members do, and how they are affected by the social organization of household and kin.[31] It has revealed far more complicated relationships within family and between family and other social formations than had previously been understood.[32] And all by asking one fundamental question, as stated earlier, and that is not only what do women do for the family, but what does the family do for women? *A cui bono?* A useful question for any interrogation in the social sciences. And a validation of a major feminist insight: The personal is political.

Notes

1. Christopher Lasch, *Haven in a Heartless World: The Family Besieged* (New York: Basic, 1977).

2. Michael Anderson, *Family Structure in Nineteenth Century Lancashire* (Cambridge, England: Cambridge University Press, 1971).

3. Carol B. Stack, *All Our Kin: Strategies for Survival in a Black Community* (New York: Harper & Row, 1974); and Leo Grebler, Joan W. Moore, Ralph C. Guzman, *The Mexican-American People* (New York: The Free Press, 1970), chap. 15.

4. Neil Smelser, *Social Change in the Industrial Revolution* (Chicago: University of Chicago Press, 1959).

5. Jane Humphries, "Class Struggle and the Persistence of the Working-Class Family," *Cambridge Journal of Economics* 1 (1977): 241–58; and Bettina Berch, *Industrialization and Working Women in the Nineteenth Century*, forthcoming.

6. Catherine Silver, in *The Empirical Study of Social Change: The Case of Frédéric Le Play* (Chicago: University of Chicago Press, forthcoming), sees Le Play as a liberal rather than as a conservative thinker, and analyzes his complex theory in detail.

7. Lutz K. Berkner, "Recent Research on the History of the Family in Western Europe," *Journal of Marriage and the Family* 35, no. 3 (August 1973): 395–405. A generally useful article with extensive bibliography.

8. George Schwägler, *Soziologie der Familie, Ursprung und Entwicklung* (Tübingen: Heidelberger Sociologica, no. 9, 1970). Excellent review of the history of family studies, but limited by its major focus on German scholars.

9. Max Horkheimer, *Studien über Autorität und Familie* (Paris: Felix Alcan, 1936), now available in English in *Critical Theory*, trans. J. Cummings (New York, 1972). The argument was revived in recent years by Alexander Mitscherlich, *Auf dem Weg zur vaterlosen Gesellschaft* (Munich, 1963) which appeared in English as *Society Without the Father* and by Lasch in *Haven in a Heartless World*.

10. The classical works for this position are W. F. Ogburn and M. F. Nimkoff, *Technology and the Changing Family* (Boston: Houghton Mifflin, 1955); and Talcott Parsons and Robert F. Bales, *Family, Socialization and Interaction Process* (Glencoe, Ill.: Free Press, 1955).

11. The current literature on family history is too extensive to be listed here. Useful surveys can be found in Schwägler, *Soziologie der Familie*; Peter Laslett, *Household and Family in Past Time* (London: Cambridge University Press, 1972); Berkner, "Family in Western Europe"; Louise Tilly, Joan Scott, and Caludia Kselman, "A Bibliography on Women, Work and Family in France and England since 1700" (manuscript from Center for West European Studies, University of Michigan, June 1977); Michael Gordon, ed., *The American Family in Social-Historical Perspective* (2nd ed.; New York: St. Martin's, 1978); Rayna Rapp, Ellen Ross, and Renate Bridenthal, "Examining Family History," *Feminist Studies* 5, no. 1 (Spring, 1979); Amy Swerdlow, Renate Bridenthal, Joan Kelly, and Phyllis Vine, *Household and Kin: Families in Flux* (New York: Feminist Press and McGraw Hill, 1980); and the special issue of *Daedalus* (Spring 1977) on the family.

12. Jack Goody, *Production and Reproduction: A Comparative Study of the Domestic Domain*, vol. 1 (London: Cambridge Studies in Social Anthropology, Cambridge University Press, 1976).

13. This is Laslett's position in *Household and Family in Past Time* and representative of the Cambridge school. Laslett admits their "*animus* against 'the myth of the extended family' " traceable to the defensive posture of some foreign scholars against the implication that its nuclear family organization uniquely disposed England to industrialization, pp. 5–10.

14. Beginning with Marx and Le Play, with opposite evaluations, as noted, the controversy extends into the present. Major proponents include William Goode, *World Revolution and Family Patterns* (New York: Free Press, 1963, 1970); Edward Shorter, *The Making of the Modern Family* (New York: Basic, 1975); Fred Weinstein and Gerald Platt, *The Wish to Be Free* (Berkeley: University of California Press, 1969); as well as more recent prophets of family dissolution, such as Lasch, *Haven in a Heartless World;* and Kenneth Keniston, *All Our Children: The American Family under Pressure* (New York: Harcourt Brace Jovanovich, 1977). Louise Tilly and Joan Scott effectively challenged Shorter's sexual liberation thesis in "Women's Work and the Family in Nineteenth Century Europe," *Comparative Studies in Society and History* 17, no. 1 (1975): 36–64.

15. See note 12. Tamara Hareven also criticized the so-called modernization thesis, which relates family structure to industrialization, in "Modernization and Family History," *Signs* 2, no. 1 (Autumn 1976). However, the interpretation persists. See Eli Zaretsky, *Capitalism, the Family and Personal Life* (New York: Harper Colophon, 1976); and David Levine, *Family Formation in an Age of Nascent Capitalism* (New York: Academic, 1977). Aristocratic family patterns are traced by Lawrence Stone, *The Family, Sex and Marriage in England 1500–1800* (New York: Harper & Row, 1977); and Randolph Trumbach, *The Rise of the Egalitarian Family* (New York: Academic, 1978).

16. For analyses of the way in which capitalism expands its need for female labor, see Veronica Beechey, "Some Notes on Female Wage Labour in Capitalist Production," *Capital and Class* 3 (Autumn 1977): 45–66; and Gabriel Kolko,

"Working Wives: Their Effects on the Structure of the Working Class, *Science and Society* 42, no. 3 (Fall 1978): 257–77.

17. Rayna Rapp, in "Examining Family History," *Feminist Studies* 5, no. 1 (Spring 1979), and "Family and Class in Contemporary America: Notes Toward an Understanding of Ideology," *Science and Society* 42, no. 3 (Fall 1978): 278–300.

18. Among the major works emerging on this topic are Jessie Bernard, *Women, Wives, Mothers: Values and Options* (Chicago: Aldine, 1975); idem, *The Future of Motherhood* (New York: Penguin, 1975); Nancy Chodorow, *The Reproduction of Mothering: Psychoanalysis and the Sociology of Gender* (Berkeley: University of California Press, 1978); Dorothy Dinnerstein, *The Mermaid and the Minotaur* (New York: Harper & Row, 1976); Lila Leibowitz, *Females, Males, Families: A Biosocial Approach* (North Scituate, Mass.: Duxbury, 1978); Adrienne Rich, *Of Woman Born: Motherhood as Experience and Institution* (New York: Norton, 1976); and various essays in Rayna R. Reiter, ed. *Toward an Anthropology of Women* (New York: Monthly Review Press, 1975), and in Michelle Z. Rosaldo and Louise Lamphere, eds., *Woman, Culture and Society* (Stanford: Stanford University Press, 1974).

19. There is a burgeoningliterature on childhood. Major items include Phillipe Ariès, *Centuries of Childhood*, trans. by Robert Baldick (New York: Vintage, 1965); Lloyd de Mause, ed., *The History of Childhood* (New York: Psychohistory Press, 1974); John R. Gillis, *Youth and History* (New York: Academic, 1974); and articles by John Demos, Etienne van de Walle, David Rothman, and C. John Sommerville in Theodore K. Rabb and Robert I. Rotberg, eds., *The Family in History: Interdisciplinary Essays* (New York: Harper Torchbooks, 1971).

20. Two feminist historians have questioned the value of a rigid application of the public/private sphere model without, however, eliminating it. Elizabeth Pleck, in "Two Worlds in One: Work and Family," *Journal of Social History* (Winter 1976), proposes that scholars examine the intersections between these two worlds and how individuals reconcile them. Tilly and Scott, in *Women, Work and Family*, show old family forms being adapted to new demands of the larger economy, but also accept the basic division.

21. For preindustrial societies, see Rosaldo and Lamphere, *Women, Culture and Society;* Reiter, *Anthopology of Women;* and Rich, *Of Woman Born.* For modern planned socities, see Karen Wald, *Children of Che: Childcare and Education in Cuba* (San Francisco: Ramparts, 1978); Barbara Wolfe Jancar, *Women Under Communism* (Baltimore: Johns Hopkins University Press, 1978); and Gail Warshofsky Lapidus, *Women in Soviet Society* (Berkeley: University of California Press, 1979); both find child-care services in socialist countries lagging behind demand but superior to such provisions in nonsocialist countries. On child rearing in the mixed economy of Sweden, see Elisabet Sandberg, *Equality Is the Goal* (Stockholm: Swedish Institute, 1973); and Lillemor Melsted, *Swedish Family Policy* (New York: Swedish Information Service, 1979).

22. R. Bridenthal, "The Dialectics of Production and Reproduction in History," *Radical America* 10, no. 2 (March–April 1976): 3–11; and idem, "Examining Family History," *Feminist Studies* 5, no. 1 (Spring 1979).

23. Gayle Rubin, "The Traffic in Women: Notes on the 'Political Economy' of Sex," in Reiter, *Toward an Anthropology of Women*, pp. 157–210.

24. Chodorow, *Reproduction of Mothering*, and in Rosaldo and Lamphere, *Woman, Culture and Society;* and Dinnerstein, *Mermaid and Minotaur.*

25. Juliet Mitchell, *Psychoanalysis and Feminism* (New York: Pantheon, 1974), pp. 401–6; and Jessica Benjamin, "Authority and the Family Revisited: Or, a World Without Fathers?" *New German Critique,* no. 13 (Winter 1978): 35–57.

26. Major contributions to this debate are Mariarosa Dalla Costa and Selma James, *The Power of Women and the Subversion of the Community* (Bristol, England: Falling Wall Press, 1972), which became the basis for the Wages for Housework movement; Margaret Benston, "The Political Economy of Women's Liberation," *Monthly Review* 21, no. 4 (September 1969): 13–27; Lise Vogel, "The Earthly Family," *Radical America* 7, nos. 4 and 5 (July–October 1973): 9–50; Wally Secombe, "Housework under Capitalism," *New Left Review,* no. 83 (January–February 1974): 47–58; Margaret Coulson, Branka Magaš, and Hilary Wainwright, "Women and the Class Struggle," *New Left Review,* no. 89 (January–February 1975): 59–71; Wally Seccombe, "Domestic Labour—Reply to Critics," *New Left Review,* no. 94 (November–December 1975): 85–96; Jean Gardiner, "The Role of Domestic Labour," *New Left Review,* no. 89 (January–February 1975): 47–58; Maxine Molyneux, "Beyond the Housework Debate," *New Left Review* 116 (July–August 1979): 3–28; *On the Political Economy of Women,* CSE Pamphlet No. 2 (London: Conference of Socialist Economists, 1975); Susan Himmelweit and Simon Mohun, "Domestic Labour and Capital," *Cambridge Journal of Economics* 1 (1977): 15–31; Martha E. Gimenez, "Structuralist Marxism on 'The Woman Question,' " *Science and Society,* vol. 42, no. 3 (Fall 1978). A good review of the debate, which centers on interpretations of Marx's definition of value producing labor and the political implications for women, can be found in Joan B. Landes, "Women, Labor and Family Life: A Theoretical Perspective," *Science and Society,* vol. XLI, no. 4 (Winter, 1977–1978).

27. See special issues of the *Review of Radical Political Economics:* July 1972, Spring 1976, and Fall 1977. For a full bibliography on housework, its economics and sociology, see Amy Swerdlow, ed., *Feminist Perspectives on Housework and Child Care* (Bronxville, N.Y.: Sarah Lawrence College, 1978).

28. Ruth Cowan, "The 'Industrial Revolution' in the Home: Household Technology and Social Change in the 20th Century," *Technology and Culture* 17 *(January 1976): 1–23; and idem, "Two Washes in the Morning and a Bridge Party at Night: The American Housewife between the Wars,"* *Women's Studies* 3 (1976): 147–72. Also Barbara Ehrenreich and Deirdre English, *For Her Own Good* (New York: Doubleday Anchor, 1978) esp. chap. 5.

29. Ann Oakley, *Woman's Work: The Housewife, Past and Present* (New York: Pantheon, 1974).

30. Ellen Ross, "Examining Family History," *Feminist Studies* 5, no. 1 (Spring 1979).

31. For further bibliography and an overview of historical change in, contemporary patterns of, and alternatives to the family, see Amy Swerdlow, ed., *Household and Kin: Families in Flux* (New York: Feminist Press and McGraw Hill, 1980).

32. A new line of questioning, exploring relations of the family and the state, is opening again, explicitly for the first time since Engels. Elizabeth Wilson, in *Women and the Welfare State* (London: Tavistock, 1977), argues that family policy is the keystone of the welfare state.

Index